U.S.
Unilateral Arms Control Initiatives

Recent Titles in
Contributions in Military Studies
Series Advisor: Colin Gray

U.S. Unilateral Arms Control Initiatives

WHEN DO THEY WORK?

William Rose

Contributions in Military Studies,
Number 82

GREENWOOD PRESS
New York • Westport, Connecticut • London

Library of Congress Cataloging-in-Publication Data

Rose, William, 1947–
  U.S. unilateral arms control initiatives : when do they work? /
William Rose.
      p.   cm.—(Contributions in military studies, ISSN 0883–6884
; no. 82)
  Bibliography: p.
  Includes index.
  ISBN 0-313-25787-6 (lib. bdg. : alk. paper)
  1. Nuclear arms control—United States.   2. Nuclear arms control—
Soviet Union.   I. Title.   II. Title: US unilateral arms control
initiatives.   III. Series.
JX1974.7.R577 1988
327.1'74'0973—dc19   88–17774

British Library Cataloguing in Publication Data is available.

Library of Congress Catalog Card Number: 88–17774
ISBN: 0–313–25787–6
ISSN: 0883–6884

First published in 1988

Greenwood Press, Inc.
88 Post Road West, Westport, Connecticut 06881

Printed in the United States of America

The paper used in this book complies with the
Permanent Paper Standard issued by the National
Information Standards Organization (Z39.48–1984).

10 9 8 7 6 5 4 3 2 1

Contents

Abbreviations

ABM	antiballistic missile
ACDA	Arms Control and Disarmament Agency
ASAT	antisatellite
BMD	ballistic missile defense
CMEA	Council for Mutual Economic Assistance (also known as Comecon)
CTB	comprehensive test ban
ENDC	Eighteen Nation Disarmament Committee
ER	enhanced radiation
ERDA	Energy Research and Development Administration
ERW	enhanced radiation weapon
FOBS	fractional orbital bombardment system
IAEA	International Atomic Energy Agency
ICBM	intercontinental ballistic missile
INF	intermediate-range nuclear forces
IRBM	intermediate-range ballistic missile
JCS	Joint Chiefs of Staff
LTB	limited test ban
MFN	most favored nation
MFR	Mutual Force Reduction
MIRV	multiple independently targetable reentry vehicle
MLF	Multilateral Force
MRV	multiple reentry vehicle

NATO North Atlantic Treaty Organization

NTM   national technical means

PVO   Protinvovzdushnaia Oborona Strany (anti-air defense of the country)

RV   reentry vehicles

SAC   Strategic Air Command

SALT Strategic Arms Limitation Talks

SLBM submarine-launched ballistic missile

SRF   Strategic Rocket Forces

TFT   tit-for-tat

TNW   tactical nuclear weapons

Preface

What can the United States do to encourage the Soviets to agree to sensible arms control proposals? This book examines the utility of one diplomatic bargaining tool: the unilateral initiative. Proponents of initiatives often cite examples where U.S. restraint in weapons testing or deployment may have helped obtain reciprocal Soviet restraint. Others counter, however, that the tactic rarely works. The harshest critics accuse the advocates of being naive idealists who don't understand that the Soviet Union is a hostile state that has and will continue to exploit signs of U.S. weakness.

A clear definition of the tactic and a full overview of Soviet responses to U.S. unilateral initiatives reveal a pattern of outcomes more complex than these views suggest: the tactic occasionally has helped to induce Soviet reciprocation and sometimes it may be the best or only way to limit a particular arms competition, but it has failed at other times and using it can have costs. If the United States is to use the tactic productively, therefore, it should understand the conditions favoring success, as well as the benefits and costs of using the tactic. With this basic knowledge, the United States could develop promising policies to help achieve arms control objectives. This book is intended to help accomplish these tasks.

Not all readers are interested in how I have used theories of international relations and foreign policy to deduce hypotheses about potentially important conditions, or about the complexities of understanding Soviet foreign policy. Readers unconcerned about these issues can skim chapters 2 and 3, and refer back to them if understanding later chapters requires it.

Robert Pickus inspired me to write this book. I learned about the unilateral initiative tactic from him, and he urged me to contribute to our understanding of when and how the United States could use it to help reach agreements with other countries.

This book is based in part on my dissertation, completed at the University of California at Berkeley. I owe special thanks to Kenneth Waltz, chairman of my dissertation committee. His writings and comments contributed the most to my understanding of the methodology and method I needed to formulate the question and to conduct the research. I am also beholden to the other committee members: George Breslauer, Wallace Thies, and Walter McDougall. Finally, I wish to thank the United States Arms Control and Disarmament Agency, which provided both financial aid and encouragement through the Hubert H. Humphrey Doctoral Fellowship in Arms Control and Disarmament.

This book represents a complete reworking of my dissertation and much additional research. Aside from updating theories, chapter 2 and most of chapter 3 are completely new, as are three of the five case studies and chapter 10 on applications of knowledge.

When working on various parts of this book, I received helpful substantive comments from Robert Strong, Steven Van Evera, Jeffery Porro, George Breslauer, Holt Ruffin, Robert Jervis, Alan Sherr, George Weigel, Robert Woito, and William Frasure. I also benefited from the advice of Mildred Vasan, my editor at Greenwood Press, Rosemary Rodensky, and Susan Rose. The final product is my own. If it has any problems or deficiencies, they are entirely my responsibility.

At Connecticut College, Elliot Schwalb and Thomas Hutton, two of my star students, helped to verify my footnotes. I am also grateful for the support I received from the Government Department: work-study funds for Elliot and Tom, postage and duplication of drafts, Elina Sharp's help in typing part of the manuscript, Wayne Swanson's assistance in securing me a semester's leave to work on this book, and Marion Doro's and Wayne's efforts to procure financial assistance for me from the Bernstein Fund and other sources. In addition, I want to thank Dean Frank Johnson, President Oakes Ames, and the Board of Trustees of Connecticut College for awarding me a "capstone grant"—a course remission enabling me to complete the project.

Writing this book required emotional as well as intellectual support. The deepest emotional support came from my wife, Sue. With her in my life I was able to concentrate my intellectual energy productively. She tolerated my six- or seven-day workweeks, and helped me keep my sanity on weekends by rescuing me from the library and "making" me go on walks. I dedicate this book to Sue, to our family, and to our future—which I hope will be less burdened by the threat of war and the expenses of the arms race.

U.S.
Unilateral Arms Control Initiatives

1

The Controversy

Frustrated with traditional arms control negotiations, which often seem to be outpaced by technological developments and the collection of bargaining chips that are not "cashed in," a number of writers plead for an alternative approach:

We should . . . try a policy of restraint, while calling for matching restraint from the Soviet Union.

Paul Warnke, 1975.[1]

[The] policy might involve acts of deliberate restraint on weapons research, development, testing, or acquisition—transforming the bargaining chip into a peace initiative. Weapons that complicate verification or are destabilizing could be withheld from the testing phase, signaling our interest in a stable deterrence pending agreement to control such weapons.

Robert Bresler and Robert Gray, 1977.[2]

Such unilateral steps would create an atmosphere of confidence which in turn would make it easier to negotiate and implement more far-reaching common security measures.

Jerome Wiesner, 1983.[3]

The leaders of the United States and the Soviet Union should attack the arms race with a method that has been used effectively in the past toward the achievement of lasting arms control agreements—reciprocal national restraint.

Herbert Scoville, Jr., 1985.[4]

As President Kennedy successfully did in stopping nuclear explosions above ground in 1963, a Democratic President will initiate temporary, verifiable, and mutual moratoria, to be maintained for a fixed period during negotiations so long as the Soviets do the same. . . . These steps should lead promptly to the negotiation of a comprehensive, mutual, and verifiable freeze.

Democratic Platform, 1984.[5]

Will such an approach work? Many doubt it. Here are several of its detractors:

The little evidence that can be gleaned . . . gives little encouragement to those who would argue that "arms control by example" or unilateral denial by the United States is likely to induce similar behavior by the Soviet Union or pave the way to a successful accord.

Albert Carnesale and Richard Haass, 1987.[6]

From 1969 to 1974, the U.S. exercised deliberate restraint in the development of warhead accuracy so as not to threaten Soviet assured destruction capability. . . . In a pattern that was to be repeated again and again during the course of the decade, the Soviets failed to reciprocate the United States's gesture of unilateral restraint— its "self-denying ordinance."

Patrick Glynn, 1984.[7]

In the naive hope that unilateral restraint by the United States would cause the Soviet Union to reverse [its vast buildup of nuclear arms], the Carter-Mondale Administration delayed significant major features of strategic modernization our country needed.

Republican Platform, 1984.[8]

As these quotations illustrate, debate on the issue rarely gets beyond the question of advocacy: Does the tactic work or doesn't it?[9] Only a few scholars use a contingent analysis, which assumes that the tactic can succeed but only under certain conditions.[10]

So who is right? The answer is important to U.S. interests. If the tactic rarely or never works, then pursuing it might detract from more promising ways to secure the national interest. If it does work, at least under circumstances that we can predict, it would be a useful or perhaps even a necessary technique for controlling the U.S.-Soviet arms race.

The Soviets find the tactic useful, both for facilitating reciprocal U.S. restraint and for projecting an image that they are actively pursuing peaceful relations. In August 1983, for instance, General-Secretary Yuri Andropov declared a moratorium on the testing of antisatellite (ASAT) weapons and proposed an ASAT ban.[11] President Ronald Reagan wished to test and deploy an ASAT system more advanced than the Soviet system. In light of the Soviet initiative and a different strategic analysis, however, Congress wanted an agreement and put restrictions on the Air Force's ability to test the U.S. ASAT. Faced with this constraint, Secretary of Defense Frank Carlucci canceled the program in February 1988.[12]

In August 1985, to increase the prospects for a comprehensive nuclear test ban agreement, General-Secretary Mikhail Gorbachev announced a moratorium on underground testing.[13] For various reasons President

Reagan opposed a comprehensive test ban (CTB).[14] Although the House of Representatives disagreed and tried to constrain U.S. testing, the Senate affirmed the president's policy and Congress did not block U.S. tests. This time the Soviets were unsuccessful with their initiative, and they resumed testing early in 1987. The issue is not dead, however. In June 1987, for instance, the Massachusetts state legislature passed a resolution calling on the president to agree to a CTB.[15]

The United States has been only reactive in this process. Why not regain the initiative, or at least be an equal player? If U.S. unilateral initiatives can help to change aspects of Soviet defense policy, the United States should use them to increase the prospect that the momentum of arms control serves U.S. as well as Soviet interests. Moreover, if we can take seriously the recent Soviet claim that "the security of some cannot be ensured at the expense of the security of others," U.S. initiatives might encourage such revisions of military doctrine.[16] In the longer term, perhaps the tactic could help create other military, political, and economic conditions conducive to global security and peaceful change.

To use the tactic productively, the United States should understand the conditions under which it is likely to succeed as well as the advantages and disadvantages of using it, and then apply that knowledge as it formulates and implements its policy. This book is intended to help accomplish these tasks.

In this chapter we will define the tactic and describe how it is supposed to work. The historical record, which we will explore in our research, shows that unilateral initiatives succeed only sometimes. Consequently, our major purpose is to contribute to our understanding of the identity and relative importance of the conditions favoring success. We will deduce potentially important conditions in chapter 2, elaborate in chapter 3 on the ones that are influenced by the domestic nature or international situation of the Soviet Union, see which factors appear to be relevant as we conduct our research in chapters 4 through 8, and discuss our principal findings in chapter 9. Then in chapter 10 we will illustrate how this basic knowledge—tentative as it may be—can be applied to predict whether or not a unilateral initiative will succeed, as well as to prescribe when and how to use it successfully.

Let us begin by seeing where unilateral initiatives fit on the map of various methods to further the commonly accepted objectives of arms control (i.e., to make war less likely, to minimize the destructiveness of war should it occur, and to minimize the costs of military preparations). Sometimes a state undertakes actions for purely national purposes. For example, placing missiles on submarines decreases the vulnerability of deterrent forces and thus makes war less likely; forgoing development of "doomsday" devices or cobalt bombs avoids having a force posture that is particularly uncontrollable or unnecessarily destructive; and phasing out obsolete systems or deploying only systems that are cost-effective saves money. Other activities are geared toward reaching agreement with an adversary through a bargaining process. Explicit bargaining involves formal negotiations between states. Tacit bargaining involves one state acting to influence the behavior of another in a direction of mutual, informal restraint. Explicit bargaining emphasizes words; tacit bargaining emphasizes deeds. Unilateral initiatives are used in tacit bargaining, or in a combination of tacit and explicit bargaining.

A unilateral initiative is an action of military restraint undertaken by a government. It is done without prior agreement by the other country to reciprocate that restraint, but the publicly stated purpose is to induce the latter to change its military policy.

There can be other purposes for unilateral initiatives, such as to change economic or political aspects of Soviet policy, or to help reduce Soviet misperceptions of U.S. intentions.[17] In order to do an adequate job of research in this book, however, we will focus only on those whose major publicly stated purpose is to help, in a direct manner, to convince the Soviets to agree to U.S. arms control proposals.

An initiative is part of the unilateral initiative tactic, whereby a state signals to another its intention to control an arms competition and thus to advance basic arms control objectives. In this study U.S. actions are the signals, and they are supposed to influence Soviet policy by demonstrating how U.S. behavior is related to Soviet behavior. The United States hopes to alter Soviet expectations of the consequences of their own actions in order to influence their policy preference; the United States wants them to calculate that current and prospective circumstances favor the Soviet Union agreeing to exercise mutual restraint.

The tactic incorporates a promise to continue U.S. restraint as long as the Soviets exercise comparable restraint. It may or may not include a threat to stop exercising restraint if the Soviets fail to cooperate. If it does, it is a conditional unilateral initiative. If it does not include such a threat, it is an unconditional initiative; the United States would still tell the Soviets it hopes for cooperative behavior, but it would not require that they reciprocate the restraint.

The purpose in using the tactic can be to dissuade a state from beginning or escalating a particular arms competition; to compel it to stop the testing, production, or deployment of a weapon the United States finds against its interests; or to compel it to make another concession that is a precondition for an agreement, such as more intrusive verification.

So far we have set out to explore only situations where a state uses the tactic to encourage cooperative behavior; but a government may have other purposes. The most frequently discussed ulterior motive is to use an initiative as a propaganda ploy. That is, a state might undertake an initiative that, if reciprocated, would result in an agreement causing net harm to the other's security interests. Accusation of this motive can be expected, fairly or unfairly, when the Soviets do not want to comply with U.S. desires. If a country implements such a propaganda initiative, it could hope that its conditional restraint will dispose third countries to exert pressures for reciprocation; alternatively, it might just want to make itself look good and the other look bad.

A state can also abuse the tactic in a manner not discussed by other authors: It could use it to manipulate its own domestic actors. In this case it would implement what I call a "counterfeit" unilateral initiative, one doomed to fail but which serves as a trick to help secure funds for a weapon that otherwise would not be obtainable. Since the United States has not abused the tactic in this manner, we cannot explore the subject in a case study. We will return to the subject in chapter 10, however, and discuss how to detect a counterfeit unilateral initiative.

2

Theory and Method

In this chapter we will construct a theoretical framework to define important concepts and to suggest ideas about the identity and relative importance of the factors favoring successful initiatives. Then we will turn to our method of research, "structured, focused comparison." Since the research entails describing and explaining the pattern of Soviet foreign policy, we must then operationalize our factors from the Soviet perspective; this is a task for chapter 3.

THEORETICAL FRAMEWORK

To explain the outcome of bargaining (the dependent variable), our theoretical framework takes into account several types of causal factors (independent and intervening variables) and their relative importance. This analysis yields eleven obvious factors, eleven potentially relevant factors, and a controversial speculation about the relative importance of the factors. Saving the term "hypothesis" for factors or speculations that are controversial, nonobvious, or obvious but usually overlooked, this analysis produces thirteen hypotheses. The research in chapters 4 through 8 corroborates at least moderately the validity of three of them.

Beginning with an analysis of the bargaining process, we will examine ideas on how a state (state A) can best implement the unilateral initiative tactic in order to influence the behavior of another (state B) in the direction of mutual restraint. As we turn to the international and domestic environment of bargaining, we will first focus on the military, political, and economic factors that may influence state B's calculations. Then we will focus on other factors in the environment of bargaining that may interfere with the rationality of the calculations or otherwise influence policy outcomes. Finally, when considering the relative importance of the conditions, we will examine the major competing views.

As note 10 of chapter 1 illustrates, scholars differ widely in their opinions on the identity and relative importance of the factors. We will take their ideas into account. Because many of the ideas overlap, however, it is unnecessary to repeat all their arguments. Instead we shall examine the obvious and potentially important causal factors organized in the categories listed above.

The Bargaining Process

The ideas of Thomas Schelling, Robert Axelrod, and several others supply us with two obvious factors and six hypotheses on how best to implement the unilateral initiative tactic. Schelling was a pioneer in developing a useful model of bargaining between states.[1] Our definitions of unilateral initiative and unilateral initiative tactic draw from his ideas, as do our first two conditions.[2]

Schelling wants to help us understand the process by which states limit wars and arms races. His model focuses our attention on a bargaining process where state A tries to influence the behavior of state B by creating mutually consistent expectations of the relationship between their behaviors. His emphasis is on examining the influence of A's deeds on B's behavior, as deeds often convey stronger messages about A's commitments than its verbal promises or threats.

For Schelling's model to apply to real-world situations, two initial conditions must be reached: a "bargaining situation" exists (i.e., the ability of one party to gain its ends depends to an important degree on the choices that the other party will make), and the parties must have "mixed motives" (i.e., both conflicting and common interests). He also assumes the parties are rational: Each is a unitary actor whose policy choices are motivated by a cost-benefit analysis.

During bargaining, when A makes a strategic move (i.e., implements the tactic), A intends to show the interdependence of A's and B's policies. Thus A attempts to influence B's calculations about the advantages and disadvantages of B's subsequent response. State A hopes that B's cost-benefit calculus will dispose it to act in their common interest and therefore to agree to limit an arms competition.

Schelling's purpose is heuristic, to highlight how one party can manipulate factors under its control in order to influence the behavior of another party. It suggests optimal performance as a benchmark to compare with actual behavior. He says that if the benchmarks are caricatures of reality and thus do not aid our understanding, the model should either be rejected or incorporated into a broader framework if it then helps us to understand observed behavior.

Convergent expectations on the interdependence of behaviors have requirements on both sides of the communication process. Consequently, from his model we can deduce two obvious factors. First, the more clearly state A communicates the tactic's connection to B's behavior and communicates A's commitment (i.e., intention and ability) to enforce conditional aspects of the tactic, the greater is the prospect that B will make the concession desired by A. Second, success is favored when state B correctly receives and interprets A's signals.

Writing more recently, Axelrod focuses on unilateral initiatives more than does Schelling, uses not only game theory but also simulation, and adds future and past time dimensions to our analysis.[3] Without going into all the intricacies of game theory and explaining—for instance, how the "prisoners' dilemma" game operates—we can summarize his basic ideas and deduce several hypotheses.

Axelrod explores the evolution of cooperation in mixed motive situations. He argues that to elicit cooperative behavior from others, the best strategy (i.e., specification of what to do in any situation) is reciprocity. State A should begin with a cooperative act (a unilateral initiative in our case), and then respond to B's reaction in a "tit-for-tat" (TFT) manner. TFT requires state A to respond to B's cooperation with another cooperative action, and to respond to B's uncooperative reaction ("defection" in game theory terms) with a matching defection. Thus he emphasizes conditional over unconditional unilateral initiatives, and he agrees with Schelling's emphasis on clear signaling.

In discussing two additional requirements for success, Axelrod highlights the periods after and before a bargaining interaction. First, the "shadow of the future" must be sufficiently large. This means that the benefits of subsequent cooperation must be more important than the short-term risks of cooperation or benefits of defection.[4]

State A can attempt to enlarge the shadow of the future for state B. First, the TFT strategy establishes a direct connection between present behavior and expected future consequences. Second, state A can disaggregate its restraint into many small stages.[5] This could involve a series of conditional unilateral initiatives, where A lets B know that B's reciprocation is a prerequisite for A to implement additional initiatives. Such a behavioral modification technique would tend to make B feel that subsequent interactions would come sooner than otherwise, and consequently the next move should loom larger in B's calculations. It would also contribute to A's reputation for following the TFT strategy. This reasoning leads to our first hypothesis.

Hypothesis 1. A series of conditional unilateral initiatives is more likely to succeed than an isolated initiative.

Axelrod's other requirement for success is that the parties should be able to recognize the history of their previous interactions, so that they have the same understanding of when the last moves occurred, who cooperated and who defected, and how much was at stake. Without this understanding, state A might implement an initiative that it views as a sacrifice deserving of B's reciprocation, but which B views differently. B might, for instance, interpret A's move as penitence reflecting guilt for a past defection, or as a gesture resulting from A's weakness; neither interpretation would dispose B to reciprocate.

Steven Van Evera argues that such misinterpretations are the usual outcome of a tactic involving a concession as the first move.[6] If he is right, then a successful unilateral initiative would require state A to go to great lengths to overcome the propensity. Consequently he urges that not only should state A accompany its initiative with an elaborate analysis that includes an objective history of the antagonism and bargaining interactions, but it should also describe where the tactic fits into this vision of history and the national strategy, explain why A's expectations for B's reciprocation are legitimate, and clearly say how and why A will not permit B to exploit A's initiative. Finally, to increase the prospect that B will receive the signals and take them seriously, he says that A should repeat the messages frequently, consistently, and in a variety of forums. Although it seems obvious that success is favored when these efforts accompany an initiative, Van Evera claims that this factor is usually and unfortunately overlooked. Consequently, let us highlight the historical factor as an hypothesis:

> *Hypothesis 2:* Success is favored when the parties have the same understanding of the history of previous bargaining interactions. Such a mutual understanding (and success) is more likely than otherwise to occur when state A accompanies its initiative with an objective analysis that relates its bargaining tactic to the previous history.

Axelrod adds that state A can orchestrate its bargaining moves to aid the formation of a common understanding of the history of interactions, especially those in the recent past. Its task is to act so that B can distinguish A's action or reaction as cooperative, as an appropriate defection, or as an exaggerated and threatening defection.

If state B does not reciprocate a conditional unilateral initiative, state A must match B's uncooperative behavior to affirm its reputation for following its strategy. In doing so it must decide when and how strongly to respond. These issues lead to hypotheses 3 through 5, which should be particularly applicable in situations where state A implements or intends to implement more than one initiative.

Axelrod says that state A should respond quickly in order to send the right signal. In particular, since B may act in ways that appear to probe the limits of a formal or tacit agreement, the sooner A responds the better. Waiting for unpunished defections to accumulate risks a need for a larger response, which could lead to more trouble.[7] Since others call for patience in the timing of matching defections, this hypothesis is controversial.[8]

> Hypothesis 3. Success is favored when state A quickly matches B's defection than when A is slow to respond.

Axelrod is also concerned about an "echo effect," where B defects and then overreacts to A's subsequent response and reciprocal escalatory behavior results. To dampen this effect and still provide an incentive for B to cooperate, he advises that A respond to B's defection in a limited manner—such as by matching B's defection with only nine-tenths of a defection.[9] Since others might argue that B is more likely to reciprocate when it knew that its defection would lead A to respond in an exaggerated, harmful manner, we can treat Axelrod's idea as an hypothesis:

> Hypothesis 4. Success is favored when A responds to B's defection slightly less than proportionately.

Robert Jervis, writing in a similar tradition, brings in a qualitative dimension to this discussion. He suggests that cooperation is more likely to evolve when states protect their security with defensive measures—ones that provide a state with security but that do not threaten an adversary's security.[10] When this is done, escalatory spirals arising out of insecurity are less likely to occur than otherwise.

Therefore, success is favored when state A responds to B's defection in a way that protects A's security but does not threaten B's security. This conclusion is controversial, however, as some authors claim that state A gains bargaining leverage when B expects that its uncooperative behavior will lead A to act in ways that decrease B's security.[11]

> Hypothesis 5. Success is favored if state A responds to B's defection defensively rather than in an offensive manner that decreases B's security.

Axelrod does not directly deal with problems posed by complex and ambiguous force postures. For example, state A may exercise restraint in the testing and deployment of a certain weapon, but B may see the move as strategically insignificant. Or state A may simultaneously improve other parts of its force posture, leading *B* to conclude that *A*'s overall behavior reflects defection.

Three coauthors writing in an issue of *World Politics* devoted to exploring game theory mention this problem: George Downs, David Rocke, and Randolph Siverson.[12] They conclude that when complex force postures are involved, formal negotiations are more likely to succeed in reaching an agreement than tacit bargaining, because negotiations can set up a package of trade-offs that takes into account different valuations of weapons. A corollary of this argument is that success is favored when force postures are relatively simple and when the unilateral initiative involves only one type of weapon. This proposition is consistent with Schelling's claim that when bargaining involves issues in the "same currency," success is favored because the interdependence between *A*'s and *B*'s behaviors is obvious.[13] Following this general logic we can infer a less obvious correlation: when the issue is not salient, the unilateral initiative tactic is more likely to succeed when implemented as a campaign approach (i.e., simultaneous restraint in several categories of weapons).

> *Hypothesis 6.* When the significance of a unilateral initiative is ambiguous, it is more likely to succeed when implemented along with other initiatives than when it is implemented alone.

These game-theoretic ideas suggest aspects of the bargaining process that may be important in explaining the outcome of bargaining. They do not, however, direct our attention to important domestic and international constraints on the bargaining process—constraints that may lead to outcomes different than these ideas lead us to expect.[14]

A state's policy-making process is complex. Ideology, previous experiences, organizational procedures, bureaucratic politics, and other domestic factors influence policy choices to varying degrees.[15] These factors constitute the domestic environment of statesmen involved in international bargaining.

Game-theoretic models also underplay external factors that may affect bargaining outcomes, such as the relative interests at risk in political and military conflicts, the distribution of power in the international system, and the stability of the strategic environment.[16] Furthermore, a state's military doctrine influences how it interprets these circumstances.

The weaknesses of bargaining and game theory are not so great that we should reject the ideas. Rather, they are more likely to be useful if we incorporate them into a broader framework that takes into account the importance of both the bargaining process and its environment. Let us now turn to the environmental factors, beginning with those that are the subject of rational cost-benefit calculations.

State *B*'s Cost-Benefit Calculations

We can expect *B* to reciprocate *A*'s unilateral initiative if *B* calculates that it has more to gain than lose; that is, compared to nonagreement, the proposed agreement promises net military, political, and economic advantages.

Let us begin by considering the direct security consequences of an agreement. Obviously, states tend not to do things that they think will undermine their security. Our analysis is complicated, however, because security means different things to different people, depending on what conceptual framework guides their thinking. In chapter 3 we will operationalize what security means to the Soviet Union. Until then, we can generalize that *A*'s initiative is likely to succeed only if *B* calculates that its reciprocation would enhance its military capabilities or would help to prevent the degradation of these capabilities. Success is also possible if the security consequences are minimal or ambiguous.

State *B* must also take into account the impact of its bargaining behavior on its military relationship with third countries. If a proposed agreement would help to prevent third countries from reaching *B*'s level of power (i.e., if it would strengthen "barriers to entry" at *B*'s level of capability), or if it would decrease or at least would not increase the military threat posed by a third country, then *B* is more likely than otherwise to reciprocate.

When adversaries are parties to an agreement that affects their military capabilities, they obviously want to be able to verify that the other side is not cheating and gaining a unilateral advantage. State *B*'s preference between "national technical means" and "on-site inspection" to verify compliance probably varies from country to country and with particular circumstances. Once again, we must wait until chapter 3 before we can become more specific about Soviet propensities.

State *B*'s ability to achieve its foreign policy objectives is affected not only by relative military capabilities, but also by the nature of relations with and among other countries. Thus *B* has interests in minimizing hostilities from third countries, as well as in minimizing the cohesion of political-military relations among its adversaries and maximizing the cohesion of its own alliance network.[17] Its response to *A*'s unilateral initiatives can influence these political relations. Thus we can generalize that the more a proposed agreement would enhance state *B*'s political ties with third countries or undermine political relations among its adversaries, the greater is the prospect that *A*'s unilateral initiative will succeed.

Prestige is another aspect of political calculations. This should be obvious, since great powers tend to care about their reputation for power and resolve. This concern for prestige is affirmed when an agreement embodies norms of reciprocity and equal status.[18] Consequently, the more a proposed agreement affirms state B's prestige, the more success is favored.

State B also has economic interests, with both domestic and international aspects. Obviously, the more money a proposed agreement could save state B, the greater is the prospect of success. Likewise, if B expects significant economic benefits from improved relations with A or A's allies, and if B thinks that an arms control agreement would enhance these economic relations, then the initiative's success is favored.

Other Environmental Factors

The above cost-benefit calculations assume that state B acts and reacts like a unitary, rational actor concerned with surviving and thriving in an anarchic international environment. However, some authors posit that certain domestic and international situations interfere with the rationality of B's calculations or otherwise influence its decisions. Let us begin by examining potentially important domestic factors: psychological proclivities of leaders, organizational procedures and bureaucratic politics, succession politics, and the balance of political forces.

Joseph de Rivera and John Steinbruner discuss psychological factors that inhibit "rational" foreign policy making.[19] For instance, a person's assumptions and beliefs about the world affect the content of his or her perceptions. In particular, a person's worldview tends to limit what is seen to what the person expects to see, and it influences the significance given to what is perceived—unless the person is exposed to and listens carefully to inputs that counter previous beliefs. In addition, the number of policy options a person considers and the quality of evaluations of the options are constrained by factors that inhibit creative insight, such as the general climate of opinion, the person's worldview and biases, the experience of stress, "noise" that might interfere with the proper analysis of information, the time available, and tendencies of a decision-making group to reject ideas and advocates of ideas that go against the opinion of most group members. Finally, after a policy has been formulated and implemented, similar pressures inhibit searching for feedback to test the desirability and practicality of the policy.

These psychological propensities may influence the course of bargaining in several ways. First, they could influence state B's ability to perceive and interpret A's signals correctly. Second, they may gain in importance during times of stress, such as during a crisis or other period of high international tension. Then again, perhaps the clear dangers associated with a crisis would tend to refocus one's attention on important factors previously ignored. Since we will not be discussing the potential impact of international tension until later in this chapter, let us postpone formulating an hypothesis on that topic.

Deborah Larson writes in the psychological tradition.[20] Drawing on Charles Osgood's ideas and her own research on the Soviet strategy to elicit U.S. cooperation in creating a neutralized Austria, she suggests that overcoming cognitive impediments to reciprocity may require a more elaborate bargaining strategy than the simple behavioral modification technique of reciprocity. State A should accompany its initiatives with a clear public elaboration of its intentions; diversify the initiatives; carry out a sequence of initiatives on schedule even if B does not reciprocate; and implement at least one initiative that involves a noticeable sacrifice of threatening capabilities. This approach may help to shatter a stereotype held by B's leaders that A is hostile and untrustworthy. To guard against exploitation by B, A should hold other series of initiatives in reserve as rewards if B begins to reciprocate.

We have already covered many of these ideas in our previous discussion. What is new is that state A may want to continue to implement additional initiatives despite no reciprocation by B. This idea adds a temporal dimension to hypothesis 6, which had simply said that success is favored in complex situations when an initiative is implemented along with other initiatives. A variation on this hypothesis, then, is that success is favored when A's campaign of initiatives is not completed all at once. To avoid redundancy, the testing of hypothesis 6 will include an evaluation of this variation.

Research by Graham Allison and Frederic Morris shows that as a weapon progresses along the weapons procurement process, it tends to accumulate an organizational constituency that favors its retention.[21] This suggests that the farther along the weapon is toward deployment, and especially if it is deployed extensively, the more difficulty state B's political leaders will have giving it up. The military, to protect its organizational interests (i.e., budget and missions), will tend to argue against giving up the weapon simply to reciprocate A's unilateral initiative.

Robert Art's and Stephen Ockenden's study of the U.S. cruise missile suggests we qualify Allison's conclusion.[22] The authors note that even though the cruise missile promised to be cost-effective at accomplishing key military missions and its development proceeded, major groups in the military resisted its deployment. They feared it would interfere with the tradition of using manned bombers to accomplish missions. The military finally accepted cruise missiles when political pressures from central authorities became sufficiently strong.

Combining their studies, we can expect that the level of bureaucratic support for a weapon is high when (1) it is widely deployed, and forgoing it would not result in acquiring a similar, substitute system; (2) it is or promises to be effective at fulfilling traditional missions; (3) the military services agree the weapon is valuable; and especially if several of these conditions apply. Consequently, the less B's military services value a weapon that is a target of A's unilateral initiative, the greater is the prospect of success.

Gerald Steinberg, recognizing the importance of institutional actors, makes the controversial argument that the nature of the international bargaining process is the key factor in determining the outcome of bargaining.[23] Formal negotiations, he claims, require extensive intraparty negotiations and thus are time consuming and inflexible internationally. Informal negotiations, in contrast, can be done with much less domestic negotiation and compromise, and they tend to minimize bureaucratic pressures to retain weapons. Consequently, with the added flexibility accompanying informal negotiations, a chief executive can make sensible compromises even if they hurt bureaucratic interests. The speedier process also helps to control weapons undergoing technological changes that might increase the weapon's bureaucratic momentum.

Steinberg adds that informal international bargaining, involving tacit bargaining and verbal communication through high-level but personal channels, also helps avoid a problem associated with prestige. He says that in prolonged negotiations, reputation for resolve is more important than otherwise, and consequently the parties tend to fear that making a concession is a sign of weakness. Thus in formal negotiations, states have a greater reluctance to make incremental concessions than in informal negotiations. Furthermore, the ambiguity associated with informal bargaining helps to avoid the problem of retracting a "trial balloon" that was rejected by the other side.[24] Steinberg's analysis is not unchallenged: Some argue that formal negotiations are sometimes necessary to conclude an agreement when complex force postures are involved.[25]

Since we are concerned with situations involving unilateral initiatives, where state A explicitly tells B what sort of reciprocation it wants, the remaining variable is whether the verbal communication takes place in simultaneous formal negotiations, through informal communication (e.g., "back channel" negotiations), or a combination. Steinberg's analysis thus leads to another hypothesis:

> Hypothesis 7. A unilateral initiative is more likely to succeed when accompanying verbal communication is conducted informally rather than formally.

Art's criticism of Allison emphasizes the strength of the chief executive relative to the bureaucracy.[26] But what if the chief executive's authority is weak or vulnerable to challenge? It is well known that U.S. presidents sometimes support a military buildup for domestic political reasons such as to gain the support of the electorate or Congress.[27] Under conditions like these, we would not expect the president to make controversial concessions to the Soviets. A similar phenomenon may occur in the Soviet

Union. Since we have not yet examined Soviet politics, let us state the premise as an hypothesis:

> *Hypothesis 8.* If A's unilateral initiative requires a controversial concession, then success is favored when the authority of B's chief executive is secure.

A related, dynamic aspect of policy making is not highlighted by the bargaining model: A's bargaining tactic may influence the balance of political forces within B's policy-making structure, strengthening the arguments of one faction and weakening others. This factor would be particularly important when the concession demanded was controversial, when the chief executive's tenure was under challenge, and when the tactic supported his or her arguments for arms control. This image of domestic politics presumes some degree of political pluralism, which may not be present in all countries. Consequently, let us state it as an hypothesis:

> *Hypothesis 9.* The more A's tactic strengthens the arguments of political leaders in B who support arms control, the greater is the prospect of success.

Now let us turn to three factors in the international environment of bargaining that may affect the rationality or context of state B's decisions: the level of international tension, the stability of the strategic environment, and the system's polarity.

Most scholars agree that arms racing is both a cause and a consequence of political conflicts and tensions, although they often disagree on the emphasis. Charles Osgood's analysis represents the extreme view where the level of tension and correlated social-psychological factors are much more important than the on-going political situation.[28] His critics tend to reverse the priority.[29] If Osgood is right, however, and the level of tension is correlated with the intensity of arms racing, then during periods of low tension we would expect more arms collaboration than during periods of high tension.

The reasoning propounded in the psychological literature discussed above may support the same conclusions. That is, when stress is intensified, such as during periods of high tension, suspicions and biases are expected to assume more influence in decision making than otherwise. Thus in a hostile environment, with a lower level of trust, it should be difficult to recognize cooperative acts and to reach agreements.

The psychological thesis does not suggest that misperceptions cannot occur when tensions are low. It simply implies that misperceptions and miscalculations tend to occur more often during periods of high tension and that this tendency reduces the prospect that an initiative will succeed. In effect, the level of tension is alleged to act as an intervening variable between psychological tendencies and the outcome of bargaining.

This analysis leads us to expect that an agreement would be unlikely when *B* perceives the level of tension to be high. Since not all scholars agree with the premise, we can formulate an hypothesis:

> *Hypothesis 10:* The lower state *B* perceives the level of international tension, the greater is the prospect that *A*'s unilateral initiative will succeed.

Another potentially important factor is the stability of the strategic environment. Robert Jervis argues that in an anarchic, self-help international system, cooperation is more likely to emerge between states when each acts to protect its security in ways that do not threaten the other. Also, they are more likely to act this way in a "stable" strategic environment, which has two criteria: The defense (i.e., a force posture to preserve the status quo) has the advantage over the offense, and defensive weapons and actions are distinguishable from offensive ones.[30] Steven Van Evera adds that in a situation dominated by what he calls "the cult of the offensive," states are likely to have misperceptions that undermine conditions favoring the evolution of cooperation.[31]

The "defensive advantage" criterion corresponds to "crisis stability"—a situation where even during a confrontation the parties have no military incentive to attack first, because it is obvious that neither has the capability to accomplish war aims at costs acceptable to itself. The converse situation is one in which the side that strikes first wins. In it, Axelrod's so-called shadow of the future would be short, because the parties would tend to calculate that the short-term advantages of defection and disadvantages of unreciprocated or asymmetrical cooperation are high relative to the long-term benefits of cooperation. This circumstance does not favor arms control concessions.

The second criterion is relevant because the weapons a state procures are an indicator of its intentions. If offensive and defensive weapons are indistinguishable, then compared to a situation where weapons are distinguishable, even a status quo state would have difficulty signaling defensive intentions. If a state procures offensive weapons when defensive ones are available, then the other state would tend to assume the state had offensive intentions and therefore cooperation would be less likely to emerge.

In adversarial relationships, where the parties frequently use "worst-case analysis" to estimate each other's central capabilities and hence to guide their weapons procurement policies, the more important of the two criteria is assumed to be "defensive advantage" because it emphasizes capabilities.

Whether defense literally refers to weapons and strategies utilizing forces in the classic protective sense, or to concepts such as mutual deterrence, depends on specific circumstances that need not concern us until we look at the particulars of Soviet and U.S. forces in chapter 3.

In summary, a stable strategic environment favors the success of a unilateral initiative. Moreover, these authors argue that if B defects in a stable strategic environment, A is more likely to respond defensively, B is more likely to interpret this response as defensive, and thus an "echo effect" of escalating defections is less likely to occur.

This factor may affect the level of political tension between countries, but the evidence suggests it also has some independent importance. For instance, political tensions between Germany and Britain declined after the 1911 Agadir crisis, but many problems associated with an unstable strategic environment persisted.[32]

As is the case with the hypothesis about international tensions, what counts is state B's perception of the strategic environment. This is more important and practical than trying to determine what both A and B perceive; this latter approach focuses on the relationship aspect of stability. Our focus is only on B's perceptions, which is sufficient for our purpose of explaining Soviet foreign policy. Not all agree with the premise that the strategic environment matters. Some might even argue that the more threatening B perceives the environment to be, the more incentive it will have to cooperate.[33] Hence we will treat the idea as an hypothesis:

Hypothesis 11. The success of a unilateral initiative is favored when B perceives an acceptable stable strategic environment (i.e., one in which an attack by A is unlikely to defeat B at costs acceptable to A, even if A attacks first). Secondarily, success is favored if B can easily differentiate defensive and offensive weapons, and A is procuring only defensive weapons.

The final potentially important factor that may affect the outcome of bargaining is the polarity of the international system. Kenneth Waltz forwards this argument as he explains variations in state behavior that correspond to a change within the anarchic system (i.e., to a fundamental shift in the distribution of capabilities, which involves an interchange between a multipolar and a bipolar world). Taking the distribution of power into account helps to explain different patterns of balancing behavior.[34]

Both bipolar and multipolar structures involve interdependent decision making, but Waltz expects some differences in outcomes in each. For instance, from the systemic perspective, he expects that if two great powers have a direct common interest in mutual arms limitations, they are more likely to reach an agreement in a bipolar world than in a multipolar world.

In a bipolar world they would be superpowers, where each was the other's main security threat; consequently, they do not need to be as concerned about restraint by lesser powers. In a multipolar world, in contrast, if a third party is also a great power, it could threaten A's or B's security if it did not exercise restraint. Therefore, an agreement in a multipolar world would more often have to involve more than the two parties; with more than two states in negotiations, with more conflicting interests, agreement would be less likely, even between the two wanting an agreement. Taking bargaining into account, we can state the idea as a nonobvious hypothesis.

> *Hypothesis 12:* If two great powers have direct common interests in limiting part of their arms competition, and if the international system is bipolar, then a unilateral initiative that focuses on those weapons is more likely to succeed than when the system is multipolar.

Relative Importance of Causes

The above discussion suggests a number of factors that may influence the outcome of bargaining. Which factors are most important? Does their weight vary with circumstances? If so, what circumstances? I have said it is obvious that states tend not to do things they think will harm their security. Let me take this idea a step further: When security is clearly at risk, then a state will tend to choose a policy that protects its security—despite the presence of other factors that dispose it to choose differently. The other factors may influence the timing of B's choice or details of its implementation, but security calculations will tend to determine the general thrust of the policy. This argument raises several questions: What is the linkage between the rational actor image and complex policy making within B? Isn't the important factor what the dominant coalition thinks it is? This confusion arises because we are talking about two different levels of abstraction.

The rational actor formulation is useful because it suggests what the outcome of domestic bargaining will be when the security consequences are salient. It suggests little, however, when security consequences are minimal or are ambiguous. Under this latter condition, we can expect other factors to assume more importance. For example, if an agreement served principally to reduce the economic or environmental costs of an arms race, and it had little effect on continued quantitative or qualitative improvements in force postures, then domestic interests and secondary national interests would tend to be more important than otherwise in B's calculations. This argument is consistent with conclusions of balance of power theory, as well as with other systemic research into bargaining.[35]

Not all scholars agree that security calculations are most important. For instance Allison and Morris, when discussing bureaucratic politics, say that although "actions of foreign governments and uncertainty about the intentions of other countries are obviously important, the . . . weapons in the American and Soviet force postures are predominantly the result of factors internal to each nation."[36] Steinberg would agree, although he emphasizes the intervening variable of the degree of formality of the negotiating process.[37] Others emphasize different factors: signaling (Schelling and Axelrod), the strategic environment (Jervis and Van Evera), psychological propensities and the level of international tension (Osgood), and the balance between common and conflicting political interests (Osgood's critics). Since the issue is controversial, let us state it as an hypothesis that highlights the importance of security:

> *Hypothesis 13.* If A's tactic clearly influences B's security calculations, then B will tend to make the concession or not make it, depending on which reaction will give B the greatest security—despite the presence of contrary factors.

Summary

In searching for conditions that might favor successful unilateral initiatives, we found twelve hypotheses (i.e., factors that are controversial, nonobvious, or obvious but usually ignored), ten obvious factors, and a final hypothesis about the relative importance of the various factors. Table 2.1 lists and categorizes the potentially important conditions.

METHOD OF TESTING HYPOTHESES: STRUCTURED, FOCUSED COMPARISON

Before proceeding with our research, we must answer a key question of method: what sort of research best serves to test the hypotheses? I used the method of "structured, focused comparison."[38] In all my historical case studies, I asked the same questions and tested the same hypotheses. This method is more reliable than using game experiments to conduct research on the unilateral initiative tactic.[39]

The tactic has been used a number of times during the nineteenth and twentieth centuries.[40] Given a wish to do an adequate job of research within the constraints of a page limit, as well as a desire to provide basic and applied knowledge to American analysts as they ponder ways to control the U.S.-Soviet arms race, I prefer cases that meet the following criteria:

1. A U.S. unilateral initiative is directed at the Soviet Union.
2. The proposed agreement involves a weapon or a component of a weapon that is directly related to the U.S.-Soviet balance of power.[41]

Table 2.1
Factors Favoring Successful Unilateral Initiatives

1.	A sends clear signals, and bargaining is in the "same currency"	Obvious
2.	B receives and interprets signals correctly	Obvious
3.	A implements a series of initiatives	Hypothesis
4.	A accompanies its initiative with a history of bargaining interactions	Hypothesis
5.	When B defects, A responds quickly	Hypothesis
6.	When B defects, A responds moderately	Hypothesis
7.	When B defects, A responds defensively	Hypothesis
8.	In a complex military situation, A implements a campaign of initiatives	Hypothesis
9.	Security is enhanced or at least is unharmed	Obvious
10.	Security vis-a-vis third countries is enhanced	Obvious
11.	Verification means are acceptable	Obvious
12.	Alliance picture is improved	Obvious
13.	Prestige is affirmed	Obvious
14.	Money is saved	Obvious
15.	International economic benefits	Obvious
16.	B's military services are not upset	Obvious
17.	Verbal communication is informal	Hypothesis
18.	If proposal is controversial, B's chief executive is secure in his authority	Hypothesis
19.	Initiative strengthens pro-arms controllers	Hypothesis
20.	B perceives low international tensions	Hypothesis
21.	B perceives acceptable strategic environment and can differentiate A's weapons	Hypothesis
22.	Both want arms limitations, and the international system is bipolar	Hypothesis

3. The United States told the Soviets what sort of reciprocation or other concession it desired.[42]
4. The outcome of bargaining is clear.[43]

Five cases involving six separate initiatives meet these criteria: (1) restraint on placing weapons of mass destruction into orbit (1962–63); (2) restraints in testing nuclear weapons (January and June 1963); (3) deactivation and destruction of B-47 bombers (1964–65); (4) restraint on spending funds to begin to produce and deploy an antiballistic missile (ABM) system (1967–68); and (5) deferral of neutron bomb production (1978).

Each of these case studies constitutes a chapter of research. The easy part is describing the sequence of bargaining interactions. Because of three problems, however, the more lengthy and difficult part of each chapter is explaining Soviet reactions to U.S. unilateral initiatives. First, fewer records tend to exist for tacit bargaining than formal negotiations, and several of the cases involve little formal negotiation.

Second, our knowledge of policy making in the Soviet Union is limited. Few primary sources exist that give us reliable insight into Politburo deliberations, so my analysis of Soviet intentions uses a substantial amount of secondary sources, indirect evidence, and inferential logic.

Third, statements by Soviets often have a propaganda purpose. For instance, in attempting to understand Soviet security calculations, we should approach with caution the official pronouncements on military doctrine and policy. As we will see in chapter 3, the pronouncements concern the political aspect of doctrine. It has, among other purposes, an internal and external propaganda role. Doctrine also has a military-technical side, and this literature is written primarily by military people for military people and does not have a propaganda function. If the two aspects conflict, the political side is supposed to predominate. But then again, it is sometimes difficult to know how much of the political statements are propaganda. Finally, the memoirs of the defector Arkady Shevchenko are probably more reliable for explaining past Soviet policies than official sources.[44]

The most reliable indicator of Soviet intentions is the pattern of their international conduct. Thus I seek information about their diplomatic behavior, weapons procurement and arms control policies, and military operations and training.

Given our restricted knowledge about Soviet policy making and the limited number of case studies, my degree of certainty is not as high as otherwise. My aim is modest, however: I want to offer a plausible, convincing analysis, one based on a sound theoretical framework and supported by systematic historical research.

3

Soviet Foreign Policy

In chapter 2 we deduced twenty-two factors that may be important in accounting for the pattern of Soviet behavior. They were derived from theories and models of international relations and foreign policy, none of which was tailored to the Soviet Union as an international actor. Consequently, before we proceed with our case studies, we must first operationalize the twelve factors that are influenced by the nature or situation of the state engaging in bargaining. Seven concern Soviet calculations about military relations with the United States and third countries, as well as verification, political relations, prestige, and domestic and international economic benefits. Three focus on the domestic environment of bargaining: bureaucratic interests, succession politics, and the balance of domestic political forces. The last two are in the international environment of bargaining, but their impact is mediated by the perceptions of Soviet leaders: the level of international tension and the stability of the strategic environment.

Before examining these factors, we should briefly state the major determinants of Soviet foreign policy. As any great power in the anarchic international state system, Soviet behavior is influenced by its vital interests of military security, geographical integration, political sovereignty, and regime survival. It also has secondary, medium-range national interests: prestige, extension of influence, and economic betterment.[1] Many of these interests affect Soviet responses to unilateral initiatives in ways that we will discuss later in this chapter.

The principal internal determinants of Soviet foreign policy emphasize the "Soviet" nature of that policy: ideology and domestic politics. Ideology has four functions that influence foreign policy in different ways.[2]

One function is "analytic," where ideology serves as a conceptual framework for viewing the world. It highlights what is important (e.g., economic structures of states) and suggests what causes what (e.g., class conflict moves history, capitalist states cause imperialism and war, and socialist states are peace-loving). As long as class struggle exists (i.e., until all states are socialist), conflict—but not necessarily confrontation—is assumed to be normal and, in the long run, progressive. During the Khrushchev and Brezhnev eras, for instance, this latter assumption influenced the Soviet interpretation of "normal" relations with the West and hence their perception of the level of international tension. Revisions in ideology would, of course, affect the corresponding worldview.

The analytic function of ideology influences how the Soviets view their cost-benefit calculations about arms control concessions. That is, their policy is greatly influenced by their perception of the "correlation of forces," the relative military, political, and economic strength of the "progressive forces of history." The concept indicates the key trends in international relations, which in the long term are expected to favor the forces of socialism. It also suggests constraints and opportunities for Soviet policy.[3]

A second function of ideology is pragmatic, to guide policy. Thus we expect the Soviets to attempt to preserve and spread socialism, although their preferred means may vary with the prevailing ideological line and particular circumstances. Ideological tenets also influence Soviet domestic political structures and processes; we will explore this later when we examine the domestic environment of bargaining.

Third, ideology has a "utopian" function, where it suggests basic values (e.g., an emphasis on equality over liberty) and long-term goals (e.g., a classless society or world revolution).

Finally, ideology has a propaganda function, whereby it can be used to justify actions taken for other reasons or to justify sacrifices the population must make. It is also a major basis of the regime's legitimacy.[4]

Ideology and national interests may sometimes conflict. As guides to policy, for example, if they suggest incompatible prescriptions, national interest calculations tend to predominate when Soviet military security is clearly at risk.[5] Many times they do not conflict, however. For example, preserving socialism in the Soviet Union complements the vital interest of protecting Soviet borders. We are also looking at different time-lines, where the utopian goal of world revolution may remain operational but in the long-term background of short- and medium-term planning.

Likewise, the worldviews suggested by national interest thinking and ideology can conflict. For instance, the Soviets may be so suspicious of a capitalist state that they might not recognize a cooperative gesture. Thus ideology may sometimes dispose the Soviets to misinterpret benign U.S. intentions as hostile when the United States implements a unilateral initiative.

The remaining domestic factors that influence Soviet foreign policy are the interests of Soviet military services, succession politics, and the identities and relative importance of the political actors involved in foreign policy decision making. We will discuss them in depth later because they directly bear on Soviet arms control bargaining behavior. Now let us elaborate upon the factors in the environment of bargaining that influence Soviet behavior, beginning with their cost-benefit calculations.

SOVIET CALCULATIONS ABOUT THE CORRELATION OF FORCES

The Soviets should reciprocate a U.S. unilateral initiative if they expect a net gain. The correlation of forces framework suggests that they will accept a proposed agreement only if it promises net military, political, and economic advantages, or at least no net disadvantages.

Military Security

The Soviet conception of security is most heavily influenced by their military doctrine.[6] As Defense Minister A. A. Grechko said in 1975, doctrine "is a system of views on the nature of war and methods of waging it, and on the preparation of the country and army for war, officially adopted in a given state and in its armed forces."[7] The evidence suggests that it provides guideposts for the formation of strategy and the development of weapon systems. For example, we find a high correlation between preferred weapons capabilities described in 1962 and the force posture a decade later—when weapons designed in 1962 that proved capable of accomplishing their missions finally would have entered into the operational inventory.[8] Consequently doctrine can help us understand under what conditions the Soviets would be willing to forgo what type of weapon. Since aspects of doctrine have changed over time, let us begin with the 1960s.

First Secretary Nikita Khrushchev presented the modern doctrine in January 1960. Before then, the "revolution in military affairs" (i.e., breakthroughs in nuclear weapons and ballistic missiles) was not a part of Soviet doctrine.[9] Minister of Defense R. Y. Malinovskiy summarized the doctrine in 1961: Any world war would be started by the imperialists, and it would inevitably take the form of a devastating nuclear war where ballistic missiles were the decisive weapon. The key task of the armed forces is to be ready to repulse the surprise attack. The objects of Soviet nuclear strikes would be everything that feeds war, such as military forces, industrial centers, and communications junctions. If war broke out, the socialist camp would win and capitalism would be destroyed forever.[10]

The next year Malinovskiy elaborated further by saying doctrine has two sides, the political and the military-technical.[11] The political side concerns the avoidance of world war, which he and Khrushchev said was possible since the Soviet Union had forces so formidable that the imperialists would not dare unleash aggression. War is to be prevented by a foreign policy designed to reduce the risks of war, backed by military forces capable of dissuading potential aggressors from attacking. Finally, a decision to initiate nuclear war would be made only by the political leadership.

The military-technical side of doctrine concerns military operations should war occur. In that circumstance, the purposes of the armed forces are to limit damage to the Soviet Union and its allies and to attempt to win the war. In this light, the Soviets apparently saw no trade-off between preventing nuclear war and fighting to win the war.

Several revisions occurred in the mid- to late 1960s. First, a war with the imperialists might not involve nuclear weapons. Original formulations considered escalation from conventional to intercontinental nuclear war "inevitable." As early as 1965, however, some Soviets began to posit that it was possible (although unlikely) that a major war might remain limited.[12] An implication was greater attention to nonnuclear forces, particularly in the European theater. Thus the second change was a more balanced development of the armed forces, instead of Khrushchev's emphasis on nuclear-armed rockets.[13] In the early 1970s this shift extended to improve Soviet power-projection capabilities, which complemented their global power role.[14] Third, the Soviets changed their expectation of how nuclear war might begin.[15] Through the mid-1960s, they apparently thought the most probable path to nuclear war would be a U.S. "bolt from the blue," with no strategic or tactical warning. The former type of warning provides evidence that the United States is preparing to attack, and the latter indicates that the attack is under way. After the mid-1960s they apparently thought that the most likely path would be U.S. first-use or planned first-use, which might occur during a conventional war or crisis war that would provide strategic warning. Thus Soviet forces would be able to move to a more survivable, "generated alert" status and, if necessary, preempt the U.S. attack.

Beginning in 1977, doctrinal statements stopped calling for Soviet strategic superiority.[16] Related changes were explicit rejections by political leaders of "first-use" and "preemption" policies. Apparently the military was unhappy with these shifts but did not publicly contradict them.[17]

Within the Soviet Union controversy continues to surround several questions: What is the likelihood that a nuclear or nonnuclear theater war will escalate to global war? Would a nuclear war be short or protracted? Is victory possible?[18] The question of victory is particularly important to us, because the answer will influence Soviet weapons procurement and arms control policies. Military writers take the position that even in the nuclear age socialist victory is possible. Beginning in 1976, however, political spokespersons began to emphasize the opposite. By late 1981, all statements by political leaders denied the possibility of victory. Military writers may have subsequently toned down direct appeals for a strategy of victory, but they have not rejected it and they continue to call for warfighting capabilities.[19]

Soviet spokespersons in 1987 talked about a "new foreign policy philosophy" that takes into account not only conflicting interests between socialism and capitalism but also their "interdependence." Hence "the security of some cannot be ensured at the expense of the security of others." Furthermore, without neglecting its defense capability, "the Soviet Union is bringing to the fore political means of ensuring its security" (e.g., arms reduction agreements, confidence-building measures, and avoiding confrontations). Finally, "sufficiency" is now a part of military doctrine. Consequently, although the Soviet Union will retain the means to rebuff any aggressor, it may engage in nonsymmetrical responses to "destabilizing" U.S. deployments or, when appropriate, asymmetrical force reductions.[20]

Despite our knowledge of what the Soviets say about their doctrine, Western analysts disagree over how seriously to take their statements. We will focus on an aspect of this controversy that seems particularly relevant for understanding Soviet defense and arms control policy: What is the relative importance of denying the United States a first-strike capability (i.e., assured retaliation) and providing the Soviet Union with a damage limitation capability that could increase the prospect for socialist victory? This is perhaps best illustrated in the classic debate between Raymond Garthoff and Richard Pipes.[21] Garthoff argues that the Soviets accept the inevitability of mutual deterrence and therefore give assured retaliation priority over damage limitation; Pipes claims the opposite. Unfortunately, the direct evidence on the topic is scarce and is subject to competing interpretations.[22] We cannot resolve the debate here, but we can draw some tentative conclusions.

Logic takes us only a little ways. We should be able to agree, for instance, that prior to 1976 or 1977, when the Soviets stopped calling for strategic superiority and began to argue about the possibility of victory, they may have seen no conflict between preventing nuclear war and having forces capable of fighting to win the war. Political and military leaders alike may have wanted the country to have forces able to accomplish both objectives. Given scarce resources and, in the nuclear age, obvious constraints on an effective damage limitation capability, it is plausible but not certain that denying the United States a first-strike capability had a higher priority than deploying damage limitation capabilities. This priority would have been manifest only when they conflicted.

The political and military aspects of doctrine began to conflict openly in 1976 or 1977 over the issue of victory and the value of war-fighting capabilities. The political leadership's rhetoric suggests that if a conflict between assured retaliation and damage limitation emerges, if necessary they will sacrifice damage limitation capabilities in order to deny the United States a first-strike capability. Soviet offers in 1986 and 1987 to trade their superiority in heavy offensive missiles for continued U.S. adherence to the 1972 ABM Treaty, as well as to agree with the U.S. "zero-option" for intermediate-range nuclear forces (INF) in Europe, are consistent with this observation.[23] Finally, on the question of socialist victory, the least common denominator among the political and military leadership from 1977 onward seems to be that if nuclear war occurred, at a minimum the Soviet Union should not lose it. This objective still has war-fighting requirements, although not as many as the objective of victory.

Indirect evidence seems to support the priority for assured retaliation. Jack Snyder suggests that to produce findings that cannot easily be discounted with an alternative explanation, a "testing strategy should focus on evidence that is unambiguously at the political level of doctrine, and on behavior that is too important to be used for purposes of disinformation. Only Soviet crisis diplomacy and coercive bargaining meet these criteria."[24] Snyder's review of the evidence, which is too complex to summarize here, shows little correlation between Soviet behavior and relative war-fighting capabilities—a situation not supporting the contention that war-fighting capabilities are most important to the Soviets.

In sum, we can tentatively say that when assured retaliation and damage limitation missions conflict, priority goes for denying the United States a first-strike capability. When they do not conflict, the Soviets probably try to maintain or improve their positions for both missions. Beginning in 1977, the potential for conflict between them became more salient.

Turning to our focus on arms control bargaining, with these understandings of what security means to Soviet leaders, we can conclude that a unilateral initiative's success is favored when the Soviets calculate that their concession would enhance their military capabilities or would help to prevent the degradation of these capabilities.

The Soviet Union, as a superpower in a bipolar world, also has security interests in strengthening "barriers to entry" at the level of power possessed by itself and the United States. Thus it is obvious that if an agreement proposed by the United States would strengthen such barriers to medium-power adversaries such as West Germany, China, Britain, and

France, then the Soviets are more likely than otherwise to reciprocate a U.S. initiative.

Like any great power, the Soviet Union does not want to be party to an agreement affecting military capabilities that it honored but the other side did not. It would like to be able to verify that the United States did not cheat and gain a unilateral advantage. The U.S. free press and pluralistic political system constrain the U.S. government from extensive cheating, however. On the choice between mutual on-site inspection and "national technical means" (NTM), most observers say that the Soviets prefer the NTM approach, because on-site inspection is too intrusive, is associated with espionage, and goes against traditions of secrecy and a closed society.[25] The Soviet signing of the 1987 INF Treaty, with its extensive provisions for on-site inspection, casts some doubt on the generalizability of this alleged propensity.[26] It is fairly obvious, however, that with other factors equal the Soviets tend to favor NTM.

Political Concerns: Alliance Cohesion and Prestige

Soviet calculations about the political effects of proposed agreements concern both the cohesion of their own alliance network and the cohesion among their adversaries. Until the split between the Peoples Republic of China (hereafter called China or the PRC) and the Soviet Union became obvious in October 1962, the Soviets wanted to maintain the appearance of unity among socialist states in order to enhance Soviet bargaining power in negotiations with the West. This situation acted as a constraint on Soviet accommodation with the United States, because the Chinese insisted on militance toward the imperialists. After October 1962, however, the Soviets wanted to isolate China. This new situation favored accommodation with the United States, because cooperation highlighted China's recklessness. U.S. involvement in the Vietnam War and President Jimmy Carter's later "normalization" of relations with China had detrimental effects on Soviet calculations about the political consequences of arms collaboration with the United States.[27] When relevant to our case studies or in speculations about the future, we will examine particular Soviet calculations.

Soviet calculations also take into account the impact of an arms control agreement on the cohesion of the North Atlantic Treaty Organization (NATO). In general, the Soviets would gain politically if a U.S.-Soviet agreement would improve the Soviet image and hence relations with West European countries, or if a proposed agreement would create tensions within NATO. They would lose politically if *not* agreeing made them appear more threatening to the West, a situation when NATO's cohesion would likely increase.[28]

These generalizations do not hold in every instance, however. For example, some Soviet political calculations in 1967–68 disposed them to reach a detente with Western Europe but not with the United States. This circumstance acted as a minor constraint on the Soviets agreeing to the U.S. proposal to limit ABMs.[29]

Prestige is another aspect of political calculations that the Soviets take into account as they consider how to respond to a U.S. unilateral initiative. Success of the initiative is favored when the proposed agreement affirms norms of reciprocity and equal status. In the postwar world where the two countries are in a league by themselves, reciprocity means that an agreement should demand no more sacrifices from the Soviet Union than from the United States. Affirmation of equal status has three components: an agreement should not constrain the Soviet Union from reaching or maintaining military parity with the United States; it should not require the Soviet Union to forgo influence in the world (i.e., to forgo its role as a global power); and it should not involve interference in Soviet domestic affairs.[30] As we will see in the case studies, all of these aspects of prestige are not invariably relevant to particular Soviet calculations.

Economic Calculations

Because of the predominant concern for security, the Soviets are unlikely even to consider a reallocation of funds away from defense without the existence of strategic parity. If this necessary condition for reallocation among sectors of the economy is not met, then economic calculations would likely center only on the possibility of avoiding an increase in the defense burden or on allocating funds within the military budget. Once parity is achieved, reallocation is favored during periods of low gross national product (GNP) growth rates. We will examine particular contingencies in our case studies.

The prospect of improved economic relations with the West is likely to favor the Soviets making an arms control concession when the concession is directly or indirectly linked to trade with the West and when one necessary and at least one of two supportive conditions obtain. The necessary condition is that the Soviet Union needs to trade with the West. Supportive circumstances are when the United States dominates a large share of the market, and the West (especially the United States) presents a trade-stimulating environment so that the Soviet Union is more likely than otherwise to be able to afford the imports.[31] This analysis, which is based solely on economic considerations, yields answers that constitute a first-order approximation that should be sufficient for our purpose of describing changing Soviet evaluations of their international economic interests.

The Soviets compartmentalize their trade, emphasizing imports of industrial products from Western Europe and Japan and grain from the United States.[32] They have to obtain industrial products from Western Europe and Japan over the United States for two reasons: these countries present a more trade-stimulating environment, and the United States does not dominate these markets. Let us begin by examining trade in grain, where the Soviets have the greatest economic interest in trade with the United States. The Soviet desire to import grain is sensitive to annual production shortfalls, because in the post-Stalin era the leadership wants to avoid alienating the population by seriously curtailing the most basic product—food.

Climatic conditions, systemic constraints associated with central controls, losses due to spoilage, and inefficient use of seed grain are the major causes of chronic shortages. Despite generally larger harvests over time, however, shortfalls from Five-Year Plan targets continued to occur and even became worse. The principal reason is that a growing Soviet population is eating more products from livestock that are fed grain. Per capita meat consumption, for instance, rose from 26 kilograms per year in 1950 to 40 in 1960, 48 in 1970, and 58 in 1980. Since Soviet geography is not conducive to growing corn, the Soviets use about half of their available wheat for livestock. Moreover, since wheat is a less-efficient feed grain than corn, the Soviets use 8 tons of grain to produce 1 ton of meat, compared to 5 tons of grain in the United States.[33]

When overviewing the 1960–87 period, we find serious production shortfalls of at least 15 million metric tons in 1963, 1965, 1967, 1972, 1975, 1977, and from 1979 on. The Soviets shifted from being a net exporter of grain to a net importer. At first the shift seemed temporary (1964-66), but it became permanent in 1972 (see Table 3.1).

The Soviet ability to import grain is influenced by the economic environment that grain exporters present. Particularly helpful are favorable prices, barter arrangements or credits to help finance the purchases under the usual situation where the Soviets run a balance-of-payments deficit and thus have a shortage of foreign exchange, and nonpoliticization of commercial arrangements.

Economic incentives for purchasing U.S. grain are strong when the Soviet Union needs large quantities of imported grain and when the two supportive conditions obtain: the United States dominates a large share of the global market, and the United States presents a trade-stimulating environment. It also has a moderately strong economic incentive to purchase U.S. grain when it has a production shortfall and when one of the supportive conditions obtains fully but the other does not. In our case studies we will examine particular Soviet calculations.

Table 3.1
Soviet Grain Production and Trade, 1960–87
(millions of metric tons)

Year	Plan	Harvest	Surplus	Exports	Imports	Net Exports
1960	--[a]	126	--	6.8	0.2	6.6
1961	--	131	--	7.5	0.7	6.8
1962	--	140	--	7.8	0.0	7.8
1963	--	108	--	6.3	3.1	3.2
1964	--	152	--	3.5	7.3	-3.2
1965	164-80	121	-43[b]	4.3	6.4	-2.1
1966	167	171	4	3.6	7.7	-4.1
1967	167	148	-19	6.2	2.2	4.0
1968	167	170	3	5.4	1.6	3.8
1969	167	162	-5	7.2	0.6	6.6
1970	167	187	20	5.7	2.2	3.5
1971	195	181	-14	8.6	3.5	5.1
1972	195	168	-27	4.6	15.5	-10.9
1973	195	223	28	4.9	23.9	-19.0
1974	195	196	1	7.0	7.1	-0.1
1975	195	140	-55	3.6	15.9	-12.3
1976	215-20	224	9	1.5[c]	20.6[c]	-19.1[c]
1977	215-20	196	-19	2.3	18.9	-16.6
1978	215-20	237	22	2.8	15.6	-12.8
1979	215-20	179	-36	0.8	31.0	-30.2
1980	215-20	189	-26	0.5	34.8	-34.3
1981	238-43	158	-80	0.5	46.0	-45.5
1982	238-43	187	-51	0.5	32.5	-32.0
1983	238-43	192	-46	0.5	32.9	-32.4
1984	238-43	173	-65	1.0	55.5	-54.5

Year	Plan	Harvest	Surplus	Exports	Imports	Net Exports
1985	238-43	192	-46	1.0	29.0	-28.0
1986	250-55	210	-40	1.0	30.0	-29.0
1987	250-55	195 est	-55	--	--	--

Source: Harvest and trade statistics from Marshall I. Goldman, *Gorbachev's Challenge: Economic Reform in the Age of High Technology* (New York: W. W. Norton, 1987), 32–33; and Bill Keller, "Gorbachev Urges Expansion of Family Farms," *New York Times,* July 1, 1987. Plan figures are from the Current Digest of the Soviet Press, trans., *Current Soviet Policies III: The Documentary Record of the Extraordinary 21st Congress of the Communist Party of the Soviet Union* (New York: Columbia University Press, 1960), 47; and selected volumes of the same series: *V, 23rd Congress,* 101; *VI, 24th Congress,* 124; *VII, 25th Congress,* 82. See also U.S. Department of Agriculture, *Assessment of the Soviet Food Program* (Washington, DC: n.p., February 1986), 5.

[a]Unlike succeeding economic plans, the 7th (1959–65) cites not average yearly figures but only the goal for 1965.

[b]When the plan target is a range of figures, the surplus equals the harvest minus the lower plan figure.

[c]Data for years beginning with 1976 are for a July through June period.

The Soviet interest in importing Western industrial products is directly related to the problem of decling GNP growth rates and the leadership's strategy for stimulating growth. Slowing growth rates began to become an issue in the late 1960s, when limits to the extensive approach (i.e., quantitative increases in capital, labor, and land) were starting to become apparent. This strategy worked fine during most of the 1950s, which averaged almost 6 percent growth per year. As the economy matured, however, diminishing returns on inputs occurred and in general the limitations of central planning became serious. The Soviets then shifted to a strategy of intensive growth (i.e., qualitative improvements to make production more efficient).[34]

To obtain the technology necessary for this "scientific and technical revolution," the Soviets can choose among three approaches. First, they could attempt to reform their economy to make it more "rational" and hence conducive to efficiency. Second, they could try to organize the Council for Mutual Economic Assistance (Comecon or CMEA—the trading bloc that includes primarily the Soviet Union and Eastern Europe) with a division of labor conducive to the production and export of high technology. Third, they could import it from the West.[35]

Consequently, the Soviets want to purchase Western industrial products under conditions of low economic growth and a lack of success of the other two options for improving GNP growth rates (i.e., domestic economic reform, and the importation of advanced machinery from Comecon countries). They are more likely to be able to make such purchases when the West presents a trade-stimulating environment (e.g., improved or at least nondiscriminatory access to Western markets, sufficient credits to help finance the sales, and various sorts of barter arrangements to help overcome chronic Soviet balance-of-payments problems).[36]

The purchase of U.S. industrial products was probably important only from 1972 to 1974, a period that does not coincide with any of our case studies. Average growth rates had declined; the Soviets did not have high expectations for domestic economic reforms (as they did with the "Kosygin reforms" of the mid- to late 1960s); expectations were also not high for efforts to get East European countries to specialize and to export substantial amounts of high technology products to the Soviet Union; and the United States seemed to present a trade-stimulating environment.[37]

The last circumstance listed above, involving a stimulating U.S. trade environment, obtained only in the 1972–74 period.[38] The first time the United States had seriously considered granting the Soviet Union most favored nation (MFN) status was from 1966 to 1968. This status guarantees that its possessor will not have to pay more tariffs to export a product than other MFN holders. However, congressional displeasure with Soviet behavior in Vietnam in 1967 and 1968, and especially in Czechoslovakia in August 1968, led President Johnson to abandon the idea. The second and, to the Soviet Union, the most hopeful U.S. push was from 1972 to 1974. During these years the parties agreed on an economic package. The Soviets would settle their lend-lease debts to the United States, and they expected to receive MFN status and access to substantial amounts of credit. The deal collapsed by early 1975, however, because of Congress's human rights linkages—the Jackson-Vanik and Stevenson Amendments to the 1974 Trade Reform Bill. President Carter raised these economic issues for a third time, but human rights problems in 1978 and the Afghanistan invasion in 1979 ended this possibility. Furthermore, Carter's 1980 sanctions included a partial embargo on high technology sales. President Reagan pushed for even stronger restrictions on technology transfers.[39]

In contrast, as the Soviet Union considered trade with Western Europe and Japan, it faced a trade-stimulating environment that had existed since the 1950s, when these countries gave it MFN status. Moreover, the United States does not dominate a large share of the market in high technology goods. Consequently, the Soviets had a much greater economic interest in purchasing industrial products from them than from the United Sates. Of course the level of Soviet interest changed with the ebb and flow of expectations for their domestic economic reform and Comecon policies.

We need not describe the changing levels of Soviet interest in trade with Japan and Western Europe, because for three reasons this concern has little bearing on U.S.-Soviet arms control negotiations. First, it has less relevance to our case studies than trade in grain, for the Soviet Union tended to compartmentalize its trade and to rely on the United States only for grain. Second, the Soviet Union is not particularly trade-dependent. Only 2.5–3.0 percent of its GNP is involved in trade, and about 60 percent of that is with Comecon countries. That leaves only a 1.0–1.5 percent trade dependence on the West, and only a tenth of that is with the United States.[40] Third, the connection between Soviet arms control behavior and trade patterns with Western Europe and Japan seems largely to be indirect—that is, for strictly bilateral arms control issues, Western Europe and Japan are unlikely to alter their trade patterns unless their U.S. ally gets extremely upset and succeeds in pressuring European countries to change. Alternatively, for issues that would involve them directly (e.g., restraints on theater weapons), the connection would be somewhat stronger—although weaker than the U.S. approach to linkage.[41]

OTHER ENVIRONMENTAL FACTORS

Domestic Politics

In our earlier discussion of ideology, I mentioned that Soviet domestic politics is influenced by several tenets. One is "democratic centralism," which protrays how politics should be within the Communist Party: cooperative and without institutionalized factions. The other major tenet is "the leading role of the Communist Party," which describes the relation between the party and society: Because only the Communist Party is sufficiently knowledgeable about the "laws of history" to guide the government and society, it shall be the only party. Moreover, the reasoning goes, in a one-class society like the Soviet Union, only one party should be needed to represent the interests of everyone.[42] Within this context, we must speculate about how or under what conditions the United States can influence the domestic determinants of Soviet foreign policy.

The least controversial domestic factor is bureaucratic politics, which largely concerns Soviet military services and their views on the effects of proposed arms control agreements on their organizational interests. Obviously, the less the services value a weapon that is the target of a U.S. unilateral initiative, the greater the prospect of success. In our case studies we will become specific as we examine the services' interests and responses to particular proposals.

The second important domestic situation is succession politics, which in the Soviet Union has been characterized by a lack of formal, institutionalized mechanisms for selecting a new general-secretary. George Breslauer and Grey Hodnett argue that when someone becomes general-secretary, until he gains ascendancy over his political rivals he seeks to bolster his authority by appealing to the traditional interests of the most important bureaucratic actors—the military, heavy industry, and party bureaucracy. Since they have interests in an image of a dangerous international environment or in high military spending, this alliance is unfavorable for arms control concessions. After becoming ascendant, which seems to take at least several years, he is less constrained by these vested interests and serious concessions become possible.[43]

In the post-Stalin era, however, even when ascendant, his authority is not absolute. To retain power when he cannot use terror to prevent the development of opposing opinions, he needs the support of key leaders on the Politburo and Central Committee. Otherwise he may be removed, as Khrushchev was in 1964. At that time, Khrushchev was deposed when a number of his "hare-brained" schemes clearly hurt the interests of the Soviet Union and key institutional actors.[44]

Breslauer claims that the historical record supports the premise that after their first several years in power, both Khrushchev and Brezhnev advocated less confrontational, more collaborative styles of competition with the United States. This is not to say that Khrushchev, for instance, always acted in ways consistent with his 1956 "peaceful coexistence" policy. Sometimes he acted in a confrontational manner, such as by placing missiles in Cuba in 1962. The important point, however, is that apparently he took this "hare-brained" action against the advice of the military. Once ascendant, the general-secretary is freer to enact controversial policies. This constraint would be unimportant when Soviet leaders agree.

The premise is controversial. Some scholars argue that the system remains totalitarian and consequently no significant pluralism exists.[45] Others claim that extensive pluralism exists, so that the general-secretary's official view reflects not his personal opinion and level of ascendance, but rather the majority view in the leadership.[46] Taking into account the particular nature of political succession in the Soviet Union, we can therefore restate hypothesis 8 as follows: If a U.S. unilateral initiative requires a controversial concession, then the Soviet Union is unlikely to make the concession if the general-secretary is not ascendant.

The third domestic political factor is the balance of political forces within the elite group of policy makers, and the impact of a U.S. unilateral initiative on the balance. Many scholars argue that this sort of politics is possible in the post-Stalin era, although they use qualifying terms such as "crypto-politics" and "institutionalized pluralism" to describe it.[47] Supporters of high military spending and thus opponents of arms control are alleged to be the military, managers and party functionaries for heavy industry, and scientists associated with defense and nuclear energy agencies. Supporters of decreased military spending or improved economic relations with the West, and hence supporters of arms control, are supposed to be managers and party functionaries for light and consumer industries, other scientists, and the foreign affairs intelligentsia.[48]

The hypothesis is that a conditional unilateral initiative that serves the interests of both countries will strengthen the position of arms control supporters and weaken that of opponents, thus favoring the initiative's success. Conversely, an initiative that clearly favors the United States would strengthen the relative position of arms control opponents and success would be unlikely. A less obvious conclusion is that an unconditional or unverifiable initiative may strengthen an argument for nonreciprocation or for official reciprocation but actual noncompliance. As with the previous factor of succession politics, the assumption of pluralism is controversial and consequently so is the relevance of this factor.

Soviet Perceptions of International Tensions

Our purpose here is to describe and explain Soviet perceptions of the level of tension between the United States and the Soviet Union. This task is a prerequisite to learning if or to what extent Soviet perceptions of tensions and their negotiating behavior are linked. It is hoped that the research in chapters 4 to 8 will shed some light on the controversy.

To the Soviets, the phrase "level of tension" describes their perceptions of Soviet-U.S. relations and the likelihood of war between the two states. Since we are concerned only with the period when the two countries are nuclear-armed superpowers in a predominantly bipolar world, relations are likely to vary only between a cold war and a detente. Worse relations (a hot war) and better relations (an entente, alliance, or merger) are unlikely to occur.[49]

We will use inductive and deductive methods to determine Soviet perceptions of this factor. First we have the indicator of what they say about U.S.-Soviet relations, the likelihood of war, and related concerns about United States intentions and politics within the United States. If their statements and perceptions are highly correlated, then when they perceive tensions as high we would expect their statements to emphasize a relationship with many more conflicting than common interests, a high danger of war, a United States with aggressive intentions, and a U.S. leadership dominated by a single hostile clique or by "madmen" instead of "realists."[50]

A common problem in Soviet studies, however, is that the regime is able to manipulate its communications media for international or domestic propaganda purposes. We know, in particular, that the "war scares" depicted in Soviet statements in 1927 and early in 1957 did not reflect real perceptions of a heightened danger of war; rather, the assertions were largely manifestations of the "zigzags" in Soviet foreign policy generated from domestic politics associated with leadership succession struggles.[51] More recently, Sewern Bialer plausibly argued that the war scare portrayed in the Soviet media during the early 1980s was caused by a combination of President Reagan's belligerent rhetoric and high defense budget and a self-awareness of economic and political vulnerabilities at home (especially Andropov's illness). In this situation, Bialer argued, the Soviets wanted to stir up Soviet patriotism and to create an image of a Soviet Union that will not allow itself to be coerced.[52] Consequently, our faith in the accuracy of relevant Soviet statements should be more suspect than usual during periods when the general-secretary has not yet consolidated his political authority, and especially if at the same time he is gravely ill.

The other method for inferring Soviet perceptions of the level of tension is deductive. It draws on the perceptions of an "objective" outside observer who assumes that the Soviet leadership views tensions as high when the United States challenges them in regions or issues of vital interest, and with means containing a high potential for escalation. Low tensions would correspond to U.S. actions that, if at all threatening, are only in regions or issues challenging nonvital interests, and with means not involving U.S. military power.

This formulation assumes that the Soviets view Soviet-U.S. relations on a continuum of competition—from confrontational to collaborative styles of competition—rather than as either a confrontational or cooperative relationship.[53] Evidence supporting its validity includes statements by Khrushchev, Brezhnev, and Gorbachev about peaceful coexistence and detente: The superpowers should avoid confrontations and nuclear war and, if possible, accommodate in areas of common interest; at the same time the political-ideological competition will continue.[54]

Soviet leaders have interjected their own nuances as they have interpreted the competition. Khrushchev and Brezhnev were optimistic about revolutionary developments and a further progressive shift in the correlation of forces, but Gorbachev takes a more sober view. Likewise, compared to Gorbachev, Khrushchev and Brezhnev were more interested in pursuing unilateral advantages than in exercising mutual restraint or furthering common interests. Finally, they were more willing than Gorbachev to assist revolutionary movements with means that the United States considers unfair, such as arms transfers and the use of proxy troops. Gorbachev seems to want a durable detente, one that will not collapse like the detente of the 1970s. Just as all of the implications of his "new thinking" in foreign policy remain to be seen, however, so do the prospects that it will become deeply imbedded in the Soviet leadership and remain institutionalized.[55]

If hypothesis 10 is correct and subsequent research demonstrates an inverse relation between the level of tension and the Soviet willingness to reciprocate unilateral initiatives, then we would expect a low level of tension to favor the success of the tactic, a high level to be unfavorable, and a moderate level to have no or an ambiguous effect. A low-moderate level would be moderately favorable, and a moderate-high level would be moderately unfavorable.

In our case studies we will describe particular Soviet perceptions of international tensions. I do not claim a high level of certainty, but it should be greatest when the inductive and deductive methods both suggest the same conclusion and when the general-secretary has consolidated his authority. During periods when the leader's authority is not yet consolidated, I give greater weight than otherwise to the deductive approach. When the approaches lead to different conclusions, the range of uncertainty is noted in the text.

Soviet Perceptions of the Strategic Environment

The final factor is the stability of the strategic environment. Since its importance is controversial, our task here is simply to help understand Soviet perceptions of it. Hypothesis 11 is that the success of an initiative is favored when state B perceives an acceptable strategic environment (i.e., one in which an attack by A is unlikely to defeat B at costs acceptable to A, even if A attacks first). Secondarily, success is favored if B can easily differentiate defensive and offensive weapons, and A procures only defensive weapons.

Beginning with the primary criterion for strategic stability—the Soviets perceive an acceptable strategic environment—operationalizing what "acceptable" means to them requires that we summarize aspects of their military doctrine which heavily influence their perceptions on security issues.

Their doctrine aims to dissuade adversaries from attacking by having a force posture, a command and control network, and an operational policy that together are capable of denying an enemy the ability to carry out a successful invasion or disarming first strike. This objective directly corresponds to the primary criterion for a stable strategic environment. The other component of doctrine is that effective Soviet damage limitation capabilities would be another disincentive for an enemy to attack.

For three reasons, this analysis assumes that only the first component of doctrine is relevant to our understanding of the primary criterion for stability. First, as we discussed earlier in this chapter, the damage limitation component of doctrine seems to be secondary to the assured retaliation requirement. Second, a desire for extensive damage limitation capabilities is incompatible with the relationship aspect of stability. Although the Soviets might feel most secure when they had both assured retaliation and extensive damage limitation capabilities, such a combination would enable them to attack first and win unscathed. From the U.S. perspective, then, the strategic environment would be highly unstable and unacceptable. In the nuclear age the only feasible environment acceptable to both countries is where both have assured retaliation capabilities. This requires that neither have effective damage limitation capabilities. Third, taking the second component into account would complicate our analysis more than is necessary for the modest degree of certainty that we seek.

Consequently, for the central strategic relationship with the United States, the Soviets would perceive an acceptable strategic environment when the United States is unable to carry out a disarming first strike. The following conditions characterize an ideal situation: (1) an ability to ride out a U.S. first strike and then launch; (2) durable Soviet early-warning sensors able to provide the tactical warning necessary to preempt a U.S. attack; (3) other intelligence means able to provide strategic warning that the United States was preparing to attack (which would enable the Soviets to upgrade their forces' alert status and perhaps preempt); (4) Soviet defenses able to protect strategic weapons and command and control facilities; and (5) U.S. defenses unable to prevent Soviet warheads and bombs from reaching their targets. In the worst situation, none of these conditions would obtain. Since neither party ever had effective defenses against the other's nuclear weapons, our analysis does not consider the last two conditions.

Beyond such extremes, we must define what we mean by acceptable, unacceptable, and ambiguous environments. These three categories of descriptive terms provide a first-order approximation of Soviet perceptions, which is sufficient for our purposes. In an acceptable environment, the United States would be unable to degrade the Soviet ability to retaliate and carry out most missions, and U.S. damage limitation efforts would yield minimal benefits. If the Soviets gave priority to civilian targets, they would be able to kill 30–50 percent of the U.S. population and destroy 60–75 percent of the U.S. industrial capacity.[56] Priority to military targets and political-economic assets that contribute to the U.S. war potential would probably result in smaller although substantial loss of life (e.g., tens of millions dead).

In an unacceptable environment, a U.S. attack against Soviet strategic nuclear forces could seriously diminish their ability to retaliate. After the

U.S. first strike, even with a countercity retaliation the Soviets would be able to kill only a few tens of millions, while the Soviets would lose several times as many people. In other words, the United States would emerge from the war noticeably better off than the Soviet Union. An ambiguous strategic environment would be between these situations: After a U.S. attack, with countercity targeting the Soviets could kill only from a few tens of millions to somewhere under 100 million Americans.

The historical record, which we will explore in our case studies, suggests that the Soviets probably perceived a strategic environment that was unacceptable through the early 1960s, ambiguous in the mid-1960s, and acceptable beginning in the late 1960s. These periods are consistent with the conventional wisdom. Unfortunately, the evidence is too inconclusive to state precise transition dates.

The secondary criterion for a stable strategic environment is that offensive and defensive weapons are distinguishable, and the parties procure the defensive weapons.

Attempting to determine Soviet perceptions of this criterion is more difficult than for the first criterion, because it is not obvious if or how the Soviets distinguish offensive and defensive weapons. On the one hand, if the Soviets literally do not discriminate between forces necessary to deter aggression and forces useful for fighting and winning a war, then we would have little basis to operationalize this criterion. On the other hand, if they respond more intensely to some U.S. forces than to others (i.e., if they are sensitive to arms race instability), then we would have a basis for differentiation. A final consideration is that this criterion may be so unimportant relative to the first that proceeding is not worthwhile.

This analysis assumes the topic is worth pursuing and that the Soviets are more threatened by some U.S. weapons, doctrines, and operational practices than others (i.e., they are more threatened by weapons capable of destroying their strategic nuclear forces than by weapons that cannot). Evidence for this conventional view includes a quote from the 1963 edition of Marshal V. D. Sokolovsky's *Soviet Military Strategy:* "A strategy which contemplates attaining victory through the destruction of the armed forces cannot stem from the idea of a 'retaliatory' blow; it stems from preventive action and the achievement of surprise."[57] Thus they would feel reassured if nuclear forces for offensive and deterrent missions are clearly distinguishable, and if the United States buys only the deterrent weapons. Offensive weapons are capable of destroying both protected (hard) and unprotected (soft) targets; they significantly threaten Soviet strategic weapons and hence the balance of nuclear forces. Deterrent weapons can destroy only soft targets and hence are single-purpose weapons that do not have extensive counterforce capabilities.

Soviet perceptions of U.S. bombers and missiles are of course influenced by the weapons' specific characteristics. Weapons more useful for a disarming first strike than for a second-strike countervalue retaliation would have high accuracy and yield, a short flight time to target, and low detectability.

U.S. weapons also interact with particular Soviet circumstances, which influence the assessment of their capabilities. For example, if Soviet forces are unhardened or if the United States does not know their location, then high accuracy is less important than otherwise. If Soviet military and non-military assets are co-located, then the flight paths of U.S. weapons would be the same and differentiation would be difficult. If Soviet sensors are unable to differentiate flight paths to different types of targets, the problem would be functionally equivalent to co-location.

This second criterion also takes into account Soviet perceptions of U.S. doctrine and operational practices. For example, a U.S. doctrine emphasizing a mutual deterrence relationship would be less threatening than an offensive strategy with extensive damage limitation requirements. As evidence for this assertion, the Soviets reacted strongly against Secretary of Defense Robert McNamara's "no-cities" counterforce policy, Secretary of Defense James Schlesinger's later statements on limited and selected nuclear options, and President Carter's Presidential Directive Number 59 (PD-59), which formalized Schlesinger's ideas.[58] Furthermore, strategic training and operational patterns that did not appear to maximize the prospects for a successful first strike would be less threatening than ones that did. Given that U.S. declaratory and action policies do not always coincide, the Soviets may take U.S. deployments and operational practices more seriously than doctrine.[59]

In sum, the Soviets are most likely to perceive defensive U.S. intentions when the following conditions obtain: (1) few U.S. strategic forces are dual capable (i.e., able to destroy both soft and hard targets); (2) U.S. weapons are not sufficiently fast to destroy unready Soviet forces; (3) the Soviet intelligence system is sufficiently accurate and reliable to give tactical or strategic warning; (4) Soviet sensors can differentiate flight paths of U.S. weapons; (5) U.S. doctrine does not suggest prompt counterstrategic nuclear force missions; and (6) neither do U.S. operational practices. If none of these conditions obtain, the Soviets would likely perceive U.S. intentions to be highly offensive.

The Soviets could theoretically see U.S. motives as defensive, offensive, or ambiguous. In our case studies we will see how U.S. intentions probably never seemed defensive; they seemed either to be offensive or, from 1968 through the early 1970s, to be ambiguous.

Considering the two criteria together, the strategic environment should appear stable when the primary criterion obtains fully (i.e., the environment is acceptable) and when the secondary one (i.e., U.S. intentions seem defensive) obtains fully or is ambiguous. The Soviets would perceive an unstable environment when the environment was unacceptable and U.S. intentions seemed offensive or ambiguous. The situation would be ambiguous when both criteria are ambiguous. It would be moderately relevant when the two conflict, and when the primary one is ambiguous and the secondary one is not.

4

Case Study: Orbiting
Nuclear Weapons (1962–63)

Neither the United States nor the Soviet Union has orbited nuclear weapons. This mutual restraint is largely due to decisions made during 1962 and 1963, and a U.S. unilateral initiative contributed to it. Let us begin our history by describing the bargaining interactions that led to the agreement, and then spend the bulk of the chapter explaining Soviet responses to the U.S. tactic.

BARGAINING INTERACTIONS

On September 5, 1962, the United States announced its first unilateral initiative in strategic bargaining with the Soviets. In a speech before midwestern industrialists and academics, Deputy Secretary of Defense Roswell L. Gilpatric said:

The United States believes that it is highly desirable for its own security and for the security of the world that the arms race should not be extended into outerspace.... Today there is no doubt that either the United States or the Soviet Union could place thermonuclear weapons in orbit, but such an action is just not a rational military strategy for either side for the forseeable future.

We have no program to place any weapons of mass destruction into orbit. An arms race in space would not contribute to our security. I can think of no greater stimulus for a Soviet thermonuclear arms effort in space than a U.S. commitment to such a program. This we will not do.... We will of course take such steps as are necessary to defend ourselves and our allies, if the Soviet Union forces us to.[1]

Gilpatric's announcement represented significant changes in U.S. policy. Previous U.S. proposals to ban nuclear weapons from space were always part of a disarmament package, and they explicitly required on-site inspection to verify compliance.[2] The new policy was the outcome of a debate within the executive branch, prodded by President John Kennedy's interest in arms control.[3]

The Soviets did not respond directly to the unilateral initiative. On October 17, Arms Control and Disarmament Agency (ACDA) Director William Foster proposed a joint ban on orbiting weapons of mass destruction to Soviet Foreign Minister Andrei Gromyko and Ambassador Anatoly Dobrynin. Gromyko reacted the same way the Soviets had in the past: A space ban must be part of a disarmament package that included limits on forward-based systems (i.e., nuclear weapons of one superpower based near the territory of the other).[4] The United States was unwilling to accept such a linkage.

Albert Gore, U.S. representative to the United Nations (UN) in a speech on December 3 was more explicit on the conditional nature of the unilateral initiative:

Even though it is now feasible, the United States has no intention of placing weapons of mass destruction into orbit unless compelled to do so by the actions of the Soviet Union. The draft treaty for general and complete disarmament . . . includes a provision against the placing of weapons of mass destruction into orbit. . . . Nonetheless, while the difficult negotiations continue for the actual elimination of nuclear weapons and means of delivering them, it is especially important that we do everything now that can be done to avoid an arms race in outer space— for certainly it should be easier to agree now not to arm a part of the environment that has never been armed than later to agree to disarm parts that have been armed. My government earnestly hopes that the Soviet Union will likewise refrain from taking steps which will extend the arms race into outer space.[5]

Until a breakthrough on September 4, 1963, the Soviets continued to be unresponsive. That day Raymond Garthoff met with Igor Usachev. Garthoff was a high-level official in the Kennedy administration, and Usachev was a veteran Soviet diplomat. Usachev acknowledged Foster's earlier probe, and he said he thought the proposed agreement required on-site inspection and covered ballistic missiles as well as orbiting bombs. Garthoff assured him that it would not limit ballistic missiles and that national means of verification were sufficient. Usachev then became very interested.[6]

On September 19, Gromyko responded positively in a speech to the UN General Assembly:

The Soviet Government deems it necessary to reach agreement with the United States Government to ban the placing into orbit of objects with nuclear weapons aboard. . . . We are aware that the United States Government also takes a positive view of the solution to this question. . . . The Soviet Government is ready.[7]

The next day, President Kennedy publicly reaffirmed the U.S. position.[8] The Soviets were willing to formalize the agreement in a treaty, but Kennedy preferred a less-formal arrangement in order to minimize the prospect of domestic resistance to the agreement.[9] On October 17 the UN General Assembly passed Resolution 1884. It welcomed Soviet and U.S. declarations not to orbit weapons of mass destruction and encouraged them to continue their moratorium.[10] Although nonbinding, it was effective.

On May 7, 1966, President Lyndon Johnson proposed a treaty banning military activities on the moon and other celestial bodies. The Soviets agreed and went even further: They proposed that the treaty also ban nuclear weapons from orbit. The Americans accepted their suggestion, and the parties formalized the agreement in the 1967 Treaty of Principles Governing the Activities of States in the Exploration and Use of Outer Space, hereafter called the 1967 Outer Space Treaty. This treaty, which is still in force, obliges the parties "not to place in orbit around the Earth any objects carrying nuclear weapons or any other kinds of weapons of mass destruction, install such weapons on celestial bodies, or station such weapons in outer space in any other manner."[11]

EXPLANATION

Why did the Soviets reciprocate the U.S. unilateral initiative, and why did they wait a year to do it formally? Let us begin our analysis by examining the bargaining process. U.S. behavioral signals were clear: The United States was not placing weapons of mass destruction into orbit, and its restraint was in the "same currency" as the requested Soviet restraint. Verbally, it promised to continue this restraint as long as the Soviets reciprocated, and it threatened to match or counter Soviet behavior if the Soviets failed to reciprocate. A serious problem concerned what it did not say about verification, but it clarified this in September 1963. The United States was somewhat clear about the scope of the proposed agreement, particularly that it wanted a ban separate from general and complete disarmament. Apparently it was not sufficiently explicit about whether or not ballistic missiles would also be banned.

Garthoff speculates that the Soviets thought the proposal was only a variation of earlier proposals to ban all objects "sent through outer space."[12] Yet Gore in his December 3 speech (quoted above) was explicit when he talked about "a provision against the placing of weapons of mass destruction *into orbit*," called on the parties to "do everything now that can be done to *avoid* an arms race in outer space," and said "it should be easier to agree now not to arm a part of the environment that has *never been armed* than later to agree to disarm parts that have been armed" [emphasis added]. At any rate, by mid-1963 these U.S. signals were clear and the Soviets apparently interpreted them correctly.

During the year preceding formal reciprocation, the Soviet response was informal reciprocation (i.e., they placed no nuclear weapons into orbit). Thus the United States did not have to respond to a Soviet "defection," beyond saying the U.S. would match or otherwise counter any such Soviet action.

U.S. bargaining involved additional initiatives, but apparently not until 1963.[13] First, to encourage Soviet concessions on verification of a comprehensive test ban, President Kennedy announced on January 26 the postponement of a planned series of underground nuclear tests. The initiative failed and the United States resumed testing on February 8. Second, in a speech at American University on June 10, Kennedy said the United States would conduct no atmospheric nuclear tests so long as the Soviets similarly refrained. This initiative succeeded and the parties agreed on a limited test ban the next month.

I found no evidence that the United States accompanied the outer space initiative with an objective history of previous bargaining interactions or explained how the initiative fit into its overall political-military vision. The United States did discuss its military doctrine, but not with an explicit linkage to the outer space initiative.[14]

The closest the United States came to presenting an objective historical context was Kennedy's June 10 speech.[15] At best, however, it constituted only a partial history and therefore did not obviously favor the initiative's success. The nearest Kennedy got to describing arms interactions was a very general statement: "We are both caught up in a vicious and dangerous cycle with suspicion on one side breeding suspicion on the other, and new weapons begetting counter-weapons." Specific examples of such interactions would have helped, as would have examples of negotiation interactions. Furthermore, although Kennedy made conciliatory statements (e.g., "Let us re-examine our attitude towards the Soviet Union and towards the cold war," and "We are not here . . . pointing the finger of judgment"), he continued to blame them (e.g., "The communist drive to impose their political and economic system is the primary cause of world tensions today"). Had he admitted that the United States shared some of the blame for cold war interactions, his speech would have more closely approximated an objective history.

The Soviets knew about and apparently interpreted correctly both the January and June test ban initiatives. We will discuss the complexities of this assessment in chapter 5.

Now let us explore how Soviet cost-benefit calculations affected their response to the proposed agreement. Mutual restraint in outer space would have had no immediate consequences to Soviet security. It would not have increased or decreased Soviet military power, for neither party (nor any third party) had orbiting bombs or, apparently, plans to deploy them. We can only speculate, but Soviet leaders may have agreed with the Joint Chiefs of Staff statement in October 1963 that "there are no military objections to this arrangement," or with Cyrus Vance's testimony in 1967, when he was deputy secretary of Defense: "Our studies show that these systems have technical and economic drawbacks in addition to safety and command disadvantages. They would, if deployed now, be inaccurate, costly, and dangerous, and they would be less effective than present intercontinental ballistic missile (ICBM) systems."[16]

If Vance's opinion was shared by Soviet planners, then the system offered only marginal advantages such as a short flight time for missiles launched from space. However, since such missiles would have been inaccurate, the system would have added little to their ability to fulfill the doctrinal mission of damage limitation.

Much more important to the Soviets was their continued freedom to deploy ICBMs. During 1962 and 1963, they were behind the United States in all categories of strategic delivery vehicles. Their military doctrine emphasized the importance of ballistic missiles, and their force planning focused on a buildup in ICBMs, particularly after the humiliation of the Cuban missile crisis.[17] They probably calculated that relying on ICBMs was the most cost-effective way to dissuade the U.S. from attacking and, should the United States attack, to fight back. Because ballistic missiles would have been more accurate than bombs or rockets launched from a moving platform in orbit, they were better able to limit damage to the Soviet Union. In addition, they were more promising as a means to catch up with the level of U.S. strategic power than building many more bombers or orbiting nuclear weapons.

Supporting this speculation is the correlation between increased Soviet interest in the U.S. proposal and Garthoff's clarification that ballistic missiles would not be restricted. The agreement also put no restrictions on the fractional orbital bombardment system (FOBS) on which the Soviets were working.[18] Soviet antiaircraft and antimissile defense programs were also unrestricted.

Soviet reciprocation would have had no security costs, but how would nonreciprocation have affected their security? The evidence suggests it would have had unfavorable long-term consequences, and therefore that reciprocation had some security benefits. The United States had said both publicly and privately that its continued restraint required Soviet reciprocation. Soviet planners considering orbiting weapons therefore had to calculate the military consequences of both parties deploying them. Deductions from Soviet military doctrine suggest a negative net assessment of such a prospect. As already mentioned, Soviet military gains would have been only marginal. However, orbiting nuclear weapons would have made more difficult the mission of limiting damage to the Soviet Union. Soviet

ICBMs might be able to destroy some U.S. ICBMs in their silos, but the Soviets had no means to destroy orbiting weapons or missiles launched from them.[19] Moreover, the United States would have responded to a Soviet orbiting nuclear bomb system with its own anti-satellite system.[20] This would present a new threat to Soviet space assets and challenge them to deploy their own ASAT system.

The U.S. Air Force wanted an ASAT system. Political leaders decided, however, that it was unnecessary because it was not needed to intercept orbiting nuclear weapons or to match a Soviet ASAT, and because a U.S. ASAT probably would have stimulated the Soviets to deploy one. Consequently, the same day UN Representative Albert Gore made his speech (December 3, 1962), the Department of Defense announced that it was "reorienting" the satellite interceptor project SAINT. The project was not totally canceled, but its priority was decreased. In addition, Secretary of Defense McNamara testified at 1963 Posture Hearings that he saw no military requirement for the Dyna-Soar space shuttle. These and other restraints on U.S. ASAT capabilities were vaguely made conditional on continued Soviet restraint regarding orbiting nuclear weapons. For example, after saying it was not U.S. policy to orbit nuclear weapons, Gilpatric warned that the United States "will of course take such steps as are necessary to defend ourselves . . . if the Soviet Union forces us to."[21] This analysis suggests that security calculations led the Soviets to expect few benefits but definite long term costs if they orbited nuclear weapons. Thus this factor was probably moderately supportive of mutual restraint.

Before Garthoff's clarification on September 4, 1963, the Soviets apparently thought that the United States demanded intrusive inspection procedures. Previous formal proposals had this requirement. For instance, the section of a 1962 U.S. disarmament proposal that called for a ban on orbiting nuclear weapons said the parties should be able to inspect space vehicles and missiles before their launch to ensure they would not place weapons of mass destruction into orbit.[22] Usachev's positive response to Garthoff's clarification suggests the Soviets preferred national means of verification to on-site inspection.

Soviet calculations of the political effects of the proposed agreement involved both the cohesion of their own alliance network and political relations among their adversaries.

When the United States first announced the initiative in September 1962, concerns about the PRC did not favor public Soviet reciprocation. At the time, the Soviets had not given up hope that the Sino-Soviet split might be contained, and to enhance their bargaining power with the West they wanted to maintain the appearance of unity in the socialist bloc. This disposed them to go along with the Chinese desire to avoid accommodation with the United States; to do otherwise might have disposed the Chinese to charge openly that the Soviet Union was unfit to be the leader of the world communist movement.[23] Sino-Soviet relations deteriorated rapidly during October, so that by the end of the month this political consideration favored arms control collaboration.

In 1962, a principal objective of the Soviet Union was to prevent China and West Germany from acquiring nuclear weapons. On August 25 the Soviets told the Chinese that they supported the concept of a nonproliferation treaty. The Chinese responded angrily in notes on September 3 and October 20. The latter note coincided with a Chinese offensive against India, a country with close ties to the Soviet Union, as well as with the Cuban missile crisis. The missile crisis ended on October 25 when the Soviets yielded. Related Chinese comments shifted from support for the Soviets during the crisis to—for the first time—open ridicule after it. Apparently the Soviets then reevaluated the situation: They did not expect to prevent China from obtaining nuclear weapons; direct confrontation with the United States was too dangerous and some accommodation was in order; and accommodation with the West could help to isolate China as a dangerous and reckless state.[24]

Calculations about the consequences of the proposed agreement on NATO's cohesion favored Soviet reciprocation over the entire period. Public reciprocation would have contributed to the Soviet appearance of reasonableness, which would have marginally improved relations with West European countries. In turn, facing a less obvious threat, NATO's cohesion would have marginally declined. Because the Soviets continued informal restraint, however, not reciprocating formally would have cost the Soviets little political capital.

Reciprocation also would have marginally enhanced Soviet political relations with neutral and Non-Aligned nations, although not reciprocating would have cost the Soviets little because of their tacit reciprocation. Some sparse evidence from *Documents on Disarmament* supports this argument. Between September 1962 and September 1963 only one Non-Aligned nation was reported to have said anything about orbiting nuclear weapons. That was Mexico, on June 21, 1963, and its position was similar to the U.S. view.[25] On October 17, 1963, the UN General Assembly passed a resolution welcoming the superpower moratorium.[26]

Prestige calculations should have favored the proposed agreement, which affirmed norms of reciprocity and equal status. For the first year, however, the Soviets mistakenly thought that the proposal required them to limit ballistic missiles and thus their ability to reach parity with the United States—which would have gone against the norm of equal status. Even this exchange would have been reciprocal, however, so overall they probably expected a mixed impact on prestige.

Domestic economic calculations probably neither favored nor opposed the Soviets' reciprocating the U.S. unilateral initiative. Since strategic parity was far off, they were not considering reallocation away from defense to consumption or investment.[27] Moreover, since the Soviets deployed no orbiting nuclear weapons and apparently had no plans to deploy them, the proposed agreement offered no substantial economic savings.

A decision to deploy such a system, however, would have necessitated some increases in defense spending in order to match or counter expected U.S. responses (e.g., an ASAT system and perhaps orbiting nuclear weapons). In turn these costs would have required an increase in the defense burden or an allocation away from other, more promising defense projects. Since the Soviets apparently had no plans to deploy such weapons, however, we can say that domestic economic issues probably were unimportant.

When the United States announced the outer space initiative in September 1962, the prospect of improved economic relations with the United States was unimportant. The Soviet harvest was fine and they needed to import no Western grain.[28] When the Soviets reciprocated publicly in September 1963, U.S. grain may have been moderately important to them. From the beginning of the crop year in mid-1963 to the beginning of the next in mid-1964 (i.e., in 1963/64), they purchased about 10 million metric tons of wheat from Canada and the United States. During 1964 the United States delivered 1.8 million tons, its share of the total.[29] The U.S. facilitated this trade by announcing the approval, in October 1963, of Export-Import Bank (Eximbank) guaranteed loans to help finance it. This was part of Kennedy's and then Johnson's "bridge-building" strategy, where a few U.S. trade concessions were intended to help improve East-West relations.[30] I found no evidence suggesting when the Soviets first learned Kennedy was seeking Eximbank loans. This analysis makes the plausible assumption that when they reciprocated formally in September, they knew about his efforts.

U.S. wheat reserves were not particularly important to the Soviet Union, however. The U.S. share of the global wheat market was only 39–40 percent, and the Soviets needed only about 11 percent of the wheat exported globally. A greater U.S. market share in coarse grains (especially corn and soybeans) was unimportant, because Soviet grain imports in 1963 and 1964 were 99-100 percent wheat.[31] U.S. grain was probably only moderately important from an economic standpoint, because just one of the supportive conditions obtained fully: Although the United States apparently presented them with a trade-stimulating environment, the United States did not dominate the wheat market.

Soviet calculations and behavior are sometimes affected by factors in the domestic and international environments of bargaining. We will complete this chapter by examining these potentially important factors.

Once the United States clarified its proposal in September 1963, the Soviet military probably did not oppose reciprocation. Since no orbiting nuclear weapons were deployed, no organization stood to lose a mission or significant budgetary allocations. The Strategic Rocket Forces (SRF) continued to develop FOBS. More important, all services but the Army had their budgets increased. After the Cuban missile crisis, Khrushchev increased the rate of production of SS-7 ICBMs and accelerated development and testing of the SS-9 and SS-11. He also increased funds for an ABM and for a Polaris-type submarine that could carry submarine-launched ballistic missiles (SLBMs).[32] The international bargaining was informal, but I found no evidence to indicate the effects of this situation on Soviet negotiating behavior. This factor may also have been unimportant, as no evidence emerged that the military or other bureaucratic actor really wanted to orbit nuclear weapons.

By 1962 Khrushchev had been in power for almost a decade—plenty of time to have consolidated his authority. As indirect evidence for this assertion, his late domestic and foreign policies antagonized too many Soviets to be the product of majority voting, and the changes in many policy directions and styles following his ouster in October 1964 indicate that he had considerable power over policy. To make these changes they had to remove Khrushchev; they could not make the changes by majority vote.[33] Therefore he would have had the political capacity to push through a controversial policy he supported.

No evidence suggests the issue was controversial, however, and apparently the Soviets were not planning to orbit nuclear weapons. If it was controversial, it probably would have been so only prior to September 4, 1963. Before then, the benefits of a more formal mutual ban would have had to be weighed against costs of possible on-site inspection and limitations on ballistic missiles. Since these disadvantages were more serious than the advantages, we can assume that not much controversy surrounded the issue.

After the September clarification, significant potential disadvantages of an agreement would have dissipated. If any leaders still argued for orbiting nuclear weapons or keeping open the option to orbit them, then the U.S. approach probably weakened their case and strengthened the arguments of those supporting arms control. I found no evidence suggesting any conflict of opinion, however.

In September 1962 the Soviets probably perceived a high level of international tension. The deductive approach suggests that tensions seemed high since the 1960 U-2 crisis, and that subsequent events probably kept them up.[34] First, they probably felt that their vital interests in Central Europe were threatened by the proposal for a Multilateral Force (MLF). If implemented, they would have faced a new force of ships carrying nuclear-armed missiles and manned and controlled by mixed crews drawn from various members of NATO. The Soviets strenuously opposed any nuclear sharing within NATO, especially if it led to some German control over nuclear technology. Second, the Soviets were also threatened by developments that affected the general balance of power and their interests in Central Europe: a large increase in U.S. defense spending for strategic weapons and conventional forces, as well as U.S. declarations emphasizing the new flexible response policy, the military buildup, and the drive for strategic superiority. Third, the United States had responded firmly to the Soviet reopening of the Berlin crisis and to the Soviet resumption of nuclear testing. Finally, during 1961 the United States supported the ill-fated Bay of Pigs proxy invasion of Cuba; this action, however, was less threatening to Soviet vital interests and did not involve the direct use of U.S. military power. It also failed. Soviet rhetoric also indicated perceptions of high tensions, as it emphasized conflicting national interests, the danger of war, and an aggressive U.S. foreign policy determined by a monolithic group.[35]

After the Cuban missile crisis the Soviets probably perceived a lower, moderate level of tension. Khrushchev apparently believed that high tensions with accompanying confrontations like the Cuban missile crisis presented too high a risk of nuclear war. He also came to see Kennedy as neither a weakling nor a warmonger, and his rhetoric toward the United States became less hostile. Although the United States continued its strategic buildup and advocated strategic superiority, NATO made no progress in implementing the MLF proposal, and the United States initiated no new challenges to Soviet vital interests.[36]

Beginning with Kennedy's conciliatory speech at American University in June 1963, the Soviets probably perceived tensions to be low.[37] When Gromyko announced Soviet acceptance of the U.S. outer space proposal on September 19, he referred to "a more favorable atmosphere" that had been generated by "the weathering of the Caribbean crisis and the signing of the . . . [Limited Test Ban Treaty]."[38]

Our final consideration is Soviet perceptions of the strategic environment. The analysis below suggests that they probably saw an unstable strategic environment when the United States first implemented its initiative, and a moderately unstable environment when they reciprocated formally a year later.

Beginning with the primary criterion for stability, in the early 1960s the Soviets most likely found the strategic environment unacceptable, and in the middle 1960s its nature probably seemed ambiguous. Since the evidence is too inconclusive to indicate precise transition dates, this analysis assumes that September 1962 was toward the end of the early 1960s, and that September 1963 was near the beginning of the mid-1960s.

During the early 1960s, the United States would have emerged from a nuclear war that it started considerably better off than the Soviet Union—an obviously unacceptable situation. It arose because the United States had significant quantitative and qualitative advantages.

The surprise Soviet launch of the satellite *Sputnik* in 1957 combined with Soviet strategic deception (i.e., exaggerations of their military capabilities) and U.S. "worst-case" analysis produced the "missile gap" controversy. U.S. weapons procurement then accelerated, and by the early 1960s a real missile gap existed—one favoring the United States, which emerged with substantial counterforce capabilities against unready Soviet strategic nuclear forces. For example, in 1960 the United States had 18 ICBMs and 32 SLBMs, and the Soviets had 35 ICBMs and no SLBMs. By 1962 the United States had 294 ICBMs and 144 SLBMs, and the Soviets had only 75 ICBMs and some SLBMs. Moreover, the estimate of 75 Soviet ICBMs is the conventional one; the lowest is four.[39]

A more detailed qualitative analysis suggests a comparable disparity. First, Soviet SLBMs could not be launched from underwater and hence were more vulnerable than the U.S. Polaris system. Second, through 1963 all Soviet ICBMs were highly vulnerable to blast because they could survive only five pounds per square inch (p.s.i.) of overpressure. Since none or only a few of them contained a storable propellant, they also took hours to fuel and then could not remain ready for long. The warheads were not even married with the missiles; they were kept at special storage facilities guarded by the KGB. U.S. ICBMs were sufficiently accurate and reliable that they could have destroyed over 90 percent of Soviet ICBMs if the United States knew all Soviet launch sites and achieved complete surprise. This brief analysis does not take into account attacks on Soviet strategic bombers. Most of those at known locations could be destroyed by U.S. missiles, but many of those subject only to U.S. bomber attack or at unknown locations would survive. It also does not consider the effects of a U.S. attack on the Soviet command and control network, which would complicate a coordinated Soviet retaliation.[40]

During the 1961 Berlin crisis and on the eve of the October 1962 Cuban missile crisis, several studies suggested that under favorable circumstances a U.S. first strike would keep its losses to about 10 million dead. These studies were inconsistent, however, with much more pessimistic studies that took into account undetected Soviet missiles. The optimistic studies also assumed complete surprise. Considering "unfavorable" circumstances led to calculations closer to 100 million Americans dead. Thus the feasibility of a U.S. attack varied. It would have been low if a conventional war were under way, which would have provided the Soviets with strategic warning and enabled them to ready more forces. It would have been better with a "bolt from the blue," but that was politically unthinkable.[41]

This analysis suggests that in the early 1960s, when the United States could seriously degrade the Soviet ability to retaliate, the Soviets should have worried about a U.S. first strike. Some evidence indicates that they did perceive an unacceptable environment. First, they intensified their policy of strategic deception. During 1960 they claimed for the first time to have military superiority. When they shot down the U-2 reconnaissance plane that year, they touted this as evidence that no U.S. bombers could reach their targets. This deception continued until October 1961, when Kennedy told Khrushchev that U.S. satellites clearly demonstrated Soviet strategic inferiority.[42] Second, just after Kennedy's revelations, Marshal Malinovskiy warned that the Soviet Union might, under some conditions, be forced to preempt. This was the first official statement suggesting preemption since 1957.[43] Third, after the October 1962 Cuban missile crisis, the Soviets increased production of their contemporary ICBM, the SS-7. They also accelerated development of SS-9s and -11s, faster reacting ICBMs that could be housed in protective silos, and they began work on a Polaris-type submarine carrying SLBMs.[44]

During the mid-1960s, the Soviets probably perceived an ambiguous strategic environment. Compared to the unacceptable early 1960s, from their perspective, the situation began to improve in 1963. The number of Soviet ICBMs rose to about 100 in mid-1963, 200 in mid-1964, 270 in mid-1965, 340 in mid-1966, and over 500 by mid-1967. In late 1963 they may have begun to deploy some missiles with a storable liquid propellant. In 1964 they began to deploy the SS-8, whose silos were hardened to 100 p.s.i. In 1965 they followed with the SS-9, which had a storable liquid propellant, was hardened to 300 p.s.i., had a warhead yield five times greater than previous missiles, and was twice as accurate. Finally, their submarine capabilities improved. By mid-1963 they had about 100 SLBMs. In 1964 they began to deploy the SS-N-5, which could be launched from underwater.[45]

As an indicator of an improving Soviet ability to retaliate, U.S. confidence in its damage limitation capabilities declined rapidly. The high point of U.S. optimism was revealed in McNamara's Ann Arbor speech of June 16, 1962, when he lauded "controlled response" and "city-avoidance." Yet just over a year later, in a speech on November 18, 1963, he said that strategic nuclear war would be "highly destructive to both sides" under "all foreseeable circumstances."[46]

In the mid-1960s the Soviets also had more effective early-warning systems, so that they would be better able to preempt a U.S. surprise attack using a launch-on-tactical-warning or launch-under-attack policy. Despite these improvements, however, they probably did not yet perceive an acceptable strategic environment. The United States still had a huge quantitative advantage, with three times as many ICBMs in 1966 and almost twice as many in 1967. As late as 1967, almost 40 percent of Soviet ICBMs did not yet have storable propellants, only one-third to one-half were hardened to 300 p.s.i., and most of their SLBMs could not be launched from under water.[47] The Soviets were not assured of an ability to prevent the United States from attacking and emerging better off than the Soviet Union. Even a countercity Soviet retaliation might kill only several tens of millions to under 100 million Americans, compared to the over 100 million Soviets that the United States could kill.

The secondary criterion for a stable strategic environment evidently did not obtain during the period of this case study. In the early 1960s, almost all U.S. behaviors indicated offensive intentions. Strategic Air Command (SAC) bombers were dual-capable weapons, intended for both counterforce and countervalue missions. The Soviets saw their emphasis on preemption, with the primary mission to attack unready military forces and then the economic-industrial base.[48] U.S. intermediate-range ballistic missiles (IRBMs) had short flight times and high accuracy, which gave them counterforce capabilities against Soviet bombers and missiles. They were also highly vulnerable, because they were at fixed, unprotected locations near the Soviet Union. Since they did not have a storable liquid propellant, they also had a slow reaction time. Consequently, IRBMs were better suited for surprise counterforce missions than for second-strike, retaliatory missions.[49] Procuring them probably contributed to the Soviet perception that U.S. intentions were offensive.

In 1960 the United States deployed its first squad of nine Atlas ICBMs, as well as two Polaris submarines—each carrying 16 SLBMs.[50] Like IRBMs, the Atlases could destroy both military and nonmilitary targets, and they did not have a storable propellant. Their longer range enabled them to hit targets throughout the Soviet Union, however.

The Polaris system had fewer offensive capabilities than land-based ballistic missiles, but particular Soviet circumstances made it difficult to distinguish as a weapon with only countervalue capabilities. On the one hand, because the Polaris submarine platform was constantly moving, the location of the launch site involved some uncertainty that decreased the accuracy of the SLBMs. Thus SLBMs had less counterforce capabilities than the land-based systems and were able to destroy only soft targets. Range limitations also meant that they could not attack some Soviet missile and bomber fields. On the other hand, because Soviet forces were not hardened against nuclear attack, SLBMs had some counterforce capability against missiles and bombers. Furthermore, from the perspective of Soviet ground-based early-warning radars, some possible SLBM flight paths were identical to paths of U.S. IRBMs and some ICBMs; this problem abated somewhat by the middle-1960s, when the United States had completed its withdrawal of IRBMs.[51]

Several additional factors contributed to the Soviets' difficulty in differentiating U.S. offensive and deterrent forces: Most Soviet strategic bases were co-located near population centers, early-warning technology was not sufficiently sophisticated to discriminate, and command and control facilities were vulnerable.[52]

U.S. declaratory doctrine did not seem defensive. McNamara's 1961 emphasis on "flexible response" continued to include the contingency of initiating general nuclear war in response to conventional aggression. He emphasized damage limitation from mid-1962 to mid-1963. His call for "city-avoidance" involved plans to use U.S. forces in a second-strike, counterforce manner. The Soviets attacked the doctrine, and even his American critics said that the forces could also be used for first-strike missions.[53]

By late 1963 McNamara downgraded the "no-cities" idea somewhat, but damage limitation was not yet clearly subordinated to assured retaliation missions. Even the term "assured destruction" was not used officially until 1964. Also by late 1963, the United States had said it would complete the withdrawal of all its IRBMs from Europe. Their removal signaled benign U.S. intentions. At the same time, however, the United States continued to augment its ICBM inventory.[54] U.S. procurement policies and declaratory doctrine did not signal a move away from offensive intentions until 1968, and we will overview the transition in chapter 7.

When the United States announced the outer space initiative in September 1962, overall the Soviets probably would have perceived a doubly unstable strategic environment: The United States had a significant offensive advantage, and it procured few weapons that were not capable of carrying out offensive missions. By September 1963, when the Soviets finally reciprocated the initiative formally, the first component probably had changed from unacceptable to ambiguous, and the second remained unchanged. Since the first is more important than the second, we can presume that overall in September 1963 they perceived a moderately unstable strategic environment.

SUMMARY

When the Soviets publicly reciprocated the U.S. unilateral initiative in September 1963, a number of the obvious factors favoring success were present. U.S. signals were both clear and complete, and apparently the Soviets interpreted them correctly.

Soviet calculations also disposed them to reciprocate publicly. Security concerns moderately favored the agreement: Although it would have had few immediate security consequences, orbiting their own nuclear weapons would have presented the Soviets with longer-term security problems (i.e., a U.S. ASAT system and orbiting nuclear weapons). The proposed verification mechanism was favorable because on-site inspection was not required. Calculations about NATO and relations with Non-Aligned countries were moderately favorable. More important, with the Sino-Soviet split now obviously irreversible, accommodation with the United States would help to isolate China as a reckless state. Because the proposed agreement called for reciprocal concessions and did not constrain their ability to attain parity and hence equal status, it affirmed Soviet prestige. Finally, the Soviet need for U.S. grain also moderately favored an agreement.

Domestically, the Soviet military stood to lose little from the proposed agreement; thus this factor also favored agreement. None of the other obvious factors discouraged agreement in September 1963, and the rest were unimportant.

Few obvious factors favored agreement in 1962, which goes a long way toward explaining why the Soviets waited a year to shift from tacit to explicit reciprocation.

Apparently U.S. signals were not sufficiently explicit about the scope of the proposed agreement or verification mechanisms. This situation may have contributed to Soviet misperceptions and expectations that an agreement would have had the security and bureaucratic disadvantages of losing ballistic missiles and intrusive inspection. Political calculations about China were also unsupportive of a formal agreement. At the time, only political calculations about NATO and Non-Aligned countries favored public reciprocation, but these considerations were obviously outweighed by the unfavorable conditions. The remaining obvious factors were unimportant or had a mixed impact.

Our case studies are also intended to help us test hypotheses about factors that may favor successful initiatives. In this chapter we find a correlation for three hypotheses. Two are associated with signaling and are moderately corroborated (a series and a campaign of initiatives). With some qualifications, for each of them neither of the circumstances alleged to favor success obtained in September 1962, and both obtained in September 1963. The other hypothesis concerns Soviet perceptions of the level of international tension. Tensions seemed high when the United States announced the initiative and low when the Soviets reciprocated formally a year later.

The hypothesis that an objective history should accompany a successful initiative is only partially confirmed. When the Soviet Union did not reciprocate formally, the United States had presented no such history. When the Soviets later reciprocated formally, it was after Kennedy's June 10 speech. It is ambiguous, however, whether or not that speech constitutes such a history.

For two hypotheses no correlations emerge, because the circumstances alleged to favor success obtained at both times (i.e., international communication was verbal, and Khrushchev's authority was consolidated). The strategic environment hypothesis was not confirmed, because supposedly unfavorable situations obtained both times (i.e., it seemed unstable in September 1962 and moderately unstable in September 1963). For the remaining hypothesized factors, either they were irrelevant or no evidence emerged.

We cannot know with certainty all the reasons why the Soviets did what they did. But at least some government participants think the U.S. tactic was helpful. For instance, Arthur J. Goldberg, chief U.S. negotiator for the 1967 Outer Space Treaty and UN ambassador, said: "Based upon this [1962] unilateral declaration by the United States, in the following year we were able to get Soviet agreement."[55]

5

Case Study:
Nuclear Testing (1963)

Twice during 1963 the United States implemented unilateral initiatives involving the testing of nuclear explosives. The first, announced January 26, failed to secure the required Soviet concession. The second, announced June 10, contributed to Soviet reciprocation and thus helped the parties to reach agreement on the Limited Test Ban Treaty. Before describing the bargaining interactions and explaining contrasting Soviet behavior, let us briefly turn to the historical background.

ATOMIC AND NUCLEAR WEAPONS TESTING, 1945-62

The United States conducted the first atomic bomb test in July 1945, and the Soviet Union followed in 1949. The first test for each side was needed to demonstrate that it could produce an atomic explosive. Thereafter other reasons for testing assumed prominence: to develop explosives of different yields, to improve particular characteristics of the explosives (i.e., yield to weight ratio, reliability, and, after the development of hydrogen bombs in 1952 and 1953, the fusion-to-fission ratio in order to develop more powerful or "cleaner" explosives that had less radioactive fallout), to test explosives designed to marry with particular delivery vehicles, and to test the effects of explosions on various types of targets.[1]

The desirability of nuclear testing did not become a serious political issue until 1954. That year U.S. tests in the Pacific exposed the Marshall Islands to fallout, and a crewman of the Japanese fishing boat *Lucky Dragon* died from exposure to the fallout. Subsequently, India's Prime Minister Jawaharlal Nehru proposed that all nations observe a "standstill agreement," and opposition to testing began to grow in the United Nations.[2] A test ban had been the subject of periodic disarmament negotiations since 1946, but not until 1958 did the United States, Britain, and the Soviet Union act to restrain their testing. In November 1958 they began a tacit, uninspected moratorium. It lasted until September 1961, when the Soviets resumed testing.

The United States followed, and for over a year the test ban negotiations made no progress.[3]

In August 1962, for instance, the United States tabled two draft treaties. One detailed a ban on all but underground tests, and it required no on-site inspection. The other was a comprehensive test ban that required on-site inspection. The Soviets rejected both drafts, the CTB because of inspection requirements and the limited test ban (LTB) because it legitimized underground testing. However, the agreement they reached the next year closely resembled the LTB draft.[4]

In November and December of 1962, the Soviets finally made some concessions.[5] They dropped a linkage between limits on testing and disarmament, which increased the feasibility of reaching agreement on a test ban. On November 13 they suggested discussions of unmanned seismic stations, and on December 10 they made the formal proposal to allow on Soviet territory two or three unmanned seismic instruments. Then on December 19 Khrushchev said that to remove an obstacle in negotiations, the Soviet Union would permit two or three inspections of suspected test sites per year. On December 28, Kennedy said that the United States had reduced its demand for on-site inspection from twelve to 20 annually to eight to ten. With the differences thus narrowed, during January the parties engaged in further discussions to attempt to reach an agreement.[6]

INITIATIVE No. 1: POSTPONEMENT OF UNDERGROUND TEST SERIES

Bargaining Interactions

On January 26, 1963, President Kennedy released a press statement that announced a postponement of a planned series of underground tests:

During the present discussions in Washington and New York on the nuclear test ban, . . . I have asked the Atomic Energy Commission to postpone underground shots in Nevada. We are maintaining the ability and readiness to resume our test program at any time. We have no intention of again accepting an indefinite moratorium on testing, and if it is clear we cannot achieve a workable agreement we will act accordingly.[7]

The wording of his announcement suggests that his intention was to encourage progress in two areas: he wanted additional Soviet verification concessions, and he wanted a treaty—not an indefinite moratorium that the Soviets could break with few costs. In reporting Kennedy's announcement, the *Washington Post* suggested two additional motives: to avoid imparing negotiations, and to avoid expected Soviet propaganda attacks when the

United States conducted the test series.[8] The article did not say which motive had priority.

The initiative failed to elicit additional Soviet concessions, and the United States began to test on February 8.[9] Soviet propaganda attacks came several days after the series began. The Soviets accused the United States of violating UN General Assembly Resolution 1762 (passed November 6, 1962), and they emphasized the resolution section urging the parties to halt all nuclear testing by the end of 1962.[10] The United States emphasized the part calling for assurances for verification, and it claimed that the Soviet offer of two or three inspections per year was inadequate.[11]

Explanation

U.S. signals about its demands and intentions were not particularly clear and hence were moderately unfavorable for the initiative's success. The United States did signal a linkage between its continued restraint and Soviet verification concessions. The U.S. demand was not in the "same currency" as the unilateral initiative, however, and an unintended signal was the *Washington Post* report that the move was in part a tactic to avoid or to minimize the effects of an expected Soviet propaganda attack. The United States also postponed its tests at a time the Soviets were not conducting tests, and it resumed testing although the Soviets had not resumed. Consequently, although the United States responded quickly when it knew the Soviets would not meet its demands, U.S. resumption of testing probably seemed like an overreaction that was not defensive in nature. The United States did not accompany the initiative with a history of previous bargaining interactions, and it was not yet conducting a series of initiatives. The closest it came to a campaign of initiatives was the previous outer space initiative, which it had announced in September 1962. The Soviets apparently received all these signals and, with the possible exception of the outer space initiative, interpreted them correctly. Their subsequent propaganda attack is evidence for this assertion.

Security calculations probably encouraged the Soviets not to agree to a CTB, although the arguments and evidence are not conclusive.

On the one hand, a CTB would have hindered qualitative improvements in explosives, such as increases in yield-to-weight and fusion-to-fission ratios. Given a desire for counterforce capabilities, the Soviets probably wanted smaller warheads with higher yield-to-weight ratios. Such warheads would permit more streamlined nosecones for the warheads so that they could reach their targets more accurately and at a higher velocity than before, and they would permit the later development of multiple warheads on launchers. Furthermore, with more efficient warheads, a given amount of deliverable megatonnage would not require so many large, expensive rockets. The Soviets may also have thought a ban would have hindered their efforts to catch up with the United States. The President's Science Advisory Commission report of 1958 suggested as much when it argued that a CTB would increase the period of U.S. superiority.[12] ACDA Director William Foster repeated this argument on March 11, 1963.[13]

On the other hand, the U.S. Joint Chiefs of Staff (JCS) opposed a CTB, saying it would hinder maintaining U.S. superiority.[14] If the Soviets agreed, security calculations would have been more likely than otherwise to dispose them to support a CTB. In addition, two Soviet actions indicate they may have seriously considered a CTB: They had been a party to the 1958-61 testing moratorium, and they made a concession in late 1962 to permit some on-site inspection.

Several lines of argument lead to the conclusion that the disadvantages of a CTB likely outweighed the advantages. First, the militaries on both sides probably opposed a CTB for organizational reasons. We know the U.S. military did and, as I shall discuss below, the Soviet military probably did. This bureaucratic situation casts some doubt on the credibility of the JCS's case that a CTB would help the Soviets.

Second, Soviet military and political calculations apparently coincided with their support for a test ban from 1958 to 1961 and their opposition to a CTB in 1963. According to Arkady Shevchenko, in February 1958 Foreign Minister Gromyko told him that Khrushchev wanted to initiate a testing moratorium largely for political purposes, despite some military opposition.[15] This was only five months after Sputnik's launch, and it is plausible they were not yet worried about developing and testing smaller, more efficient warheads. Scientists in the United States conceived of the multiple reentry vehicle (MRV) idea in 1958, and U.S. MRV deployment began in 1964—years before Soviet deployment.[16] Assuming U.S. leadership in the multiple-warhead idea and subsequent Soviet awareness of the concept by January 1963, the Soviets probably saw more military disadvantages to a CTB in 1963 than in 1958.

Soviet calculations about "barriers to entry" to its level of power would have moderately favored a CTB. On the one hand, if West Germany became a party to a CTB, the agreement would have added a technical constraint to acquiring nuclear weapons—a major Soviet foreign policy objective. On the other hand, Britain and France already had nuclear weapons, and by this time the Soviets expected China to accept no constraints on its plans to build and test such weapons.[17]

Verification requirements did not favor making the concession. The United States demanded the right to conduct a minimum of seven on-site inspections per year, compared with the Soviet maximum of three.[18] Either the United States demanded too much, or the Soviets were looking for an excuse not to make the concession. At any rate, several months later Khrushchev gave the traditional Soviet explanation for opposing more than a few (if any) on-site inspections: "The Western Governments advanced their terms on a certain number of inspections for the conclusion of a test ban agreement. What do they want? Essentially, they want Soviet territory to be opened to spies from NATO military headquarters."[19]

Political calculations favored a test ban agreement. Since the October 1962 Cuban missile crisis, China had been openly hostile toward the Soviet Union, and U.S.-Soviet cooperation would help to isolate China as a reckless state.[20] An agreement also would have marginally improved political relations with most European members of NATO. Soviet relations with France apparently would have been unaffected, however. French President Charles de Gaulle said, for instance: "We have no objection to the great powers suspending their nuclear tests; but the fact that they might change their arsenals . . . would in no way be a disarmament measure."[21] Short of general nuclear disarmament, France wanted to continue to test in order to develop its own nuclear arsenal. Finally, an agreement would have improved Soviet relations with the Non-Aligned countries, which favored a test ban.[22]

An agreement would have had mixed consequences for Soviet prestige. On the one hand, the proposed agreement would have put equal, reciprocal obligations on both parties. On the other hand, since it probably would have hindered the Soviet ability to catch up with the United States, it would have harmed the norm of equal status—another important aspect of prestige.

Domestic economic consequences would have been mixed, but overall they probably disposed the leaders to reject a CTB. On the one hand, a CTB would have permitted cutting the budget of the Soviet testing bureaucracy. On the other hand, after the humiliation of the Cuban missile crisis, achieving strategic parity became an even greater long-run imperative.[23] Therefore preventing improvements in nuclear explosives would have necessitated more expensive quantitative increases in strategic power; these additional costs would have outweighed financial savings from a CTB. International economic considerations were unimportant, because the Soviets were not yet aware that they would need to import Western grain because of a poor harvest later in 1963.[24]

The domestic and international environment of bargaining may also have affected Soviet behavior. The Soviet military probably opposed a CTB, since it would have hindered warhead improvements. Because the military would then be less able than otherwise to perform their strategic missions, they probably argued that making the concession would undermine Soviet security prospects. Evidence for this proposition is a consistent lack of enthusiasm by the Soviet military for a test ban. Their journals frequently omitted references to a test ban, and when they mentioned one they tended to link it to infeasible disarmament proposals and to emphasize the dangers of Western power.[25]

Test ban discussions were under way at the time of Kennedy's initiative, and these seemed to be informal. As evidence that they were not formal negotiations, Secretary of State Dean Rusk said that "the recent discussions have not in perhaps the most proper sense been called negotiations." ACDA's Foster also called them "private meetings which took place during the [Geneva] recess."[26] Glenn Seaborg reported that the Soviet negotiator had no freedom of action, however.[27] This lack of flexibility may have been due to one or several factors: strict prior instructions, a requirement for consultation with the leadership in Moscow, or constraints arising from the recessed Geneva negotiations; the literature did not suggest which reason. Formal negotiations resumed in Geneva on February 12, several days after the United States started testing again.[28]

Khrushchev's authority was consolidated at this time. The U.S. proposal had such serious security, inspection, and bureaucratic disadvantages, however, that the question may not have been controversial among key political actors. I found no evidence of controversy or of the initiative's impact on the balance of opinion within the leadership.

In January 1963 the Soviets probably perceived a moderate level of international tension. This was a time of transition from a high level preceding the resolution of the Cuban missile crisis and a low level beginning with Kennedy's American University speech in June.

As was discussed in chapter 4, Soviet perceptions of the strategic environment probably shifted from unacceptable in the early 1960s to ambiguous in the mid-1960s. Since January 1963 is not obviously in either period, we can say only that their perception likely ranged somewhere between the two values. Secondarily, the U.S. force posture and declaratory doctrine both indicated offensive intentions and they continued to do so through the mid-1960s. Overall, therefore, in January 1963 the Soviets probably perceived a strategic environment that ranged somewhere between unstable and moderately unstable.

INITIATIVE No. 2: MORATORIUM ON ATMOSPHERIC NUCLEAR TESTS

Bargaining Interactions

President Kennedy's American University speech of June 10, 1963, led to a major breakthrough on the test ban issue. He stated the familiar view that peace would be more likely if the Soviet Union adopted a more enlightened attitude, but he added that he believed the United States could help them to do that. He cited common interests in avoiding war, called for improved relations and increased cooperation with the Soviets, expressed hope that a CTB would be forthcoming, said that test ban negotiations would resume in Moscow, and then announced a unilateral initiative:

To make clear our good faith and solemn conviction on the matter, I now declare that the United States does not propose to conduct nuclear tests in the atmosphere so long as other states do not do so. We will not be the first to resume. Such a declaration is no substitute for a formal binding treaty—but I hope it will help us achieve one. Nor would such a treaty be a substitute for disarmament—but I hope it will help us achieve it.[29]

His speech did not coincide with a halt to nuclear testing. Neither side had tested in the atmosphere since December, and the United States was continuing to test underground. It did, however, reaffirm and further Kennedy's policy shift toward improving relations with the Soviet Union, and it officially committed the United States to refrain from testing in the atmosphere unless the Soviets resumed testing. Kennedy felt that the environmental and political gains of a LTB treaty outweighed minor military losses, and that the tactic would help to reach an agreement.[30]

Within several days of Kennedy's speech, Khrushchev welcomed its general tone and even permitted *Pravda* and *Isvestia* to publish it.[31] He responded to the specific proposal for an LTB on July 2 in East Berlin, saying the Soviet Union would seriously consider a ban on testing in the atmosphere, under water, and in outer space; previously the Soviets had not supported an LTB. In his July 2 speech, Khrushchev also linked progress toward a test ban to a nonaggression pact between NATO and the Warsaw Treaty Organization. If accepted, the pact would have implied Western acceptance of the political status quo in Europe. He soon dropped this linkage that the West would not then accept. Though Kennedy had committed the United States to halt only atmospheric tests, the following day the State Department accepted the idea of a three-environment ban.[32]

Negotiations resumed July 15 in Moscow, and the delegates initialed the Limited Test Ban Treaty on July 25.[33] After a somewhat heated debate, the Senate ratified the treaty on September 24. In the process the military obtained four "safeguards" in exchange for their support: a comprehensive and aggressive program of underground testing, maintenance of modern nuclear weapons laboratories, maintenance of a capacity to resume atmospheric tests, and improvements in verification capabilities.[34] The treaty entered into force on October 10.

Explanation

U.S. signaling was very clear. Kennedy's initiative was in the same currency as what he wanted the Soviets to do: reciprocate the restraint. He was clear in his promise not to test in the atmosphere and in his threat to resume testing if the Soviets did not reciprocate. The precedent that Kennedy had resumed testing just after the Soviets broke the earlier tacit moratorium added credibility to this threat. The public nature of his speech also indicated his seriousness. Furthermore, the tone of his speech was clearly conciliatory, so the combination of his words and deeds signaled benign intentions.

Apparently the United States did not accompany the initiative with an explicit history of test ban negotiations and other bargaining interactions. In addition, no evidence of such a history appears in *Documents on Disarmament* between the June 10 initiative and July 25, when the parties initialed an LTB agreement. As we saw in chapter 4, however, Kennedy's speech constituted a partial history of Cold War interactions. At best, therefore, we can say that it is ambiguous whether or not this condition obtained.

The United States was in the process of conducting a campaign of initiatives. Actions consistent with a campaign include continuation of the outer space initiative and a concession at the United Nations concerning Hungary. At the time the Soviet Union reciprocated the LTB initiative, the United States had not been conducting a series of initiatives. Soviet actions indicate that they correctly interpreted U.S. signals, and subsequent cost-benefit calculations disposed them to reciprocate.

Unlike a CTB, an LTB had few security consequences because underground testing was permitted. Thus the Soviet Union could continue to improve the yield-to-weight ratios of its warheads and thus enhance its ability to retaliate and degrade U.S. military capabilities. In 1962 the Soviets said that underground testing was giving them "not inconsiderable results" in developing cleaner bombs, so evidently atmospheric testing was becoming less important militarily.[35]

A Soviet statement on August 3, 1963, also indicates they saw no security losses: "Does conclusion of a treaty banning the tests alter the present balance of power? No, it does not. [We] would never have agreed to the conclusion of such a treaty if it placed us in an unequal position, if it gave unilateral advantages to the other side."[36]

As with calculations about a CTB, Soviet considerations for "barriers to entry" to the nuclear club would have moderately favored an LTB. If other Soviet adversaries became parties to the treaty, the complexity and expense of underground testing would inhibit their acquisition of nuclear weapons. Verification requirements presented no problems, for on-site inspection was not required.[37]

Political calculations continued to favor a test ban agreement. Most European members of NATO would have found Soviet reciprocation reassuring.[38] The same can be said for the Non-Aligned countries.[39] The LTB Treaty would also help to isolate China by painting it as a reckless state. As evidence to support this latter argument, consider the following statements. First, we hear the Chinese:

This treaty signed in Moscow is a big fraud. . . . The people of the world demand general disarmament and a complete ban on nuclear weapons; this treaty divorces the cessation of nuclear tests from the total prohibition of nuclear weapons. . . . [T]his treaty actually strengthens the position of the nuclear powers for nuclear blackmail and increases the dangers of imperialism launching a nuclear war or a world war.[40]

Then the Soviets responded: "All who cherish peace unanimously approve the results of the Moscow talks. . . . Those who oppose the prohibition of nuclear tests . . . show themselves to be opponents of peaceful coexistence, opponents of the line of relaxing international tensions and of undermining the forces of aggression and war."[41] The proposed agreement also affirmed Soviet prestige, because they were required to give up no more actual or potential capability than the United States.

The net domestic economic consequence of an LTB was evidently minimal. The direct economic consequence was a small increase in testing expenses, because underground testing is more costly than atmospheric testing. The agreement also contributed to a further lowering of international tensions, apparently a Soviet objective. This situation may have had an indirect economic effect of marginally helping to avoid an increase in defense expenditures and hence a decrease in consumption at a time the Soviets were striving to reach parity with the United States. Overall, this factor was probably unimportant. International economic considerations would have been unimportant if by early summer the Soviets did not yet expect the coming shortfall in grain production. Since I found no evidence indicating their level of awareness of the agricultural situation at the time, the impact of this factor ranged somewhere between unimportant and favorable.

The proposed agreement put no significant constraints on military missions or budgets, so the Soviet military, like the U.S. military, probably had few strong objections.[42]

Bargaining included formal negotiations. On the U.S. side, Kennedy structured his negotiation team to maximize his own personal control. The U.S. delegation included representatives from ACDA and the Departments of Defense and State, as well as the president's national security advisor. The Joint Chiefs of Staff and the Atomic Energy Commission were not represented. The delegates reported daily and directly to Kennedy, not to their respective agencies.[43] Kennedy had less control over the Senate ratification process, however, and the U.S. military secured the four "safeguards." I found no information on how the Soviets structured their delegation or consultation process in Moscow.

Khrushchev's authority was consolidated, but the proposal offered so many advantages that the likelihood of controvesy seems small. Some evidence suggests, however, that Kennedy's initiative may have made it easier for Khrushchev to push his policies through. Norman Cousins, editor of the *Saturday Review*, had told Kennedy that Khrushchev needed to produce some specific and effective agreement with the United States in the wake of the Cuban missile crisis. Khrushchev allegedly wanted to persuade his collegues who did not share his view that the crisis was a turning point in the Cold War.[44] Apparently such deeds by the United States would have helped his domestic prestige; although he could push policies through, his continuation in office was tenuous.[45]

This analysis suggests that Khrushchev faced little if any opposition to an LTB *after* Kennedy's American University speech. Before the speech, when many Soviet leaders probably associated any test ban with a CTB, he may have faced some opposition to a test ban. Thus Kennedy's initiative probably helped to shift the balance of political forces further in a direction favoring an LTB, although by how much is unclear.

As we saw in the Chapter 4, with Kennedy's June 10 speech the Soviets apparently perceived a low level of international tension. No international crises were under way, Soviet rhetoric took on a collaborative tone as it covered the mutual relationship and politics in the United States, and it made no references to a high danger of war.[46] Both parties also wanted to lower tensions, and their policies of mutual concessions aided the process.[47]

The secondary criterion for a stable strategic environment remained unmet, as U.S. weapons procurement patterns and military doctrine still indicated offensive intentions. Once again, the Soviet perception of the primary criterion may have been in the period of transition between the early 1960s (when the environment was unacceptable) and the mid-1960s (when its nature was ambiguous). Overall, therefore, the Soviets probably perceived a strategic environment that ranged somewhere between unstable and moderately unstable.

SUMMARY

Many more conditions favored the success of Kennedy's June initiative than his January one. U.S. signals were perfectly clear in June. In January, however, U.S. signaling was moderately unfavorable for the proposed agreement because the initiative was not in the same currency as the desired Soviet concession, and it seemed to be a propaganda tactic. In both cases the Soviets apparently received the U.S. signals correctly.

Cost-benefit calculations clearly favored a LTB but not a CTB. A CTB had too many security, verification, and domestic economic disadvantages. An

LTB, in contrast, had no significant security or domestic economic disadvantages, and it had verification and prestige advantages (in contrast to ambiguous prestige consequences in January). The Soviet military also seemed to exhibit opposition to a CTB but not to the LTB.

In both instances political calculations favored an agreement, but in January other circumstances clearly overwhelmed this condition. International economic consequences, the final obvious factor, was either unimportant in both instances or was unimportant in January and favorable in June; I found insufficient evidence to suggest which combination for June.

The research for the two cases in this chapter partially supports three hypotheses, where the expected condition obtained for one of the cases but the situation was ambiguous or unknown for the other. These concern the history of previous interactions (not present for the unsuccessful CTB case and ambiguous for the successful LTB initiative); the impact of the initiative on the balance of power within the Soviet leadership (unknown for the CTB case and possibly favorable for the LTB case); and Soviet perceptions of the level of international tension (moderate and hence perhaps irrelevant for the CTB case and low for the LTB case).

No correlation emerges for four hypotheses, because the circumstances supposed to favor or undermine success obtained in both cases: a campaign of initiatives was under way (although the campaign was sparse in January), a series of initiatives was not under way, the strategic environment probably seemed to range somewhere between unstable and moderately unstable, and Khrushchev's authority was consolidated. The relevance of the last factor is in doubt, however, because the prominence of the disadvantages and advantages was clear in each case.

The hypothesis on the formality of negotiations fails the test of research completely, because for both cases the outcome was opposite from the circumstances the hypothesis leads us to expect (i.e., negotiations were informal during the unsuccessful CTB case and formal during the successful LTB case).

Three hypotheses are difficult to evaluate. First, when the Soviets rejected the U.S. demand for more verification concessions, the United States responded quickly by resuming underground tests in February. This quick response failed to secure subsequent Soviet agreement on verification mechanisms for a CTB, but it may have added credibility to Kennedy's signals that accompanied his later, successful LTB initiative. Second and third, when the Soviets failed to accept the January proposal, the United States did not respond moderately or defensively. As expected, Soviet interest in a CTB did not increase. Despite this U.S. bargaining behavior, however, the Soviets did reciprocate Kennedy's June initiative.

6

Case Study: Medium-Range Bombers (1964–65)

During 1964 and 1965, the United States tried to use its phase-out plans for the B-47 bomber as a unilateral initiative. It hoped that the Soviet Union would agree to destroy an equal number of TU-16s, a comparable medium-range bomber, but the initiative failed to elicit Soviet reciprocation. Before explaining Soviet behavior, let us examine the bargaining that occurred.

BARGAINING INTERACTIONS

B-47s began to enter the U.S. active bomber inventory in 1954. Ultimately over 2000 were produced, and almost all were stationed overseas near the Soviet Union. As early as 1959, however, the United States began to phase them out. They were becoming vulnerable to a preemptive missile attack, and their mission was gradually taken over by intercontinental range B-52 bombers and ballistic missiles.[1]

Not until 1963 did the United States attempt to link its deactivation plans to Soviet behavior. It first proposed the mutual destruction of medium-range bombers on August 5, 1963, when representatives of the United States and the Soviet Union signed the LTB Treaty in Moscow.[2] At a news conference on January 2, 1964, Secretary of State Rusk reiterated that there had been some informal discussion of a "bomber bonfire."[3]

The Soviets had their own priorities. Their memorandum to the Eighteen Nation Disarmament Committee (ENDC), submitted on January 28, 1964, included a proposal to eliminate all bomber aircraft.[4] On March 2, Foreign Minister Andrei Gromyko publicly criticized the U.S. proposal for the first time:

An attempt is being made to confront our proposal [for the elimination of all bombers] with the United States proposal for the elimination by the Soviet Union and the United States of bombers by single type. This proposal, however, is quite useless, for every soldier is quite aware that one obsolete bomber can be replaced by another more modern one.[5]

Adrian Fisher, Deputy Director of ACDA and acting representative to the ENDC, formally made the proposal on March 19, 1964:

The United States proposes destruction by the United States and the Soviet Union of an equal number of B-47 and TU-16 bombers. We propose that this destruction be carried out at the rate of twenty per month on each side, the bombers to be taken from the operational inventory. We are prepared to continue the destruction of these bombers at this rate for a period of two years. In addition, we are prepared to increase the total number destroyed by adding to the monthly quota an additional agreed number to be taken from bombers stored and preserved for emergency mobilization. . . .

The B-47 and TU-16 are logical arms with which to begin to start the process of physical destruction of arms. The United States and the Soviet Union possess roughly comparable numbers of those aircraft. The two types have been assigned generally similar strategic roles. Thus the balance in overall force structure of the two sides would be maintained at the reduced levels resulting from their de-struction.[6]

Fisher went on to state the unilateral initiative part of his speech, where he linked details of U.S. phase-out plans to Soviet reciprocation:

The United States does have plans to phase B-47s out of its battle ready forces. I assume that the Soviet Union also has phase-out plans for the TU-16. But phasing out of aircraft does not mean destruction. Bombers in storage can be flying again in short order. What the United States is now proposing is to negotiate a rate of de-struction which, if immediately implemented would be significantly faster than its planned phase-out rate.[7]

In statements on April 2 and July 16, 1964, the Soviet representative to the ENDC, Semen Tsarapkin, continued to reject the proposal.[8] Later on July 16, acting U.S. representative to the ENDC, Clare Timberlake, said: "We are prepared to consider any lesser numbers selected by them. If the Soviet Union is not prepared to undertake destruction of any TU-16 aircraft at this time, perhaps it might suggest other types of aircraft—or other armaments—with which it would prefer to bargain."[9] His appeal for Soviet flexibility was unheeded. A Soviet memorandum dated December 7, 1964, stated that the Soviet Union would consider "bonfires of bombers" only in the context of an agreement to destroy all bombers.[10]

UN Ambassador Adali Stevenson made the next U.S. public statement on this issue on April 26, 1965. He said that despite Soviet disagreement, "the United States has initiated plans to phase out large numbers of these bombers."[11] He then put this initiative into the context of additional U.S. initiatives:

For its part, the United States has taken some actions which we hope will be reciprocated. I have mentioned the effort made by my Government that has resulted in reduction of military expenditures; I have noted the reductions in the planned production of fissionable materials; and I have commented on the program initiated to begin the reduction of B-47 strategic bombers from our active inventory.

In connection with this last point I might observe that by mid-1966 the United States will have inactivated or destroyed over 2000 B-47 bomber-type aircraft. I might also add that none have been provided as potential strategic nuclear vehicles to other countries. In addition, the United States will make a reduction during 1965 in the number of B-52 heavy-bombers in the existing operational forces. These reductions also will be accompanied by the destruction of aircraft. Moreover, the United States now plans to forgo the construction of some Minuteman missiles which were included in our plans, as well as further increments of such missiles in the future.

Those are examples of restraint on the part of a nation which is capable . . . of far greater military production. There are limits, however, to the restraints or other actions that can be taken unilaterally without reciprocity.[12]

The Soviets responded two days later with another disarmament proposal, which in part called for the elimination of all military aircraft capable of delivering nuclear weapons.[13] This remained their policy, and therefore the unilateral deactivation of the B-47 bomber fleet failed to compel the Soviets to reciprocate. The United States brought this proposal up publicly only three more times during 1965 and 1966, and then only in passing.[14] By the end of 1966, all the B-47s had been deactivated or destroyed.[15] The TU-16s, in contrast, remained the backbone of Soviet long range aviation for both the Air Force and Navy until the 1970s.[16]

EXPLANATION

U.S. signals were not obviously clear or obscure. On the one hand, its commitment to give up the B-47s was clear, as was its desire to trade them for Soviet TU-16s. On the other hand, the United States did not demonstrate a significant interdependence between the military policies of the two sides. The United States did not threaten to retain the B-47s in service if the Soviets failed to reciprocate. The threat that existed was minimal—merely to keep deactivated bombers in storage and to have a slower pace of deactivation than if the Soviets agreed.

Apparently the United States responded moderately and gradually when, in the face of no Soviet reciprocation, it implemented its threat. Two years later Fisher said that "most of the United States B-47s, although no longer operational, are still part of the United States mobilization reserve from which they could be promptly reactivated for service."[17] This response was also defensive.

The U.S. initiative was part of a series of initiatives. It followed the successful outer space and LTB initiatives, as well as the mutual, informal reductions in defense expenditures. This latter area of agreement was an idea the United States suggested in September 1963, but the Soviets were the first to announce reductions formally. Thus for 1964, the Soviets said they reduced expenditures by 600 million rubles compared to 1963, and in January the United States announced that its defense budget would be cut 1 to 2 percent. The parties continued restraint for more than another year.[18]

A campaign of initiatives was also under way. In addition to those mentioned above, the United States had implemented several that were unreciprocated at the time of the March 19 B-47 initiative. In January and February of 1964, the United States shut down four plutonium production reactors and reduced the rate of production of fissionable materials.[19] Early in March the United States also said it had concluded agreements with the International Atomic Energy Agency (IAEA) to inspect three small U.S. research and power reactors, and that IAEA inspection of a larger reactor would come later.[20]

The United States did not accompany the March 19 initiative with a history of previous bargaining interactions. On April 9, however, Fisher said the two parties had reduced military expenditures informally, but he did not say who made the first move.[21] On April 20 and 21, Johnson and Fisher elaborated on the sequence of moves involving limitations on the production of fissionable materials.[22] The only reference I found in *Documents on Disarmament* that linked the B-47 initiative to other U.S. unilateral initiatives was by Stevenson a year later (quoted above).[23] On April 26, 1965, he mentioned mutual reductions in military budgets and fissile material production, but not the outer space and LTB initiatives. He also said that U.S. initiatives to reduce the number of B-52 bombers and to forgo production of some planned Minuteman missiles had not been met with Soviet reciprocation. Obviously the United States did not present a clear, complete, and coherent image of the history of previous interactions. Since it provided some (although fragmented) history, however, it is not obvious that this condition did not obtain. Consequently, it seems uncertain whether or not the United States presented an appropriate history.

Fisher accompanied his announcement of the B-47 initiative with reference to a strategic context: The proposal would maintain the balance of power at reduced levels and ensure security for both.[24] Timberlake added on July 16 that the proposal would provide for a more equitable balance of power than the Soviet proposal to abolish all bombers.[25] Given Soviet strategic inferiority, however, the U.S. statements are not obviously objective.

The Soviets received these signals and interpreted them correctly. The various criticisms of the U.S. proposal showed that they understood its terms. They also understood that the United States was phasing out its B-47s and would continue to phase them out even without Soviet reciprocation. Tsarapkin elaborated on this theme and his opinion about U.S. motives on April 2, 1964:

It is afterall common knowledge that the United States B-47 bomber is an obsolete weapon, and that the United States Government long ago took the decision to withdraw it from service. In fact, as is clear from an announcement made by the Department of Defense of the United States on 8 November 1963, the United States has been gradually withdrawing this aircraft from service since 1959, and only half the original number now remain.

It is obvious to everyone that the United States side has made its proposal for the destruction of the obsolete B-47 aircraft, not for the purpose of disarmament, but for the purpose of accelerating the reequipment of its air force by introducing technically-superior machines . . . [such as] the F-111a bomber.[26]

Tsarapkin drew these conclusions despite awareness of other instances of U.S. restraint. On February 20, 1964, for example, he referred to the "reduction of military budgets based on the policy of 'mutual example.' . . . "[27] The Soviets of course knew about U.S. restraint in orbiting nuclear weapons, in atmospheric nuclear testing, and in the production of fissile materials.[28] When they cited instances of the policy of mutual example, however, they omitted the B-47 initiative.

The Soviets paid no direct penalty for their inflexibility, because the United States did nothing to halt or curtail its phase-out plans once it knew that the Soviets would not reciprocate. The Soviets understood U.S. signals, but cost-benefit analysis disposed them not to reciprocate. As Tsarapkin said on April 2, 1964, "the drawbacks of the United States proposal for the destruction of some obsolete bombers is becoming increasingly evident. . . . [Such measures] would in fact disturb the correlation of forces . . . to the advantage of the West."[29]

The United States claimed that destroying medium-range bombers would not harm Soviet security.[30] Given overall U.S. strategic superiority, however, the Soviets probably calculated that such an agreement would have harmed their security. Unlike the obsolete B-47s, TU-16s were vital to the Soviet nuclear force posture.[31] Technical and economic problems constrained the Soviet Union from matching the U.S. intercontinental capabilities, and medium-range bombers and missiles were needed to fulfill several missions: to dissuade NATO countries from attacking the Soviet

Union or its East European allies by holding Western Europe hostage and, if war broke out, to limit damage to the Soviet Union by attacking NATO's forces.

Specific targets included U.S. overseas bases and bases of the European NATO allies. At this time, because nuclear forces in Western Europe were vulnerable, the Soviets had a credible nuclear war-fighting capability against NATO allies in Western Europe. In addition, TU-16s were used for maritime reconnaissance and attack. Losing the TU-16s would have seriously jeopardized fulfillment of these missions. Although a new medium-range bomber, the TU-22 "Blinder," gradually began to replace some TU-16s in the mid-1960s, the TU-16 remained central to the Soviet Union through the 1970s.[32]

During 1964 and 1965, the United States had clear quantitative and qualitative strategic nuclear superiority: four times as many ICBMs and about three times as many SLBMs and heavy bombers. The Soviets were ahead only in numbers of medium-range bombers (1400 to 780 [1964] and 1400 to 580 [1965]) and intermediate and medium-range missiles (800 to 0).[33]

Given overall Soviet nuclear inferiority, trading TU-16s for the destruction of equal numbers of active and inactive B-47s would have hurt their relative nuclear capability. Moreover, given the unconditional nature of the B-47 fleet deactivation, the Soviets faced no explicit threat to their security if they failed to reciprocate.

On October 16, 1964, China tested its first atomic bomb.[34] Thus from this time on the Soviet Union clearly would face three regional adversaries with atomic weapons and medium-range bombers: Britain, France, and China. As of October 1964, Britain had 180 land-based bombers and orders in for five Polaris missile-firing submarines. France had the first eight of a planned fleet of fifty Mirage IV bombers. China had only a few obsolescent TU-4s.[35] The U.S. proposal envisioned no restrictions on the military capabilities of these countries. Therefore, if the Soviet Union gave up many of its TU-16s, its power and flexibilitiy would also have declined relative to them. "Barriers to entry" at their level of power were not relevant in this case, because the proposal would have had no significant impact on the ability of third countries to threaten U.S. security.

Verification of the proposed agreement would have required on-site inspection. As Timberlake said on July 16, 1964, "we would propose the designation of perhaps six persons each by the United States and the Soviet Union; and those persons would verify the destruction of the bomber aircraft at the designated airfield of the other party."[36]

I found no direct public statements by the Soviets about the verification requirements of the U.S. proposal. Tsarapkin did make an indirect response on the same day as Timberlake's previous statement: "The elimination of bombers should be carried out under international control since it is a real disarmament measure."[37] Note that he was not talking about the destruction of only medium-range bombers; he referred to the elimination of all bombers—a proposal the United States rejected.[38]

When the United States first announced its initiative in March 1964, Soviet concerns for China favored reciprocation. This was during the November 1962 to early 1965 period, when accommodation with the United States served to isolate China as a reckless state that opposed all East-West collaboration. Then, beginning in early 1965, when the United States escalated its military involvement in Vietnam, Soviet calculations probably reflected ambiguous political consequences. During this time when the outcome of the war was in doubt, the Soviets evidently feared that collusion with the United States might strengthen Chinese claims to be the legitimate leader of the world communist movement, and hence that North Vietnam would draw away from the Soviet Union and toward China. The situation was not clearly unfavorable for arms control, however, because accommodation with the United States still served to isolate an anti-Western China from noncommunist states.[39]

Since Soviet medium-range bombers threatened United States NATO allies, an agreement obliging only the U.S. and the Soviet Union to destroy many of these bombers would have reduced the threat to West European countries without forcing them to decrease their capabilities. Therefore, feeling less threatened by the Soviet Union, their relations with the Soviets probably would have improved. During 1964 and 1965, the only statement from these countries reported in *Documents on Disarmament* was by British Foreign Secretary Richard Butler, and it was consistent with this thesis.[40]

The Soviet position probably cost them little if any political capital with additional states, many of which considered the U.S. proposal unbalanced. From 1964 to 1966, for example, *Documents on Disarmament* reported only three statements from Non-Aligned countries that mentioned the proposal: by Burma, the United Arab Republic, and Nigeria.[41] All three felt that the proposal did not go far enough because it put no restraints on modernizing bombers, although they varied on whether or not they thought the Soviet counterproposal for eliminating all bombers was sufficient.

The proposed agreement did not affirm Soviet prestige. It was widely known that the United States considered its B-47s obsolete and planned to phase them out.[42] Since TU-16s were still a vital part of the Soviet arsenal, a destruction of equal numbers would not have been a reciprocal exchange. Moreover, because of overall Soviet nuclear inferiority, such an exchange would have made the Soviet Union even more inferior—hardly an affirmation of the norm of equal status.

For two reasons Soviet calculations about the domestic economic effects of the proposed agreement did not favor the initiative's success. First, no

matter how the Soviets responded, the United States was unlikely to inten-
sify the arms race as a result. Thus the proposed agreement would not have
saved the Soviet Union from having to increase its defense budget. Second,
the proposed agreement would have reduced Soviet military capabilities in
Europe, since no follow-on plane was ready to replace the TU-16. Consequently, to accomplish their missions, the Soviets would have had to procure additional more expensive and less reliable long-range aircraft.[43] Since
the Soviet Union had a record grain harvest in 1964, U.S. grain was unimportant to them during the 1964/65 crop year. Consequently, the proposed
agreement offered no international economic advantages or disadvantages.[44]

The domestic and international environment of bargaining did not favor
the success of the U.S. initiative. The Soviet Air Force and Navy would have
been hurt by the proposed agreement, and so they probably opposed it.
The inventories of the other services (the Army, Strategic Rocket Forces,
and Air Defense Command) would not have been directly affected. All
would have been more able to carry out their own missions during a war,
however, if the TU-16s succeeded in destroying enemy forces.

The Soviet Navy had two components with aircraft: Naval Air Defense
and the Naval Air Force. The latter used TU-16s for maritime strikes, reconnaissance, and antisubmarine warfare missions. The Air Force had three
components: Long-Range Aviation, Frontal (theater) Aviation, and Military
Air Transport. The TU-16 was central to Long-Range Aviation, with missions against U.S. overseas bases and bases of regional adversaries, as well
as against other targets to complement damage limitation missions or to enhance deterrence. It was also the main tanker aircraft. The TU-16, which
first entered into service in 1954, had a twenty-year life span. It was not due
to retire until the 1970s, and hence it formed the backbone of Long-Range
Aviation and Naval Air Power.[45] Because replacements for TU-16s would
be slow coming into service, the U.S. proposal would have resulted in both
capability and budget reductions for the two services. The Navy would
have been especially hurt, as most of its targets were not fixed and hence
could not have been destroyed by missiles.

The international bargaining began tacitly with unilateral U.S. deactivation of B-47s. The two superpowers briefly discussed the issue at the signing of the LTB Treaty, which introduced informal verbal communication.
When Fisher announced the initiative in March 1964, he introduced the
proposal to the ENDC. Apparently serious formal negotiations on the topic
never took place, because the Soviets had no interest in the proposal.

When the United States first announced the initiative early in 1964,
Khrushchev had no major rivals. He fell from power in October 1964 and
was replaced by Brezhnev, who took a number of years to consolidate his
authority.[46] This change in leadership had no apparent effect on Soviet

policy toward the U.S. proposal. Soviet policy under Khrushchev suggests he opposed it; Brezhnev either opposed it or could not or would not challenge the military's opposition to it. The evidence does not obviously suggest which, but it is plausible and probably likely that he too opposed it because the cost-benefit calculations so clearly favored non-reciprocation. Indeed, few if any Soviet leaders were probably impressed with the U.S. initiative, given the disadvantages of the proposed agreement and the low costs associated with nonreciprocation. I was unable to find evidence to back this assertion, however.

The Soviets apparently perceived a low-moderate level of international tension when the United States first announced the initiative in March 1964. This level was slightly higher than for the latter part of 1963, when the Soviets perceived tensions to be low. After Kennedy's assassination in November 1963, the Soviets apparently were less happy with Lyndon Johnson. Khrushchev, for instance, saw him as racist and anti-Soviet.[47] The United States was also gradually increasing its indirect involvement in Vietnam.

Soviet rhetoric remained optimistic. On March 5, 1964, for example, Gromyko said that disarmament is possible "if still greater use is made of the favorable opportunities resulting from the conclusion of the Moscow Treaty banning nuclear weapons' tests, and from the achievement of agreement . . . against the placing into orbit of objects carrying nuclear weapons." In the same speech, however, he discounted the U.S. proposal for mutual reductions of medium-range bombers.[48]

The Gulf of Tonkin incident occurred in August 1964, where two U.S. destroyers were allegedly attacked by North Vietnamese torpedo boats. The United States responded with a reprisal air raid, the first overt U.S. military action against North Vietnam. Evidently these actions did not greatly alarm the Soviets, however, because they expected the Vietcong to win in South Vietnam. The Soviets dismissed the Gulf of Tonkin incident as the product of Chinese provocation, although we cannot know if the Soviets were serious or were simply using the event for anti-Chinese propaganda.[49]

The Soviet mood darkened in 1965, largely because the United States began long-term operations in Vietnam using direct military power. In February the United States started a bombing campaign against North Vietnam. Soviet Prime Minister Kosygin was in Hanoi at the time and the United States publicly admitted the raid, adding insult to injury. The United States introduced combat troops in March, and during the summer Johnson announced a large troop increase. Although the Soviets probably did not expect the United States to attack their homeland or other vital territory, they may have had a renewed fear of escalation. With the United States demonstrating its willingness to use direct military power against

Soviet allies and friends (e.g., in Vietnam and, with less interest and concern, in the Dominican Republic in April 1965), the possibility of escalation to a war between the superpowers increased.[50] On its merits, this leads us to expect the Soviets to have perceived a moderate level of tension.

Soviet rhetoric indicated a perception of a slightly greater level of tension, however. They condemned U.S. behavior as aggressive, warned that it imperiled peaceful coexistence, and stopped discussing U.S. politics in pluralistic terms.[51] For instance, Nikolay Fedorenko, Soviet Ambassador to the United Nations and a representative to the ENDC, said on 24 May 1965:

> We have heard statements by the United States concerning plans for the destruction of certain obsolete bombers. . . . Yet for a realistic assessment of the measure we must listen—we cannot help listen—to the unceasing explosions of United States bombs in Vietnam. We cannot form our view of a state of world affairs on the basis of what United States diplomats tell us; we cannot regard the destruction of antiquated aircraft as a disarmament measure and as evidence of a desire for peace on the part of the United States when United States weapons are being used to shed blood in various parts of the world.[52]

Two factors can explain the divergence between the deductive and inductive indicators. First, as was discussed earlier in this chapter, the Soviets were under pressure in the communist world to at least sound militant in order to deflect charges by the PRC that they were more interested in accommodation with the United States than with the survival of an ally under attack. Second, this was during a period when Brezhnev was still consolidating his authority. Consequently, since we should give less weight than usual to Soviet rhetoric, the Soviets probably perceived a moderate level of tension.

The U.S. initiative occurred in the mid-1960s, when the Soviets probably perceived a strategic environment that was not obviously unacceptable or acceptable. As was discussed in chapter 4, their position had improved from the unacceptable period of the early 1960s, when the United States would have emerged from a nuclear war it started obviously better off than the Soviets. The situation was not yet acceptable, however, because not until later did it become obvious that the United States would emerge no better off than the Soviet Union from such a war.

The secondary criterion for a stable strategic environment continued to be unmet. From the Soviet perspective, U.S. offensive capabilities declined somewhat in 1965, but not because of benign U.S. intentions. Since the change was almost entirely the result of Soviet efforts to deny the United States a first-strike capability, they still probably perceived offensive U.S. intentions. The Soviets had deployed additional ICBMs that were more survivable and that had a higher level of readiness. They also gradually improved their early-warning radars, which enhanced their ability to provide tactical warning and to differentiate some origins and flight paths of U.S. weapons.[53] U.S. declaratory doctrine continued to advocate strategic superiority. Damage limitation continued to be an objective, although it had lower priority than assured destruction.[54] The Soviets also could not have been reassured with comments by retired SAC Commander General Curtis LeMay, who in his 1965 book advocated a U.S. first-strike capability and provided thinly veiled arguments for a preventive war.[55] Not until later did the United States signal a move away from offensive intentions. With perceptions of offensive U.S. intentions and a strategic environment that was not obviously acceptable or unacceptable, the Soviets probably perceived a strategic environment that was moderately unstable.

SUMMARY

The U.S. attempt to use its phase-out plans for the B-47 bomber failed as a unilateral initiative. This outcome should not be surprising, as only three obvious conditions favored success: the Soviet Union apparently received and correctly interpreted these signals, it would have benefited from improved political relations with West European and Non-Aligned countries, and until early 1965 the proposed agreement would have aided the Soviet foreign policy objective of isolating China.

Additional, more important obvious factors disposed them not to reciprocate the U.S. initiative, however. The proposed agreement would have harmed Soviet security with respect to the United States and smaller nuclear powers, and the effectively unconditional nature of the initiative meant that Soviet security would have been no worse off if they did not reciprocate. Verification would have required on-site inspection on Soviet territory, which they seemed unwilling to accept for agreements that did not clearly favor them. The agreement also would have harmed their prestige because it would have involved an unequal exchange and would not have affirmed the norm of equal status. Finally, the Soviet military probably opposed the proposed agreement. The remaining obvious factors were either unaffected or indeterminant.

Two of the hypotheses are supported, and in each case the expected outcome of failure occurred: The United States did not respond quickly to the Soviets' lack of reciprocation, and the Soviets probably perceived the strategic environment to be moderately unstable. Six hypotheses fail the test of research: The initiative did not work despite a moderate and defensive U.S. response to the lack of Soviet reciprocation; the United States had been implementing both a campaign and a series of initiatives; communication was informal; and for about a year following the unsuccessful March

1964 initiative the Soviets probably perceived a low-moderate level of tension.

The research is inconclusive about the hypothesis on the strength of the general-secretary, because the issue probably was not controversial. Finally, the research suggests nothing about the hypothesis on the initiative's impact on pro-arms control actors (no evidence emerged), or on the hypothesis about an accompanying history of previous bargaining interactions (the situation was ambiguous).

7

Case Study: Antiballistic Missiles (1967–68)

The Soviets were the first to begin to deploy an anti-ballistic missile system. Evidence of site construction started to accumulate in 1961 and 1962, and by 1966 they were clearly accelerating construction of a site near Moscow. In order encourage them to halt deployment and to begin negotiations to limit defensive and offensive weapons, President Johnson implemented a unilateral initiative in January 1967. The tactic failed, as the Soviets refused even to consider limitations on ballistic missile defense (BMD). Not until 1968, when the United States began to spend funds to produce and deploy its own ABM, did the Soviets indicate interest in ABM limitations and arms control talks. To understand these Soviet behaviors, we must first examine the historical background.

ABM PROCUREMENT, 1955–66

In 1955 the Soviets established the Protinvovzdushnaia Oborona Strany (PVO) as a separate military service. PVO translates as "anti-air defense of the country," and its mission is to defend against bombers and missiles.[1] It was responsible for conducting ABM research and development (R&D). U.S. R&D began in 1957, when the Army established the Nike-Zeus Guided Missile Defense System Project. In 1959 and 1960 the Army requested $1.3 billion, which included funds to begin production and deployment. President Eisenhower pared the request to $300 million for R&D only. Congress added $137 million for production, but Eisenhower refused to spend it.[2]

In 1961–62, evidence from satellite reconnaissance indicated that the Soviets were conducting an extensive ABM research, development, and testing program and were beginning site construction near Leningrad and Moscow.[3] Statements by Soviet leaders added to the impression of Soviet interest and progress in BMD.[4] In October 1961, Defense Minister Malinovsky claimed that "the problem of destroying missiles in flight has been solved." In July 1962, Khrushchev boasted that a Soviet ABM "can hit a fly in outer space."

U.S. tests of reentry vehicles (RVs) indicated that atmospheric filtering was the most reliable way to distinguish live RVs from decoys. Consequently, in 1963 McNamara ordered the low altitude, high acceleration interceptor, Sprint, to complement the longer range Nike-Zeus interceptor. This combination of Nike-Zeus and Sprint, with accompanying radars and data processors, was then called the Nike-X ABM system.[5]

The administration also increased efforts to develop offensive means to counter Soviet ABMs. Research, development, and testing of decoys and chaff to confuse ABM radars was already under way. Scientists had conceived of the multiple RV (MRV) idea in 1958; it involved putting several warheads on a ballistic missile and then during its flight releasing them shot-gun style at a target. MRVs had the advantage of not being filtered out by the atmosphere, so they increased the ability of the offense to saturate and hence overwhelm low altitude ABM interceptors. The United States deployed MRVs first, in 1964.[6] The Soviet ABM program continued. After the humiliation of the Cuban missile crisis, among other military measures Khrushchev accelerated the development of the Galosh ABM system. In a parade in November 1963, the Soviets displayed the Griffon missile, which was deployed near Leningrad. Some U.S. analysts suspected it had a BMD capability.[7]

In March 1964 President Johnson proposed a freeze on offensive and defensive strategic weapons, to be verified by on-site inspection. Soviet Foreign Minister Gromyko rejected the proposal and instead reiterated his "umbrella plan," part of the Soviet proposal for disarmament. The umbrella components were to be some ICBMs that would act as a "minimum deterrent," and ABMs and antiaircraft missiles that would serve as insurance against illegal retention of offensive delivery vehicles. The parties would retain the umbrella until the end of the last stage of disarmament.[8]

In November 1964 the Soviets displayed the Galosh missile in their military parade. It was deployed near Moscow, and the U.S. intelligence community thought it had a capability comparable to the Nike-Zeus. Satellite reconnaissance also began to detect additional signs of the Tallinn system, first noticed in 1961, though the U.S. intelligence community did not agree whether it was designed to intercept bombers or missiles.[9]

During 1965 and 1966, Johnson and McNamara continued to request funds only for research, development, and testing, despite the unanimous call of the JCS for production of long-lead-time components. McNamara argued that the cost-exchange ratio favored the offense: For every dollar put into offense, four dollars worth of defense were needed to counter it. Consequently, he emphasized offensive counters to the Soviet ABM. His opinion also reflected a shift in doctrinal emphasis from damage limitation to assured destruction missions, because he thought Soviet offensive improvements made damage limitation less feasible.[10]

The Soviets abandoned their Leningrad site but accelerated work near Moscow during 1966 and 1967. In November 1966, McNamara announced the presence of the Soviet Galosh ABM system that was deployed near Moscow. This was the first public acknowledgement of a Soviet ABM site. McNamara said that the United States would counter it by deploying an advanced Polaris-type missile (Poseidon) that could effectively penetrate any Soviet defense. He did not yet say that Poseidon would carry MIRVs—MRVs that are independently targetable.[11]

JOHNSON'S UNILATERAL INITIATIVE

The decision whether or not to deploy ABMs ultimately was President Johnson's. He had a variety of pressures encouraging and discouraging him from beginning deployment. He finally decided to use the unilateral initiative tactic because it was able to satisfy many of the major domestic actors pressuring him and, he said, he found merit in McNamara's strategic arguments.[12] On January 24, 1967, in his budget message to Congress, Johnson announced that during 1968 the United States will

continue intensive development of Nike-X but take no action now to deploy an ABM defense; initiate discussions with the Soviet Union on the limitation of ABM deployments; in the event these discussions prove unsuccessful, we will reconsider our deployment decision. To provide for actions that may be required at that time, approximately $375 million has been included in the 1968 budget for the production of Nike-X for such purposes as defense of our offensive weapon systems.[13]

When McNamara submitted his Military Posture Statement on January 25, he put the initiative into the context of U.S. strategic doctrine. If the Soviets continued to improve their damage limitation capabilities with widespread ABM deployment, then to maintain its assured destruction capability the United States would enhance its ability to penetrate Soviet ABM defenses. Should efforts to limit Soviet ABMs fail, the United States would then begin to produce and deploy ABMs to protect Minuteman missiles.[14] Within a few days Llewellyn Thompson, the U.S. ambassador to the Soviet Union, carried a special message to the Soviet Union calling for a BMD moratorium.[15]

The restraint part of the tactic failed to compel the Soviets to agree to an ABM moratorium or to begin strategic arms limitation talks (SALT). At a London news conference on February 9, Soviet Premier Aleksey Kosygin rejected the idea of an ABM ban: "Maybe a defensive system is more expensive than an offensive system, but it is not a cause of the arms race but designed instead to prevent the death of people." The best course, he claimed, was to "seek renunciation of nuclear armament and the destruction of nuclear weapons." Although five days later *Pravda* said the Soviet Union "was ready to discuss the problem of averting a new arms race, both in offensive and defensive weapons," subsequent behavior suggests they were as yet uninterested in ABM limits. In particular, at the June summit in Glassboro, New Jersey, Kosygin was unyielding.[16]

Johnson then decided that some U.S. ABM deployment was required. Domestic pressures for deployment were increasing, and he wanted to avoid an election campaign issue of an ABM gap. He also thought that beginning to deploy an ABM might convince the Soviets that they had more to gain from SALT than from an uncontrolled arms competition. He did, however, want to keep McNamara on board, so he let McNamara announce deployment in any way he chose.[17]

On September 18, 1967, McNamara gave a long speech in San Francisco. Most of it emphasized the futility and drawbacks of engaging in an arms race with the Soviets. He reiterated his view that the United States did not need to respond to the Soviet ABM with its own ABM, because offensive counters were a sufficient, less expensive remedy. He added that an extensive U.S. ABM would undermine the objectives of mutual deterrence and thus would compel the Soviets to react to maintain their assured destruction capability. He concluded by announcing the deployment of a light, anti-Chinese ABM, and that production would begin at the end of the year. He listed some concurrent benefits: protection of the population from an accidental launch of a ballistic missile by any nuclear power, and some defense of Minuteman sites against a Soviet attack. He emphasized that this deployment was not the first stage of an anti-Soviet ABM, warned against pressures to expand it into a heavy Soviet-oriented system, and said that this deployment decision was not inconsistent with the desire to limit strategic nuclear offensive and defensive forces.[18] His views were soon echoed by ACDA Deputy Director Adrian Fisher and Assistant Secretary of Defense Paul Warnke.[19] In an interview with *Life* magazine on September 29, McNamara repeated his views and first mentioned MIRVs—that MIRVs assured penetration of a Soviet ABM and that the Soviets could develop MIRVs able to saturate a U.S. ABM.[20]

Other comments and the implementation plans, however, signaled that the U.S. ABM really was directed against the Soviet Union. The JCS and several Senate leaders stated publicly that this deployment was the beginning of an anti-Soviet ABM. Johnson apparently allowed the ambiguities to remain so that McNamara and the JCS each could think that it had won the argument.[21] Johnson's approach also influenced the shape of the planned deployment, which was indistinguishable from the beginning of an anti-

Soviet area defense system. Most of the continental ABM sites were in or near major metropolitan areas and, since Chinese and Soviet ICBMs would travel in similar corridors, radars and interceptors designed to destroy Chinese warheads could also destroy Soviet warheads.[22] The Soviets did not respond directly to any U.S. signals about the American ABM.[23]

In January 1968 Johnson requested $1.2 billion for production and deployment of the ABM system, which had just been named Sentinel. An attempt in the Senate in April to delay deployment was defeated. On May 20 First Deputy Foreign Minister Vasili Kuznetsov said that the Soviet Union was ready to enter talks to limit "strategic means for delivering nulcear weaponry." On June 21 Kosygin reiterated that the Soviet Union was willing to exchange views. On June 24 the Senate defeated a second attempt to delay Safeguard's deployment. Four days later, Foreign Minister Gromyko announced that the Soviet Union would enter SALT to discuss offensive and defensive weapons. On July 1, at the signing of the Non-Proliferation Treaty, both superpowers repeated their commitment to begin SALT, although they set no starting date.[24]

Soviet behavior was consistent with this verbal interest in restraint. Although they did not declare a deployment moratorium, in August U.S. satellites detected curtailment of work on their remaining Moscow ABM site, which was two-thirds completed.[25] On August 19 Soviet Ambassador Anatoly Dobrynin finally told the Americans that the Soviet Union was willing to convene a summit on September 20 and publicly announce then that SALT would begin in several months. The Soviets intervened in Czechoslovakia on August 20, however, the day before Johnson planned to announce his trip to Moscow. Johnson then canceled his trip, and SALT did not begin.[26] Subsequent Soviet negotiating behavior demonstrates that indeed they were interested in ABM limitations.

Richard Nixon assumed the presidency in January 1969. On February 6, Secretary of Defense Melvin Laird ordered a halt to Sentinel's deployment, pending a review of U.S. strategic objectives and requirements. On February 17 the Soviets asked Nixon to set a date to begin SALT, but he was not yet ready. On March 14 he announced his decision to modify the Sentinel ABM and turn in into the Safeguard system, which would concentrate more on protecting U.S. strategic forces.[27]

Safeguard also had a political role: to serve as a bargaining chip that would encourage the Soviets to make concessions in exchange for a treaty limiting ABMs.[28] Most U.S. officials, including President Nixon, National Security Advisor Henry Kissinger, and Secretary of Defense Laird, emphasized its linkage to limits on Soviet heavy missiles. They feared increasing Soviet offensive capabilities; in particular, they worried about Soviet MRV tests on their heavy ICBM, the SS-9, which had begun the previous year. Secretary of State William Rogers continued to stress Safeguard's linkage only to the Soviet ABM.

In June Nixon told the Soviets that the United States was ready to begin SALT; in July Gromyko said the Soviets were also prepared; and in November the negotiations began. Sometime between December 1970 and May 20, 1971, the Soviets made the concession on heavy ICBMs.[29] A year later the parties completed negotiations and signed the Moscow Accords: the ABM Treaty and the Interim Agreement to limit strategic offensive arms.[30]

EXPLANATION

It is well known how Safeguard contributed to favorable changes in Soviet policy.[31] Consequently, our analysis focuses on the complex and less-explored bargaining that took place during the Johnson administration—when the Soviet response changed from initial disinterest in ABM limitations to, beginning in mid-1968, serious interest.

U.S. signals were clear and consistent about its demand for mutual limitations on ABM deployment: its threat to produce and deploy an ABM system if no agreement emerged, and its promise to continue restraint if negotiations succeeded. Late in 1967, however, U.S. signals about the purpose of its ABM system became inconsistent. For most of 1967, U.S. officials had said that continued and expanded Soviet ABM deployment would require offensive counters and, possibly, some defense of Minuteman missiles to enhance the U.S. assured destruction capability. When the United States first announced ABM deployment in September 1967 (which cannot be considered a quick response to Soviet disinterest in ABM limitations), most U.S. officials emphasized that the system was not intended to protect U.S. cities against a massive Soviet attack. Instead, they said, it was merely anti-Chinese and also would provide some defense for ICBMs. Thus they intended to signal a moderate and defensive U.S. response to continued Soviet disinterest in ABM limitations.

Beginning about the time the United States announced deployment in September 1967, however, some officials gave the conflicting message that the U.S. ABM was the beginning of an anti-Soviet system. Moreover, planned construction could also be interpreted this way. These signals suggested that a lack of Soviet reciprocation would lead the United States to deploy both MIRVs and an anti-Soviet ABM system. Since this response probably would have increased relative U.S. capabilities, these signals did not indicate moderate or defensive intentions.

During 1967–68, the United States was not implementing a campaign or a series of initiatives. It also did not accompany its initiative with an official history of previous initiatives or other bargaining preceding the initiative.

Kosygin's rejection of the U.S. proposal in February and June of 1967 indicates that the Soviets received and probably understood initial U.S. signals.[32] I found no direct evidence that they received and correctly interpreted some later signals suggesting that the U.S. response might not be moderate or defensive. Circumstantial evidence—signs of increasing Soviet interest in ABM limitations—suggests they may have.

Soviet calculations early in 1967 about the security consequences of an ABM agreement were ambiguous but probably mostly unsupportive.

Evidently the Soviets hoped their BMD would enhance their damage limitation capability. Both Gromyko (March 1964) and Kosygin (February and June 1967) emphasized the benefit of being able to protect Soviet territory from missile attack, and no one publicly questioned the desirability of deployment.[33] Apparently most Soviet leaders believed that ABMs would be able to carry out their missions, at least until the Soviets achieved parity in ballistic missiles.[34] Supporting this contention are optimistic statements in 1967 by General P. F. Batitakii (PVO commander) and General P. A. Kurochkin (a deputy defense minister).[35] The 1968 edition of *Soviet Military Strategy* also left unchanged the claim that Soviet armed forces could intercept all enemy planes and missiles.[36] Shevchenko implies the same optimistic belief when he explains that the Soviets later became interested in ABM limitations because, in part, Galosh "had proved less effective than anticipated."[37]

Some Soviet leaders were less optimistic about at least the short-term prospects for BMD.[38] Defense Minister Malinovsky said in 1966 that the Soviet ABM could cope with some but not all enemy missiles. In 1967 Marshal A. A. Grechko, soon to be defense minister, and Marshal V. I. Chuikov, head of the Soviet civil defense, said the Soviet Union did not yet possess defenses capable of intercepting all missiles and planes. Furthermore, optimistic statements about Soviet offensive capabilities suggest some awareness of BMD deficiencies. In 1967, SRF commander Marshal N. Krylov claimed that "the great speed [of ballistic missiles], together with variable trajectories, especially upon approach to target, practically guarantees the invulnerability of missiles in flight, especially when they are employed en masse."[39] Truly outspoken pessimism was not publicly expressed until after 1967, however.[40]

Despite uncertainty about the technical feasibility of BMD, by 1967 the Soviets had spent an equivalent of $4–5 billion on it, and U.S. satellites detected an acceleration of site construction near Moscow in 1966 and 1967.[41] Thus in 1967 most leaders, even those with doubts, evidently thought it might work and provide net security benefits—if not in the short term than perhaps eventually. Such hopes would have decreased their interest in negotiations to limit ABMs.

Now let us turn to Soviet security calculations in mid- to late 1968, when they curtailed work on their Moscow ABM site and said they were willing to enter negotiations to limit offensive and defensive weapons. Analysts speculate that the Soviets slowed construction of their Moscow ABM site because they doubted its effectiveness, wanted to signal interest in avoiding an ABM competition, or both.[42]

At the least we know that the leadership was sufficiently concerned about Sentinel to agree to begin negotiations, and that it was not yet so afraid of an ABM competition that it was willing to commit itself officially to a deployment moratorium. Because of mixed U.S. signals, however, the Soviets still faced uncertainty about whether or not the United States would deploy a full-scale anti-Soviet ABM in the absence of Soviet restraint. Moreover, they probably faced uncertainty about the effectiveness of their own ABM in the longer term in light of their continued R&D. This situation was not conducive to a firm stand one way or another. In the absence of an official U.S. commitment to deploy an anti-Soviet ABM, they could afford to talk and to defer completion of the Moscow site.

Security calculations probably now disposed them to exercise restraint for two reasons. First, apparently they worried about the effectiveness of their own ABM. What had changed from earlier in 1967 was that in September the United States first announced its intention to deploy MIRVs—which could saturate ABM defenses as they attacked separated targets. Evidence of decreasing Soviet confidence that their ABM could carry out a damage limitation mission is that Soviet praises of it disappeared from their newspapers.[43]

Second, they probably feared that without Soviet concessions, the United States would develop and deploy an extensive ABM system that would both neutralize their gains in strategic missiles and be superior to their ABM.[44] Such a situation, when combined with expected U.S. progress with MIRVs, would hinder the ability of their arsenal of ballistic missiles either to limit damage to the Soviet Union or, at worst, to carry out a crushing retaliation. If they paid attention to McNamara's often-repeated arguments against a heavy U.S. ABM system, at the least they would have worried about their future ability to retaliate without a substantially increased offensive capability. This assertion is supported by a Soviet book that warned about such dangers. It came out over a year later and apparently was not intended for an external audience.[45]

A related situation is that some Soviet leaders probably thought that ABM limitations would enable them to compete in areas where they were less inferior technologically, such as in ballistic missiles. This concern is consistent with the pattern of Soviet negotiating behavior that prevailed at least until the 1987 INF Treaty.[46] The Soviets knew that the United States had superior computer technology, and therefore that in an ABM race they might emerge inferior. The United States had also demonstrated a commitment to deploy an ABM that even Nixon later said "could be misunderstood as the first step toward construction of a heavy system."[47] Engaging in prudent defense planning, using "worst case analysis," the Soviets probably concluded that Sentinel was or eventually would be directed against them—despite mixed U.S. signals on this issue.

Security calculations about nuclear threats from third parties would have contributed to Soviet reluctance to ban ABMs—weapons that would have helped strengthen barriers to entry to the level of power and security of the superpowers. Newhouse speculates, in particular, that the Soviets thought BMD would provide protection against Chinese missiles. He also notes a correlation between Kosygin's inflexible position at Glassboro and, the week before, another Chinese nuclear test.[48] BMD might also have been effective against British and French missiles and served as a hedge in case West Germany became a nuclear power. Recall that West Germany was not legally prohibited from acquiring nuclear weapons until it signed the Non-Proliferation Treaty late in 1969.

Until Paul Warnke's speech on October 6, 1967, the U.S. proposal seemed to call for on-site inspection. Warnke then vaguely said that an agreement limiting strategic offense and defense "may have to depend on our own unilateral capabilities for verification."[49] Adrian Fisher said on December 12 that the Soviets did not respond to Warnke's offer.[50] Thus the verification condition did not favor the U.S. proposal until at least October 1967. Although the Soviets indicated interest in the proposal several months before this date, however, they did not formally agree to limit their ABMs.

When the United States announced the unilateral initiative early in 1967, Soviet calculations about China probably continued to have an ambiguous impact on their bargaining behavior. This was during the 1965 to early 1968 period when the United States was escalating its military involvement in Vietnam and the outcome of the war was in doubt. The Soviets were therefore under pressure in the world communist movement to avoid seeming too conciliatory with the United States. At the time, however, moderate arms control agreements still would have served the Soviet foreign policy objective of isolating China as a reckless state.[51]

Calculations about the effects of an agreement on relations with West European countries were also probably ambiguous. On the one hand, apparently in this instance the Soviet objective of weakening NATO disposed them to avoid arms control negotiations with the United States.[52] Soviet foreign policy was focusing on a detente with certain West European countries (especially France, which no longer was a formal member of NATO), instead of with the United States. A benefit of a relaxation of tensions in Europe would have been some loss of NATO's cohesion. These expectations would have worked against the proposal to enter into bilateral negotiations with the United States.

On the other hand, Soviet BMD would degrade the utility of the small nuclear arsenals of France and Britain. If this situation arose, it probably would have increased tensions between the Soviet Union and Western Europe and in consequence would have undermined this political aspect of the correlation of forces. Indirect evidence is that the British, Canadians, and West Germans all supported the U.S. proposal to limit offensive and defensive arms.[53] The French apparently said nothing about the proposal.[54]

Calculations about relations with Non-Aligned countries probably favored the proposed agreement. Evidence is that their statements about ABMs in 1967 and 1968 tended to emphasize the escalatory nature of the system.[55] The only relevant political conditions that changed in 1968 concerned China and Czechoslovakia, and the new situation increased Soviet interest in the U.S. proposal.

By the spring of 1968, following the Tet offensive and growing U.S. public disillusionment with the Vietnam War, a communist victory seemed only a matter of time. The Soviets then had less reason to fear that North Vietnam would draw closer to China.[56] Because the war continued, however, they probably still felt some minor reservations about accommodation with the United States. Overall, because they still wanted to isolate China from the United States, and because accommodation with the United States would serve this objective, calculations about China probably moderately favored the proposed agreement.

Events in Czechoslovakia during the "Prague Spring" of 1968 were also important. The government began to implement reforms that threatened the preeminence of the Communist Party—reforms that the Soviet Union refused to accept. Another probable Soviet concern was that China might draw closer to Czechoslovakia and other East European countries, which could undermine the cohesion of the Warsaw Pact. On August 20 the Soviets invaded Czechoslovakia to preempt such developments.

The Soviets obviously wanted, if possible, to moderate U.S. reactions to the invasion. This situation disposed them to seem interested in the U.S. arms control proposal (i.e., SALT had the political advantage of being a means to further decent relations with the United States). Circumstantial evidence of this SALT-Czechoslovakia connection is that two important events occurred on August 19: the Central Committee of the Soviet Union approved the invasion, and Dobrynin told the Americans that the Soviet Union was willing to convene a summit and publicly announce that SALT would begin.[57]

Initial Soviet calculations about the impact of the proposed agreement on their prestige were probably ambiguous. Since an agreement would have restricted both parties' programs equally, it seemed to affirm the norm of reciprocity. An agreement might have slowed the Soviet ability to reach strategic parity, however, because they were behind in offensive weapons; this prospect went against the norm of equal status. Since neither concern obviously dominates, the Soviets probably expected that the proposed agreement would result in no clear advantage or disadvantage to their prestige.

When the Soviets indicated interest in the proposal in 1968, calculations about prestige probably favored the initiative's success. The principal change was that they had come closer to achieving parity in numbers of ICBMs, the principal symbol of nuclear prowess. The United States reached 1054 ICBMs in 1967, and the number remained constant. The Soviets had 340 in 1966, 720 in 1967, 800 in 1968, and 1050 in 1969. Also in 1968 the Soviets began to deploy a Polaris-type SLBM and to test MRVs.[58] Thus by 1968 an agreement limiting BMD would not have seriously hampered their ability to reach parity (and hence equal status) with the United States. A relevant part of their calculations, of course, was increased doubt about the effectiveness of their ABM system.

Concern for the Soviet domestic economy was probably irrelevant in 1967 as they considered whether or not to reciprocate. They had not yet reached strategic parity, and apparently they still hoped that an ABM system would speed achievement of that objective—regardless of the cost. Their evaluation probably changed to moderately favorable late in 1967, when with knowledge of U.S. MIRVs the Soviets had more reason to doubt the effectiveness of their ABM. Thus even without reducing their defense budget, they probably wanted to avoid wasting money that could be better applied to military hardware where they had no technological disadvantage. As 1969 approached and they were about to reach parity in ICBMs, this condition probably became marginally more favorable. It was probably not highly favorable, however, because economic problems did not force the Soviets to reduce the growth rate in defense expenditures until 1976 or 1977.[59]

International economic calculations moderately favored the proposed agreement only from mid-1967 to mid-1968, and they were irrelevant at the other times. The Soviet harvest in 1967 was short 19 million tons from the plan, and harvests in 1966 and 1968 exceeded the plan.[60] Even with the 1967 shortfall, however, U.S. grain was merely moderately important to the Soviets because only one of two supporting conditions obtained. On the one hand, the United States was apparently presenting the Soviets with a trade-stimulating environment. This assertion is plausible if we assume that the trade-stimulating environment the U.S. presented in 1963/64 still obtained.[61] On the other hand, at the time the Soviets preferred to import wheat. Unlike for coarse grains, the United States did not dominate the global market in wheat.[62]

Turning to the environment of bargaining, early in 1967 the SRF and the PVO had good reasons to oppose arms talks.[63] The United States had been proposing a freeze on strategic arms since 1964, and the SRF would have resisted attempts to freeze it into inferiority and thus to constrain its ability to carry out its missions. The PVO had an obvious interest in ABMs.

The urgency of PVO objections to ABM limitations may have decreased late in 1967 as more doubts about the system's effectiveness emerged. What little evidence I found, however, suggests that the military continued to oppose SALT. For example, Shevchenko says that Defense Minister Grechko only reluctantly accepted the later opening of SALT, and even then he conducted a "guerilla effort" to stall negotiations.[64] Since SALT had not begun, all the bargaining on strategic weapons during 1967–68 was informal.

When the United States announced its initiative in 1967, Brezhnev was not yet ascendant over his rivals. Between 1964 and early 1968, he was actively competing with Kosygin.[65] During this period Brezhnev was more supportive of traditional values than was Kosygin, which made Brezhnev seem less interested in arms control than he later became. This behavior contributed to his increasing ascendance, just as it had previously for Khrushchev.

During the spring of 1968, Brezhnev emerged ascendant over Kosygin and began the process of formulating a comprehensive program. This latter task was not completed until the spring of 1971, when he presented his "peace program" at the Twenty-Fourth Party Congress.[66] Thus for most of 1968 Brezhnev seemed to have more ability than previously to make arms control concessions, but not as much ability as he would gain in 1971. I found no evidence indicating the initiative's impact on the relative strength of any Soviet arms control proponents.

From early 1965 to early 1968, the deductive approach suggests that the Soviets perceived a moderate level of international tension. Clearly their vital interests were not threatened by U.S. military behavior overseas, but the United States was fighting against the Soviets' North Vietnamese ally at a time when the outcome of the war was in doubt.[67]

Their rhetoric suggested that they perceived a moderate-high level of tension, however. For example, Alexey Roshchin, the Soviet representative to ENDC, warned in May 1967 that "international tension not only is not decreasing but on the contrary, as a result of the further escalation by the United States of the war of aggression in Viet-nam, it is continuing to increase."[68] On August 24 he added that U.S. aggression is "becoming more and more dangerous to peace."[69] On December 11 Kuznetsov even accused the United States of "using means of mass destruction, such as gas and chemical weapons which are prohibited by the Geneva Protocol of 1925."[70] The Soviets also were not discussing U.S. politics in pluralistic terms.[71]

Brezhnev was not yet secure in his authority, and the situation in Vietnam disposed the Soviets to sound militant toward the United States.[72] Consequently, since Soviet statements were less reliable than usual, I give more credence to the deductive indicator and conclude that the Soviets probably perceived a moderate level of tension to early 1968. What changed early in 1968 was that the Soviets probably saw a decline in the U.S. threat to Soviet interests in Indochina and a related decrease in the likelihood of escalation to general war. Thus they probably perceived a low-moderate level of tension. Key events were the Tet offensive in January 1968, as well as Johnson's decisions in March to halt the bombing of North Vietnam and to begin peace negotiations. Soviet rhetoric also was not as shrill, indicating a low-moderate or moderate level of tension.[73] Since a communist victory now seemed inevitable, the Soviets were less impelled by a concern for China to exaggerate their conflict with the United States. Because Brezhnev gained ascendancy over Kosygin during the spring of 1968, we can assume equal importance for the deductive and inductive methods of determining Soviet perceptions. Consequently, during the rest of 1968, the Soviets probably perceived a low-moderate level of tension.

As we discussed at length in chapter 4, during the mid-1960s the Soviets probably perceived a strategic environment that was not obviously acceptable or unacceptable. In 1968 they had over 850 ICBMs (compared to 1054 for the United States). Over half were hardened to 300 p.s.i., and three-quarters had storable propellents. Dynamic calculations of a surprise, countersilo ICBM attack also indicated a significant drop in the percentage of Soviet ICBMs that the United States could destroy. Assuming the United States knew the location of all Soviet ICBMs and that the Soviets had no strategic or tactical warning, the United States could have destroyed 85 percent in 1966 but only 72 percent in 1968 and 58 percent in 1969.[74] Since the Soviets also had many more ICBMs (about 300 in 1966 and more than 850 in 1968), their ability to retaliate improved markedly.

Some interrelated evidence supports the contention that after the mid-1960s, the Soviets no longer were obsessed with the possibility of a U.S. surprise nuclear attack (i.e., they apparently found the strategic environment acceptable). First, their doctrine shifted and no longer assumed that the most probable path to nuclear war would be a U.S. "bolt from the blue." By the late 1960s they expected the path to be escalation of a serious crisis or a conventional war, which would provide the strategic warning time necessary to preempt. Second, between 1965 and 1967, Soviet military statements shifted away from a sole emphasis on nuclear rockets and inevitable escalation of any superpower war to global nuclear war, and toward the "possibility" that a conventional war in Europe might not escalate to nuclear war. Third, their force posture began to emphasize a more balanced development of their armed forces, with greater attention to theater conventional forces. Fourth, Warsaw Pact exercises began for the first time to simulate scenarios whose beginning and early phases did not involve nuclear weapons. The first was in 1965, but such exercises were not the rule until the late 1960s.[75]

In sum, after the mid-1960s the Soviets could count on causing so much damage to the United States that even a surprise U.S. attack on their strategic forces would not enable the U.S. to emerge noticeably better off than the Soviet Union. Countercity targeting could kill at least 100 million Americans. Subsequent technological developments and military deployments have not altered this situation.[76]

Through 1967, U.S. intentions probably continued to seem offensive. The weapons the United States procured appeared capable of counterforce missions, and U.S. doctrine still called for nuclear superiority. Beginning in 1968, U.S. intentions probably seemed ambiguous. 1968 was the first year the United States deployed no additional ICBMs and ended the somewhat provocative practice of airborne alerts, and McNamara gave assured destruction even more prominence over damage limitation.[77] U.S. intentions probably did not appear defensive, however. First, the United States had not yet rejected strategic superiority as an objective. Although McNamara thought superiority had little value, other administration officials wanted it to bargain from strength and to enhance "extended deterrence" (i.e., U.S. protection of Europe and Japan). They looked to MIRVs as a vehicle.[78] General LeMay's 1968 book also repeated his call for a U.S. first-strike capability and his thinly veiled arguments for a preventive war.[79] Second, the announcement of intended MIRV deployment suggested continued procurement of weapons with counterforce capabilities, and Sentinel could easily have been interpreted as the first stage of a heavy, anti-Soviet ABM system.[80]

When the United States announced its initiative early in 1967, overall the Soviets probably perceived a strategic environment that was moderately unstable. The strategic environment was not obviously acceptable or unacceptable, but U.S. intentions continued to seem offensive. By the time they reciprocated partially in mid-1968, the environment probably seemed stable. Evidently it was acceptable, and U.S. intentions seemed ambiguous.

SUMMARY

Compared to when the United States first announced the initiative early in 1967, more conditions favored its success when the Soviets finally indicated serious interest in ABM limitations in mid- to late 1968. In 1967 only three obvious conditions favored the initiative's success: U.S. signals were clear, the Soviet Union probably received and correctly interpreted them, and an agreement would have enhanced Soviet relations with Non-Aligned countries. At the same time, however, Soviet calculations about their military security, the requirement for on-site inspection, and barriers to entry at their level of power disposed them not to meet the U.S. demands. Moreover, the Soviet military probably opposed any concessions. The remaining obvious conditions were either irrelevant or involved ambiguous consequences.

When the Soviets showed interest in the U.S. proposal in mid- to late 1968, success was favored because the Soviets recognized and correctly interpreted U.S. signals; on-site inspection evidently was no longer necessary; political calculations concerning China, NATO, and Non-Aligned countries favored the Soviets agreeing to limit ABMs; and the proposed agreement promised to affirm Soviet prestige, to permit some reallocation of funds within the defense budget, and to serve Soviet security interests vis-a-vis the United States. Situations concerning "barriers to entry" and the interests of the military services remained unfavorable for an agreement.

U.S. signals became mixed beginning in late 1967. Before that time, U.S. officials consistently signaled that the U.S. response to Soviet nonreciprocation would not be a heavy, anti-Soviet system. Then late in 1967 some officials began to say that the U.S. ABM was the beginning of a heavy system. U.S. deployment plans could be interpreted either way. Ironically, this new mixture of signals apparently helped to shift Soviet security calculations more toward support for the proposal.

The research supports the hypotheses on the general-secretary's authority and on the strategic environment. First, the issue probably became controversial late in 1967 when the United States announced it would deploy ABMs and MIRVs. Brezhnev was still competing with Kosygin at that time, and not until Brezhnev became ascendant in 1968 did the Soviets begin to make concessions. Second, the strategic environment seemed moderately unstable during 1967 when the Soviets made no concessions. By the time they finally reciprocated in mid-1968, the environment probably seemed stable.

The hypothesis about international tension is confirmed, at least partially. The Soviets apparently perceived a low-moderate level of tension when they showed interest in the U.S. proposal. Before mid-1968, tensions probably seemed to be at a moderate, perhaps uninfluential level.

The hypotheses correlating an initiative's success with a quick response to state B's defection is partially confirmed. The United States did not respond quickly to continued Soviet disinterest in ABM limitations, and the Soviets did not reciprocate in 1967. When the United States responded in September by saying it would deploy its own ABM system—nine months after announcing its initiative—the Soviets did not reciprocate right away. They did in mid-1968, however, which is why this case seems to offer a partial confirmation. Full corroboration would have resulted if the Soviets never reciprocated.

No correlations emerge for four hypotheses, because the relevant circumstances did not change during 1967–68: the United States did not provide an official history of previous bargaining interactions, neither a campaign nor a series of initiatives was under way, and bargaining was informal. For the remaining hypotheses, either the situations were irrelevant or ambiguous (moderate and defensive responses to defection), or no evidence emerged (the impact of the initiative on Soviet arms control advocates).

8

Case Study:
Neutron Bombs (1978)

On April 7, 1978, President Jimmy Carter announced deferral of neutron bomb production and linked continued restraint to the Soviets reducing their conventional or nuclear advantages in Central Europe. The unilateral initiative failed to elicit such reciprocation. Before describing the complex bargaining interactions and explaining Soviet behavior, let us briefly examine the technology of the weapon and its rationale.

HISTORICAL BACKGROUND

The technical name for the neutron bomb is "enhanced radiation weapon" (ERW). It is a nuclear device that, compared to other atomic and nuclear bombs, releases a greater proportion of its energy as prompt radiation (mostly neutrons) and less as blast, thermal radiation (heat), and residual radiation (fallout).[1] A nuclear bomb gets most of its energy from a fusion reaction, the combining of hydrogen atoms to form the heavier helium atom. Fusion releases eighty percent of its energy as prompt radiation, mostly high-energy neutrons, and twenty percent as blast. The reaction requires high temperatures that can be obtained only with a fission trigger. A fission (or atomic) bomb gets its energy from splitting heavy atoms. 50 percent of the energy is released as blast, 35 percent as heat, 5 percent as prompt radiation, and 10 percent as residual radiation. Thus a pure fusion device, "clean" in the sense of no residual radiation, has not yet been invented; the neutron bomb simply has a higher fusion-to-fission ratio than other bombs.

According to Samuel Cohen, the U.S. "inventor" of the neutron bomb, the Soviets may have conceived of the idea first and begun research and development in 1952.[2] In the United States, the technical conception for the device was in 1958.[3] The idea first appeared in the public literature in May 1959, when *U.S. News and World Report* discussed a "neutron 'death ray' bomb which would kill men with streams of poisonous radiation, while leaving machines and buildings undamaged."[4] The initial U.S. test was in 1964.[5]

Although such a device could serve a variety of uses, our discussion concentrates on the major controversy: its tactical utility in overcoming the Soviet advantage in numbers of tanks in Central Europe.[6] Tanks, of course, are useful for offensive operations, and they complement the offensive-oriented Soviet theater doctrine that prevailed through at least 1986. NATO's doctrine, in contrast, is geared toward defense of its own land instead of advance into enemy territory.[7]

The "flexible response" part of NATO's doctrine dictates that if the Soviets and their Warsaw Pact allies attack Western Europe with conventional weapons—under postwar circumstances where Pact tanks greatly outnumber NATO tanks—then if needed to prevent defeat the United States would introduce nuclear weapons. First, the United States would use tactical nuclear weapons (TNWs) on the battlefield. Then, if necessary, it would use other nuclear weapons against the Soviet homeland as part of its policy of "extended deterrence." The purpose of the doctrine is to dissuade the Soviets from ever attacking, by presenting them with a probable situation where they could not accomplish their war aims at acceptable costs.[8]

Under many scenarios for a Warsaw Pact invasion, to stop it NATO would have to use its TNWs in Western Europe, particularly in the Federal Republic of Germany (FRG). The problem, suspected when the United States introduced TNWs in 1953 and confirmed in the "Carte Blanche" exercises in 1955, is that such use of TNWs would be highly destructive to the FRG.[9]

Compared to the standard, fission-type TNW, the advantage of an ERW against tanks is that the neutrons could penetrate tank armor and kill or disable the crews while causing less collateral damage to the surrounding countryside of West Germany—particularly if low-yield devices were used. Thus the threat to use them might be more credible than otherwise and, ERW proponents argued, NATO's ability to dissuade the initial Soviet attack would thereby be stronger.[10]

The U.S. government became seriously interested in the weapon in the mid-1970s, in part from the development of a less-expensive prototype in 1974.[11] Secretary of Defense James Schlesinger's doctrinal innovations also contributed to the change. To enhance the credibility of the U.S. deterrent, he wanted a broader range of military options to respond to Soviet aggression; the neutron bomb fit well into a European application of this doctrine.[12]

By 1977 the Energy Research and Development Administration (ERDA) was ready to begin production of the ERW.[13] One model was eventually to be deployed on short-range Lance missiles, and another was to fit in eight-inch artillery shells.[14] President Carter then had to deal with political obstacles to production.[15] The major one involved alliance politics—particularly relations with the FRG, where deployment of the weapon was most important. West German Chancellor Helmut Schmidt expected military advantages with the weapon but, especially in the face of extensive Soviet propaganda, it had acquired serious political disadvantages.[16] Consequently, worried about domestic opposition to it, Carter wanted the United States first to produce to the ERW and then, as the leader of NATO, ask the FRG to deploy it. Since Carter did not want to take sole political responsibility for producing a new generation of nuclear weapons, he saw little value in production without a West German precommitment to deployment.[17]

A possible way out of this impasse was to link production to Soviet behavior where, in order to avoid facing ERWs, the Soviets might be willing to forgo current or increased advantages in tanks or in INF. In 1978 the Warsaw Pact had three times as many tanks in Central Europe as NATO. In 1977 the Soviets also began to deploy three-warhead, intermediate-range SS-20s to replace single-warhead, medium-range SS-4s and intermediate-range SS-5s, which increased the Soviet unilateral advantage in long-range theater nuclear missiles.[18]

The West forwarded its first arms control proposal involving the ERW early in the fall of 1977 at negotiations under way in Vienna since 1973. These were the Mutual Force Reduction (MFR) talks, where NATO was striving to convince the Warsaw Pact to give up its advantages in conventional forces useful for offensive attack. No progress was made with this linkage. Moreover, the Soviets continued the Pact modernization program that ran from 1965–79. Thus the quality and quantity of Soviet tanks improved, further increasing the Pact advantage over NATO.[19]

Later in the fall U.S. officials shifted the arms control focus to INF, where the United States hoped to trade its agreement not to produce or deploy the bomb for a Soviet decision to give up the SS-20s. The Soviets found out about this linkage from a leak reported by Richard Burt, not in formal negotiations.[20] The nonstrategic range of SS-20s put them in a "gray area" not subject to the SALT negotiations, and they did not fit in the MFR talks either.

The Soviets were uninterested in such linkages. On December 23, Brezhnev responded with a proposal for mutual renunciation of neutron bomb production, and he warned that the Soviets would match the United States if is proceeded with production and deployment.[21]

On March 10, 1978, Secretary of Defense Harold Brown publicly suggested trading the neutron bomb for Soviet concessions. The next day *Tass* reacted: "The Soviet Union again affirms its proposal and calls on the U.S. for a mutual renunciation of the production of the neutron weapon."

Any attempt to link the weapon with "other questions that have no relation to it" would be unacceptable.[22]

BARGAINING INTERACTIONS

On April 4 and 5, two articles suggested intense debate in the administration over whether or not to proceed with production of the weapon.[23] For various reasons, Carter faced the challenge of how to back off from ERW deployment without appearing to cancel it outright. The means he chose was a unilateral initiative. His motives had more to do with limiting damage to his reputation and to alliance cohesion, however, than with influencing Soviet behavior.[24] At any rate, on April 7, 1978, he declared:

I have decided to defer production of weapons with enhanced radiation effects. The ultimate decision regarding the incorporation of enhanced radiation features into our modernized battlefield weapons will be made later, and will be influenced by the degree to which the Soviet Union shows restraint in its conventional and nuclear arms programs and force deployments affecting the security of the United States and Western Europe.

Accordingly, I have ordered the Defense Department to proceed with the modernization of the Lance missile nuclear warhead and the eight-inch weapon system, leaving open the option of installing the enhanced radiation elements.[25]

Brezhnev responded later that day:

We resolutely reject any attempt to impose unacceptable terms on us. . . .

Faced with a mass protest movement against the plans to develop and deploy these [neutron] weapons in Europe, the United States of America and some other NATO countries are trying to mislead the peoples, pretending that they are ready to hold talks with the Soviet Union while in fact trying to make it the subject of bargaining and tying in this weapon with unrelated issues. Concealed behind all this is only one thing—a desire to go away from the clear cut and concrete proposal for mutual refusal to manufacture neutron weapons.[26]

On April 10, Vance elaborated on the desired form of Soviet reciprocation:

The kind of things that we would be looking toward are the kind of things which affect the security of the European region in such things as the tank forces in the area, the threat to the area which arises from weapons such as the SS-20 ballistic missile, and other items which it is too early yet to delineate. . . . As the president said, one of the major factors affecting his ultimate decision will be the response which we seek.[27]

The Soviet line remained unchanged. On April 25, Brezhnev said that "taking such a statement by the President into account, we will not begin production of neutron weapons either, if the United States does not do so. What comes later depends on Washington."[28] The same day Carter retorted: "The Soviets have no use for a neutron weapon, so the offer by Brezhnev to refrain from building the neutron weapons has no significance in the European theater, and he knows this."[29]

Apparently the issue was dropped in U.S.-Soviet bargaining. As evidence for this assertion, Soviet propaganda against the ERW declined substantially after May 1978. Moreover, terms such as "neutron bomb" or "enhanced radiation weapon" were not even in the indexes of the 1979 volumes of *Documents on Disarmament* or *Public Papers of the President.* In mid-1978 the Soviets began to make some concessions in the MFR talks in Vienna. I found no evidence, however, of any linkage between these concessions and Carter's decision to defer production of ERWs.

In June 1978 the Soviets agreed to elements of a 1975 U.S. proposal that called for a common troop ceiling and for a first phase of reductions that would focus on Soviet tanks and U.S. nuclear weapons.[30] On October 6, 1979, Brezhnev announced actual Soviet reductions:

Motivated by a sincere desire to take out of the impasse the efforts of many years to achieve military detente in Europe, to show an example of transition from words to real deeds, we have decided ... to unilaterally reduce the number of Soviet troops in Central Europe. Up to 20,000 Soviet servicemen, about 1000 tanks and also a certain amount of other military hardware will be withdrawn from the territory of the German Democratic Republic in the course of the next twelve months. . . . We call on the governments of NATO countries to properly assess the initiatives of socialist states and to follow our good example.[31]

In the same speech he said: "We are prepared to reduce the number of medium-range nuclear means of delivery in Western areas of the Soviet Union as compared to the present level but, of course, only in the event if no additional medium-range nuclear means are deployed in Western Europe. . . . "[32] Vice President Walter Mondale responded four days later by welcoming the speech. He said, however, that it needed to be seen in the context of Soviet advantages, military increases instead of matching NATO's restraint, and an intention to lure NATO from crucial conventional and theater nuclear force modernization.[33]

On December 12, 1979, NATO announced is "two-track decision," whereby in 1983 the United States would begin to deploy 572 single-warhead missiles (108 Pershing II ballistic missiles and 464 ground-launched cruise missiles)—if proposed INF arms control negotiations got nowhere.[34] As a part of this decision, Secretary of State Vance said: "The modernization decision that we have made here also makes it possible for us to withdraw 1000 nuclear warheads from Europe. In addition to this reduction, for each of these weapons we deploy, we will withdraw one existing weapon from Europe."[35] No mention was made of neuton bombs. Meanwhile, despite Brezhnev's offer to reduce the number of SS-20s in the western part of the Soviet Union in exchange for the United States introducing no INF missiles, the Soviets continued to increase their SS-20 deployment.[36] Clearly, the Soviets were exercising no restraint in INF.

The only references to ERWs in the 1980 volume of *Documents on Disarmament* concerned a French weapon. On June 26, 1980, French President Giscard d'Estaing announced that France had tested an ERW and that a production decision could be made as early as 1982.[37] The Soviet response was much less severe than it had been toward the Americans. For instance, in a memorandum dated September 23, 1980, the Soviets simply said they were ready to prohibit neutron weapons, "but other countries capable of developing such weapons refuse to conduct negotiations on their production."[38]

President Carter never did order ERW production, although he said that new warheads for the Lance missile would be designed to accept alternative components so that they could be converted to enhanced radiation devices.[39] On August 8, 1981, President Ronald Reagan ordered that ERWs be produced, although deployment to Western Europe would require a multilateral NATO decision. This approach did not lead to a strong Soviet reaction.[40] The United States was then able to concentrate on the INF issue, and these negotiations began on November 30, 1981.[41]

EXPLANATION

Carter's unilateral initiative to defer neutron bomb production failed to induce the Soviets to make significant concessions. Let us begin our explanation for Soviet behavior by examining the bargaining process. The concessions the United States demanded clearly involved Soviet tanks or SS-20 missiles. These demands, however, were not in exactly the same currency as neutron bombs. This asymmetry of weapons made it easier than otherwise for Brezhnev to gain propaganda points by claiming that the United States was "tying in this weapon with unrelated issues," and by saying the Soviet Union would match the U.S. unilateral initiative with parallel restraint in its own neutron bomb production and deployment.[42]

Moreover, the United States was vague about whether the Soviets were supposed to give up an advantage or merely stop increasing their advantages. During negotiations prior to the initiative, the United States had tried to convince the Soviets to give up advantages they already held.[43] In his April 7 speech, Carter simply called for the Soviet Union to show "restraint in its conventional and nuclear arms programs and force deployments affecting the security" of NATO.[44] In a speech on May 5, 1978, Carter said he would consider going ahead with ERWs "if the Soviets continue to buildup their own forces to a degree that increases the threat against the Western Europeans. . . . "[45] Finally, Mondale's lukewarm response to Brezhnev's October 1979 INF proposal and announcement of an intention to withdraw 1000 tanks from Eastern Europe suggests that the United States wanted not only reductions, but serious reductions.[46]

The promise aspect of the U.S. initiative was clear: With appropriate Soviet restraints the United States would continue to defer production of the weapon. The promise was also credible, because the huge political controversy over the weapon meant that individuals and groups with vested interests in it lacked sufficient sway to block an agreement.

The threat aspect of U.S. signals was weak, however. On the one hand, as stated in Carter's April 7 speech, the unilateral initiative sounded conditional, whereby continued U.S. restraint depended on reciprocal Soviet concessions. In the same speech, to enhance the credibility to the threat to produce ERWs in the absence of Soviet concessions, Carter said that planned modernization of the Lance warhead and eight-inch shell would be carried out so that they could be readily converted to enhanced radiation (ER)devices. On October 18 he ordered the Department of Energy to begin to produce components that could convert these weapons into neutron bombs.[47]

On the other hand, additional words and deeds detracted from the credibility of the threat and thus made U.S. restraint seem unconditional. First, the *New York Times* article reporting Carter's April 7 speech quoted an unnamed high official: "After all the trouble this thing has caused, do you think the While House will want to go through it all over again in the near future? For all practical purposes, the neutron bomb is dead."[48]

Second, in December 1979 the Senate Armed Services Committee complained that the administration had not issued a report the committee had asked to receive from the Pentagon by the end of 1978.[49] The report was supposed to specify the kind of Soviet restraint that would warrant a U.S. decision to cancel or continue to delay construction of ERWs, as well as the date by which the United States should decide whether to proceed in the absence of Soviet restraint.[50]

Third, the administration's commitment to produce ER components for TNWs eroded. In his April 7 speech, Carter said that modernization of the Lance warhead and the eight-inch artillery shell would leave open the option of installing ER components. This suggested that the components would be produced for both weapons. Subsequent volumes of the *Report of Secretary of Defense Harold Brown to the Congress* gave a different impression. In the fiscal year (FY) 1980 *Report,* Brown said that the Lance warhead would offer the option of ER features, and the eight-inch round would be able to incorporate the features "with shortened lead time."[51] The FY 1981 and 1982 *Reports* repeated that the Lance would offer an ER option, but they made no mention of the eight-inch shell.[52] Furthermore, even this limited production of components was apparently delayed. As evidence for this assertion, the *Congressional Quarterly Almanac* reported in 1980 that with standard procedures conversion could take months or years unless production of the parts began immediately.[53]

Finally, Carter never ordered production of ERWs. When Brown issued the FY 1982 *Report* on January 19, 1981, the Lance warhead continued to have only an "enhanced radiation option."[54]

The United States was not implementing an explicit campaign of initiatives. The only other unilateral initiatives that Carter implemented prior to his neutron bomb initiative involved U.S. actions in 1977 intended to limit arms transfers to the Third World. Since no administration official accompanied the ERW initiative with even a mention of this previous bargaining interaction, the most that the United States signaled was a very brief, tacit campaign of initiatives. Furthermore, because the arms transfer initiatives largely failed in their objectives, the United States was not conducting a series of initiatives.[55] Also in 1977, Carter canceled production of the B-1 bomber. This action was not a unilateral initiative, however; he did it because the bomber was not cost-effective compared to other systems such as cruise missiles.[56]

The United States did withdraw 1000 TNWs from Europe during 1980, but this was not clearly part of a sequence of initiatives. On the surface it may appear to be the third action of unilateral restraint, coming after Carter's April 1978 initiative to defer ERW production and the Soviet Union's withdrawal of some tanks from Eastern Europe following Brezhnev's October speech. I found no evidence, however, that it was intended to be part of a series of initiatives or was perceived that way by the Soviets. Cyrus Vance, who announced the withdrawl of the 1000 TNWs, had merely said that the decision was linked to the U.S. decision to deploy INF in Europe.[57] Neither he nor Carter linked it to the earlier neutron bomb initiative, nor did the Soviets publicly make such a linkage.

The Soviets probably received and correctly interpreted U.S. signals concerning the neutron bomb—including their ambivalence. The Soviets certainly must have followed the news reports and government sources I mentioned above. Their responses show they knew what Carter was proposing, and the significant decrease in related Soviet propaganda following the spring of 1978 is evidence that they correctly expected Carter not to produce usable neutron devices.

Security calculations disposed the Soviets not to meet U.S. demands. Since we have not yet discussed Soviet theater doctrine, this evaluation requires a lengthy discussion. At least through the mid-1980s, their theater doctrine emphasized an offensive strategy with superiority in many measures of military capability. Domination of the East European "buffer zone" enables the Soviets to base many of their frontline forces there, integrated with the similarly offensive-oriented forces of their allies. This doctrine gave them the ability to "refight World War II," only this time under more favorable circumstances: the Pact would be better able to preempt a mounting invasion from the West, the war would be fought outside the Soviet Union (thus limiting damage to the USSR), and the aggressor could be defeated decisively and more quickly than during the "Great Patriotic War."[58] As Col. A. A. Sidorenko wrote in 1970, "only the offense leads to . . . victory."[59] Defensive or delaying tactics were usually to be temporary, until the offensive could be resumed.

Western analysts note that an offensive doctrine has two secondary advantages. First, it offers an intimidating coersive capability so that East and West Germany would hesitate to reunify as a neutral or pro-Western state.[60] Second, it makes domination of Eastern Europe easier, both by giving the Soviets the capability to intervene, and by denying Pact allies extensive preparations for defense that could be used to hinder a Soviet intervention.[61]

Our discussion focuses first on the Soviet ground forces, whose mission was to advance rapidly and defeat the enemy. The doctrine required that they fight from advantages of numerical superiority in artillery, troops, and tanks. In order to maintain the momentum of the advance and carry the battle to the enemy's rear, tanks are essential.[62]

Offense takes different forms: the meeting and defeat of moving tank armies, the breakthrough of defenses, and the pursuit of enemy tanks. Our focus is on the breakthrough, where the Soviets planned to attack in two or sometimes three echelons. The first would have the preponderance of force, with two-thirds of the tanks and most of the artillery. Its mission was to attack until rendered ineffective. Then it was to be replaced by the second echelon, whose main mission was to exploit weaknesses created by the first and thus to maintain the momentum of the advance.[63]

This doctrine required the Soviets to have superiority in combat power. Locally, they preferred a ratio of eight to one in tanks and considered four to one a minimum.[64] The Soviets have their greatest advantage in Central Europe, which is the main strategic corridor: in 1978 approximately three to one in Pact to NATO tanks. In Southern Europe, their advantage was only about one-and-a-half to one.[65] NATO worried most about the extensive Soviet advantage in Central Europe.

To accept parity in tanks or even to give up a significant part of their advantage would have crippled the ground forces' ability to carry out its offensive missions. Breakthrough would be much more difficult, since a successful offense requires a substantial advantage; the momentum of an advance would be slowed or stopped; and decisive victory would be much more difficult to achieve. Since U.S. ERW deployment was unlikely in any event, the Soviets probably calculated that meeting Carter's demand for offensive reductions would have hurt their security—a situation obviously unfavorable for reciprocation.

What if, in the absence of a Soviet concession to forgo offensive advantages, U.S. ERW production and deployment was likely? Since military planners operate on a net assessment basis, might the disadvantages of tank reductions have been offset by the advantage of not having to face U.S. ERWs?

Certainly the Soviets were aware of the anti-tank utility of the weapons. They knew about the technical characteristics of the weapon's effects as early as 1961.[66] Subsequent writings through the 1970s demonstrated an awareness of the military utility of prompt nuclear radiation, although they did not specifically mention ERWs. In 1970 Col. Sidorenko said: "A reasonable compromise must be found here between the requirements for troop protection and the need for successful accomplishment of the combat mission."[67] Two years later Major-General G. Biryukov and Colonel G. Milnikov said:

In performing the mission of destroying armored troops on the field of battle, it is expedient to destroy such a basic element as the tank crews in and outside the tanks. This makes it possible to deprive the enemy armored troops of their combat power with a greater economy of ammunition, in shorter periods and with a high destruction ability. . . . The point is that the effective radius of a nuclear explosive is one and a half to twice as great against a tank crew (using radiation) as it is against a tank (using blast).[68]

Beginning in the late 1970s, Soviet tanks apparently began to carry shielding useful against prompt radiation (i.e., gamma rays and neutrons).[69] Before this time, protective blasts on tanks focused only on reducing damage from nuclear blasts or from contamination by nuclear fallout and a chemical or biological warfare environment. Perhaps early designers assumed that the armor provided adequate protection against prompt radiation from standard nuclear devices.

Kovriki is the Russian name of the three- to- four inch thick plastic blanket embedded with materials that absorb prompt radiation. The first type contained lead pellets that absorb gamma rays. Soviet sources imply that later types had layers of "hydrogen-trapping materials" to reduce the effects of neutrons. In 1984, armored vehicles mounting external kovriki over the roof were displayed for the first time. Their significance is controversial, however. Most U.S. military analysts think they were added in response to the prospect of U.S. ERWs. An alternative hypothesis that was popular in Europe was that they were added to defeat conventional antitank weapons depending on shaped-charge warheads. The author of my source for this information, Steven Zaloga, thinks that this latter hypothesis "does not address the increasing shift away from stand-off probes to other methods of detonation. . . . " Consequently, he supports the speculation about ERWs.[70]

Direct evidence is too thin to determine the level of Soviet concern about ERWs. Although their deployment of shielding suggests that they worried about the weapon, I found insufficient evidence to know how much they cared. Useful evidence of a serious concern would have been an observable modification of their training or military exercises in response to French neutron bombs or to the possibility of U.S. ERW deployment under Carter or Reagan. If they cared that much, they may have seen no net security disadvantages to meeting Carter's demand for trading Soviet tanks for a U.S. pledge not to deploy neutron bombs. Not making operational changes might have indicated less concern about the weapon and consequently a negative net assessment for Carter's proposal; alternatively, it might simply have been consistent with a possible Soviet procedure of not changing tactics in the absence of a clear and present danger. Although I found no evidence of changes in Soviet practices, I cannot be sure that my sources did not omit relevant information.

Kent Wisner's analytical study of Soviet doctrine and operational tactics provides some insight into what Soviet officers might have thought.[71] This indirect, largely deductive approach suggests that they expected ERWs to enhance NATO's capabilities only marginally—a situation unfavorable for reciprocation.

When a breakthrough of defenses is undertaken, forces are dispersed as long as possible, concentrate only at the last crucial time, and then disperse rapidly again. ERWs have more kill-capability than standard fission devices only when the tanks approach the line of contact with the enemy. Their utility is highest close to the line where tanks are only 50–100 meters apart. This deployment occurs three-tenths to one 1 kilometer (km) from the line. Here two 1-kiloton eight-inch shells could destroy a tank company (separated from a neighboring company by 100 meters), while three or four fission devices of the same yield would be needed. This close, however, the United States would risk killing or injuring friendly troops. At 1–3 km, where companies deploy into platoon columns 100–150 meters apart and companies are 500 meters apart, one round of either type would be necessary. At this range, the only advantage of ERWs would be that blast would be about 20 percent less. However, to work best at this range, the ERW would need to fall exactly between companies, and the Soviets could not be using terrain for cover. Beyond this range, ERWs would again have no more kill capability than standard devices, although the level of blast would be less. I found just one statement by a Soviet officer that examined how the utility of ERWs might vary. Col. G. Ivanov wrote in 1982 that ERWs had an advantage over standard nuclear weapons only against concentrations of armor, such as in the stage just before breaking through.[72]

This analysis suggests that the kill capability of ERWs is significantly greater than for fission devices only close to the front, where the risk of harming friendly troops is high and thus under conditions where they may not be used.

What about the argument that the reduced blast effects would enhance the credibility of the U.S. threat to use nuclear weapons and thus would strengthen the U.S. ability to dissuade the initial Soviet invasion? This argument might be relevant if local commanders had permission to use the weapons at the proper place during the few minutes Soviet tanks are concentrated. As of this writing, however, it takes 24 hours to obtain such permission, and the president would not easily order the "first-use" of nuclear devices.[73]

The improbability of proper use of the weapons was exacerbated by the situation where the Soviets had a nuclear war-fighting doctrine and NATO did not.[74] This is why several Western military analysts say that deployment of ERWs would be only a small step in redressing the military balance and adding to NATO's nuclear capability. If ERWs were deployed, the Soviet doctrinal notion of preemption might lead them to strike the weapon storage depots at the beginning of a conflict. Furthermore, if the United States was the first to use nuclear weapons, the Soviet political leadership probably would issue release orders that left discretion for the use of nuclear weapons to military commanders. On the battlefield, such weapons would then likely have been used to speed the rate of advance and to destroy NATO troop concentrations—in other words, massively, not in a limited manner. Therefore in battle the Soviets might have emerged with a net advantage. These arguments may have been behind Secretary of Defense Harold Brown's statement downplaying the military utility of ERWs only two days after Carter announced the initiative.[75]

Making the plausible assumption that the Soviets had conducted similar analytical studies of the military utility of ERWs and were aware of NATO's problems using them in a timely, useful manner, we can deduce that the Soviets expected that ERWs would have enhanced NATO's capabilities only marginally. Given insufficient direct evidence, however, this conclusion can only be tentative.

If our analysis is correct, the Soviets probably thought they would be better able to carry out the breakthrough mission with a tank advantage facing ERWs than without a tank advantage and not facing ERWs. Moreover, the net assessment disposing them not to meet U.S. demands would be even more obvious when considering the other two offensive missions: the meeting of moving tank armies and the pursuit of NATO tanks. Since in either case Soviet tanks would not be as concentrated as in a breakthrough, ERWs would not be particularly more capable than fission devices. The Soviets would also be less able to perform their missions if they had fewer tanks.[76] Making the decision not to meet U.S. demands was probably made much easier by the low prospect that the United States would deploy ERWs.

As the Soviets considered the U.S. proposal to trade U.S. ERW deployment for Soviet SS-20 deployment, their security calculations once again disposed them not to accept it.

Until at least 1981, their doctrine emphasized that once nuclear war is under way, the Soviet Armed Forces should seek to fight it to limit damage to the Soviet Union and to win. Allegedly in 1977 the Soviet political leadership rejected the preemption option, although this assertion is controversial.[77] The SS-20's capabilities complemented these nuclear warfighting requirements better than the predecessor SS-4 and -5. Giving up SS-20s, with their three MIRVs each, would have reduced the Soviet ability to launch quick and accurate nuclear strikes against important military targets. The mobility of SS-20 launchers also reduced the vulnerability of the missiles, thus increasing their utility in a war.

SS-20s had no direct tactical linkage with ERWs, as did Soviet tanks. Consequently, not meeting the U.S. demand to give up SS-20s would not have led to any degradation of the capability of these missiles to carry out their missions. Moreover, since the United States was unlikely to deploy ERWs in any event, at the time, keeping their SS-20s made more military sense than giving them up. In sum, meeting U.S. demands concerning either tanks or SS-20s would have cost the Soviets important military capabilities, while not meeting the demands presented no significant military costs.

Calculations about third parties also worked against the U.S. proposal. If the Soviets gave up their advantages in INF or in conventional forces, they would have had less overall capability vis-a-vis third countries such as European members of NATO. Barriers to entry at the level of power of the United States and Soviet Union were not relevant, because the proposal would have had no significant impact on the ability of third countries to threaten U.S. security.

On-site verification requirements associated with the U.S. proposal also did not favor the Soviet Union making significant concessions. U.S. MFR proposals called for inspection of one side's territory by nationals of the other side. For instance, the United States wanted inspectors at reduction area entry and exit points, up to eighteen air and ground inspection trips to the other's force reduction area per year, and the right to send observers to movements involving at least one division.[78] In contrast, the Soviets claimed that troop and equipment levels could be monitored by "national means of verification."[79] Soviet SS-20s also would have required intrusive inspection.[80]

Soviet political calculations about China may have favored the ERW initiative's success for a few months, but by mid-1978 the situation was unfavorable.[81] From the Sino-Soviet border clashes in 1969 through early 1978, the Soviets hoped that improving relations with the United States would help to restrain the development of U.S.-Chinese ties. Starting in March 1978, U.S. leaders began to say that a "strong and secure" China served U.S. interests. Apparently worried about possible U.S.-China military ties, on June 17, 1978, *Pravda* warned that alignment of the two countries "on an anti-Soviet basis would rule out the possibility of cooperation with the Soviet Union in the matter of reducing the danger of a nuclear war, and of course, of limiting armaments." In November Secretary of State Cyrus Vance said that the United States would not object to arms sales from NATO countries to China, and in December the United States and China "normalized" their relations. The next year the United States even established two intelligence-gathering stations in China to monitor Soviet missile tests. In this political context, the Soviets decided to delay by six months the summit meeting at which they and the United States had planned to sign the SALT II Treaty. Obviously this condition had become unfavorable for the initiative's success.

The Soviet calculation about NATO was moderately unfavorable, because not meeting U.S. demands presented no political costs and possibly offered some benefits. Non-reciprocation would not have strengthened NATO's cohesion. ERWs were too divisive in NATO for that, in part because the Soviets successfully played on the European's "fear of entrapment"—the fear that reckless U.S. behavior might drag European countries into a destructive nuclear war in which they had no interest.[82] The prospect of U.S. ERW deployment strengthened the "peace movement's" opposition to it in West Germany, Belgium, and especially the Netherlands. Thus if the Soviets made no major concessions, and if this Soviet behavior led the United States to increase efforts to deploy ERWs, then the political capacity of West European governments would have declined even further. Moreover, Soviet propaganda played on the asymmetry between ERWs and what they called the "unrelated issues" of conventional forces and INF. The Soviets also minimized the damage to their political relations by proposing an alternative agreement: a mutual ban on ERWS.

Agreeing to Carter's proposal would have produced mixed results. On the one hand, because Carter's policy had harmed the U.S. leadership position in NATO, meeting U.S. demands would have exonerated Carter's policy and thus would have strengthened NATO's cohesion. On the other hand, the U.S. proposal would have improved Soviet relations with West European countries, since this response would have reduced the threats posed by Soviet advantages in tanks or INF.

The Soviets also probably calculated that non-reciprocation would not harm their relations with Non-Aligned countries, largely because of the apparent success of their propaganda campaign. Meeting the U.S. demands would have improved Soviet relations with them, however, because the outcome would have been policies they apparently supported: a ban on ERWs, as well as limitations on either conventional forces or INF.[83] Overall, these calculations probably moderately favored the proposed agreement.

The proposed agreement would not have affirmed Soviet prestige, and the INF linkage probably would have harmed it. First, non-reciprocal exchanges were involved: The Soviets would have had to give up useful weapons already deployed, in exchange for a U.S. promise not to deploy a weapon that, politically, it probably could not deploy anyway. Moreover, SS-20s were not mere battlefield weapons, and an exchange involving tanks went against the MFR principle of "symmetric reductions."[84] Second, whether or not an agreement would have affirmed equal status depended on the linkage. Since the U.S. MFR linkage would not have left the Soviet Union inferior to NATO in conventional forces, the overall impact on prestige would have been ambiguous. For the INF proposal, no Western arms control proposal offered to compensate the Soviets for British and French (or Chinese, for that matter) nuclear forces that could strike the Soviet Union; overall, therefore, Soviet prestige would have been hurt.

Domestic economic calculations moderately favored the proposed agreement. If the Soviets met the U.S. demands and agreed to give up their superiority in conventional forces or to limit SS-20 deployment, they would have been able to save money. This was also in the economic era that began in 1976, in which constraining the growth of military spending was important to Soviet leaders.[85] Not agreeing would not have forced them to increase military spending, however, given both the unlikelihood of U.S. ERW deployment and our earlier conclusion that even deployment probably would have increased NATO's capabilities only marginally.

When Carter announced the initiative in April 1978, Soviet calculations about international economics may have favored the proposed agreement. This was toward the end of the 1977/78 crop year, when the 1977 Soviet grain harvest was short 19 million tons.[86] Both supportive conditions obtained as well: the Soviets wanted to import mostly coarse grains and the United States dominated over half of this market, and the United States presented a trade-stimulating environment under the 1975 Five-Year Grain Agreement.[87] With the 1978 harvest and its 22 million ton surplus, however, the Soviets did not need to import as much grain. Hence this condition was probably irrelevant in Soviet calculations from mid-1978 through mid-1979, and the ERW issue was dead by the time the Soviets needed U.S. grain again with the 1979 harvest shortfall.

Turning to the environment of bargaining, the Soviet military obviously resisted the proposed agreement. The proposal offered no important advantages to the military services, because ERWs probably would not have improved NATO's capability significantly. More importantly, it portended serious disadvantages. First, reductions in Soviet offensive forces would have hampered the ability of the ground forces to carry out missions to conquer NATO territory and to limit damage to the Soviet Union. It also would have resulted in budget reductions. Second, loss of the SS-20s would have hindered the ability of the SRFs to carry out regional damage limitation missions, and it would have resulted in the loss of sunk investments as well as prospects for future SS-20 deployments.

Most of the bargaining that took place over the ERW was informal. Late in 1977, several months before Carter's initiative, the United States brought up the ERW-conventional force linkage at the MFR talks.[88] The Soviets rejected the linkage, and apparently this item was not on the MFR agenda during 1978.[89] Thus the ERW did not fit into on-going negotiations, including SALT, and the INF negotiations had not yet begun.

Brezhnev was ascendant over his rivals at this time, as he had been since early 1968 and especially since 1971.[90] The U.S. proposal had so many disadvantages, however, that the issue probably was uncontroversial. I found no evidence of controversy, nor of the impact of Carter's initiative on Soviet moderates. I suspect that the initiative's effective unconditional nature and the successful Soviet propaganda campaign did not particularly help any moderates.

Carter's initiative occurred during the 1975 to December 1979 period when the Soviets probably perceived a low-moderate level of international tension. The deductive approach suggests that several developments increased tensions a bit compared to the heyday of detente during the early 1970s. First, since the January 1975 passage of the Jackson-Vanik amendment to the U.S. Trade Reform Bill, U.S. human rights policy had been an irritant to the Soviets. It challenged the norm of equal status and the Soviet regime's monopoly over policy. Jimmy Carter, who became president in 1977, also had human rights as a central part of his foreign policy. Second, as was discussed above, the Soviets were unhappy with Carter's improvement of relations with China. Third, the Soviets were upset with the U.S. arms control proposal of March 1977, which would have required the Soviets to give up their advantages in ICBM counterforce capability without obtaining a comparably large concession from the United States. However, these were not serious threats to Soviet vital interests, and the means the United States used had little potential for escalation to war.[91]

Tensions probably remained at a low-moderate level for most of 1979, although the parties signed the SALT II Treaty in mid-1979, about the same time Carter approved full-scale development for the MX missile. This large ICBM, with ten MIRVs having enhanced accuracy and yield, would when deployed in the mid-1980s be much more capable of counterforce missions than the contemporary Minuteman missiles. It was comparable to the Soviet SS-18 and -19 missiles. In addition, among Carter's top foreign policy advisors, the more hard-line Zbigniew Brzezinski seemed to overshadow Cyrus Vance.[92]

In 1978 and for most of 1979, Soviet rhetoric also indicated a low-moderate level of tension. Statements about superpower relations and the United States were somewhat less favorable than before 1975, as comments about U.S. domestic politics included references to "reactionary circles" and "militaristic right-wing forces" on the attack.[93] With the Soviet invasion of Afghanistan in December 1979 and U.S. reactions to it, the Soviets probably perceived a higher, perhaps moderate level of tension. We need not explore this situation, however, because it occurred after the period of this case study.

The Soviets probably perceived an acceptable strategic environment, just as they had since the late 1960s. Under all forseeable circumstances, the United States could not emerge from a nuclear war it started noticeably better off than the Soviets. They also probably perceived U.S. strategic intentions to be ambiguous or offensive. In chapter 7 we saw how beginning in 1968 the Soviets likely saw ambiguous U.S. strategic intentions. Sometime between the mid-1970s and early 1980s, they once again probably came to see U.S. intentions as offensive.

By the early 1980s, U.S. intentions obviously seemed offensive. When discussing U.S. nuclear doctrine in 1982, for instance, Secretary of Defense Caspar Weinberger said that "we are planning to prevail if we are attacked."[94] President Reagan's strategic modernization program was consistent with this doctrinal objective. In 1981 he accelerated development of the second-generation Trident SLBM, the D-5. Because its MIRV warheads would be much more accurate and have a greater yield than previous SLBMs, when deployed in 1989 it would for the first time give an SLBM a countersilo capability. Moreover, the large scope of the planned deployment would theoretically enable this system to destroy all Soviet ICBM silos.[95] Reagan also authorized deployment of the MX missile in fixed silos.[96] His resurrection of the B-1 bomber probably seemed less threatening, however, because its slower speed made it less useful for first-strike missions than the MX or D-5.[97]

Soviet perceptions of U.S. intentions in the late 1960s and the early 1980s are relatively easy to deduce. The transition date is unfortunately difficult to determine. Some might put it as early as 1974, when Secretary of Defense James Schlesinger officially began to call for a targeting policy with options to destroy hardened Soviet targets.[98] Soviet pronouncements on the "Schlesinger doctrine" were invariably hostile. They claimed that limited nuclear war ideas were an illusion that increased the likelihood of a nuclear war, one which would surely escalate to total war.[99]

Moreover, as MIRV deployment proceeded on Minuteman missiles, the U.S. ability to degrade the Soviet ICBM warhead inventory increased from a projected 40 percent destruction rate in 1970 to 50–60 percent in 1974. The percentage later dropped a bit, but the reason involved Soviet MIRV-ing and not U.S. concessions. At the same time, the United States did not in-tend to MIRV all its Minuteman missiles; the Minuteman II had only one warhead and the Minuteman III had three.[100]

Carter's policy in 1977 may have been confusing to the Soviets.[101] On the one hand, early on he forwarded the above-mentioned March 1977 arms control proposal, which would have required the Soviets to give up their advantage in ICBMs. He also spent $5 million for D-5 R&D. On the other hand, he seemed less concerned with his predecessors about limited war scenarios, and he slowed development of the MX. In 1978 he authorized $190 million for MX development, but said it would be deployed in a man-ner not optimized for a first strike: in a mobile mode, which was much more expensive than in vulnerable fixed silos. He also said the United States would not upgrade Minuteman II accuracy as much as was possible.[102] In 1979 he announced his "countervailing strategy," which furthered the "Schlesinger doctrine." Secretary of Defense Harold Brown claimed that although limited options were necessary to have a possibility for keeping a nuclear war limited, he did not expect such a war to remain limited. Unlike later in the Reagan administration, neither Schlesinger nor Brown wanted prompt and accurate capabilities equal to or greater than Soviet capabili-ties; their idea was not to prevail with "escalation dominance," but rather to deny the Soviets a monopoly on such capabilities. Overall, "essential equivalence" was sufficient.[103]

In 1979 Carter also ordered full-scale development for the MX, and deployment of the new Mark 12A warhead began. Eventually it would be on 300 of the 550 Minuteman III missiles. The Mark 12A would double the warhead's "single shot kill capability" against hardened targets.[104] In August 1980 the administration announced PD-59; it would implement the new "countervailing strategy." That month Brown also revealed progress on "stealth" technology to make future U.S. bombers invisible to Soviet radars.[105] In the "dual track" decision of December 1979, Carter announced that in the absence of a Soviet concession to forgo their unilateral advan-tage in INF missiles, the United States would develop, produce, and deploy its own—including the fast and highly accurate Pershing II missile.[106]

At some time during this 1974–82 period, the Soviets probably came to perceive U.S. intentions as offensive. More precision is beyond the scope of this work. In sum, at the time of Carter's ERW initiative, the Soviets probably perceived a strategic environment that was acceptable and U.S. intentions as ambiguous or offensive. Overall, therefore, the strategic environment probably seemed stable or moderately stable.

SUMMARY

Two obvious conditions moderately favored the success of Carter's initiative: The proposed agreement would have saved the Soviets some money and would have improved Soviet relations with Non-Aligned countries. In addition, for several months after the initiative, calculations about China and the Soviet desire for U.S. grain apparently favored reciprocation. Finally, the Soviets probably received and correctly interpreted U.S. signals. The first problem, however, is that the United States sent mixed signals, some of them with the unintended message that the initiative was unconditional. This situation was unfavorable for the initiative's success.

The remaining Soviet cost-benefit calculations worked against the initiative's success. The proposed agreement probably would have had net security disadvantages vis-a-vis the United States and third countries; it required on-site inspection; it would have had net political costs as the Soviets considered NATO's cohesion and, beginning in mid-1978, the PRC; it would not have affirmed Soviet prestige and the INF linkage would have harmed their prestige. The military services also had strong bureaucratic reasons to oppose the proposal.

The hypothesis about the formality of the bargaining process fails this case study, because the Soviets did not reciprocate despite a situation where the communication was predominantly informal. Three other hypotheses do not do well either: the Soviets probably perceived a low-moderate level of tension and a stable or moderately stable strategic environment, and Carter's previous initiatives to limit arms transfers to less-developed countries suggest that the United States was conducting a brief, tacit campaign of initiatives.

Three hypotheses receive support, because the expected outcome of failure occurred: the United States was not implementing a series of initiatives, it did not accompany the initiative with an official history of previous bargaining interactions, and it did not respond quickly to Soviet disinterest in the proposal by implementing its threat to produce ERWs.

Because the United States did not respond to the Soviet defection, the research suggests nothing about hypotheses concerning moderate or defensive reactions. The issue was probably uncontroversial within the Soviet leadership, so the status of the general-secretary's authority was irrelevant. Finally, I found no evidence about the initiative's impact on Soviet moderates.

9

Principal Findings

President Kennedy's unilateral initiative to halt atmospheric nuclear testing contributed to the Soviet decision to agree to a limited test ban. Furthermore, the declared U.S. policy not to orbit nuclear weapons, when combined with later clarifications about the scope of the proposal and verification requirements, expedited the Soviet announcement of parallel restraint. These cases illustrate that the unilateral initiative tactic sometimes works. The comprehensive test ban, bomber, and neutron bomb cases show that it also fails. Then we have the ABM case, where the Soviets were uninterested in reciprocating U.S. restraint until after the United States said it would deploy its own ABM. Yet implementing a threat not to continue unilateral restraint does not guarantee Soviet reciprocation, as the CTB and bomber cases illustrate.

How can we account for the pattern of outcomes? Our research suggests that an initiative succeeds only under certain conditions. That is, the outcome of bargaining is a function of a number of factors deduced in chapters 2 and 3 that were at least moderately corroborated by the research. This knowledge constitutes the major part of our principal findings. The other parts examine the relative weight of these conditions, offer some observations and speculations about hypotheses that received little if any support, illustrate some of the tactic's advantages and disadvantages, and discuss the connection between the unilateral initiative and bargaining chip tactics. We will finish this chapter with suggestions for further research that could help to increase the degree of certainty of our findings and to fill gaps in our knowledge.

CONDITIONS FAVORING SUCCESSFUL UNILATERAL INITIATIVES

Our major purpose is to understand when unilateral initiatives work. This requires us to learn the identity and relative importance of the conditions favoring successful initiatives. "Success" means that the Soviets complied with U.S. wishes and thus exercised restraint in their weapons policy. "Failure" means they did not comply.

Immediate success occurred only in the LTB case. The other two instances of success, involving orbiting nuclear weapons and ABMs, came more than a year after the United States first announced its initiatives. In a sense, then, the policy failed for a year. Consequently, when I discuss the five instances of failure, I include the first year of these two cases along with the three obvious failures involving the CTB, bombers, and ERWs.

Another complication is that when success finally occurred in the ABM case in mid- to late-1968, it was only partial because the Soviets did not fully meet U.S. demands. Unlike their behavior for more than a year preceding this time, they agreed to discuss ABM limitations and halted construction of their Moscow ABM site. With a complete success they would have agreed to limit ABMs and said they were engaging in a construction moratorium. Not too long into the Nixon administration, they did agree to limit ABMs; I interpret this behavior as evidence that their 1968 interest in ABM limitations was genuine although less committal than later.

Failure also is not always complete. For example, although the Soviets waited a year to agree formally to prohibit the orbiting of nuclear weapons, informally they reciprocated all along. Since something caused them to change their declaratory policy, I contrast the situation surrounding the first year—a period of "partial failure"—with the time they formally reciprocated. When I discuss failure below, I include the five instances of both complete and partial failure. The same applies for the three instances of success.

Before Soviet leaders can respond to a U.S. initiative, they should understand what the United States wants them to do and how the U.S. will react to various Soviet responses. With this information, they can rationally evaluate the probable effects of their actions on their military, political, and economic interests. Soviet military calculations take into account the U.S.-Soviet relation of forces, capabilities of third parties, and verification requirements for the proposed agreement. Politically they worry about the cohesion of their alliance network in comparison with relations among their adversaries, as well as about their prestige. Finally, they consider possible domestic and international economic consequences.

Bargaining occurs in a domestic and international environment that sometimes influences the rationality or context of Soviet calculations. An obvious factor is the opinion of the Soviet military services. The final two conditions are hypotheses corroborated by the research. These take into account the general-secretary's ability to push through a controversial policy, as well as Soviet perceptions of the level of international tension.

The discussion of each factor begins with a statement of when it favors a successful initiative. To help understand how the factor operates or to qualify the generalization, I draw illustrations from the case studies. Let us begin by examining the sort of signaling that favors success.

1. *The United States clearly signals its demands and its commitments to implement, as appropriate, its promises and threats. When possible, the U.S. initiative is also in the same currency as the new Soviet policy the U.S. desires.* The Soviets are more likely than otherwise to make a concession when this condition obtains. Of the eight instances we examined, the expected outcome occurred five times, failed to occur twice, and was difficult to predict in the B-47 case because U.S. signals were not obviously clear or obscure.

The outer space case illustrates the importance of clear and complete demands. For a year the United States did not explicitly say that its proposal would not require restraint on ballistic missiles or on-site inspection. Soon after the United States clarified its demands, the Soviets agreed to the proposal. In the successful LTB case, U.S. signals were very clear and bargaining was in the same currency.

In the unsuccessful CTB and ERW cases, different currencies were involved and that made Soviet nonreciprocation less costly politically than otherwise. U.S. signals also were not entirely clear. In January 1963 Kennedy postponed a series of underground tests at a time when the Soviets were not testing, and he resumed testing when they refused to make more verification concessions. In 1978 Carter linked U.S. restraint in ERW deployment to Soviet concessions in either conventional forces or INF. Moreover, Carter's threat to produce and deploy ERWs in the absence of Soviet concessions was not credible.

In neither ABM instance did the expected outcome occur. For most of 1967 U.S. signals were clear, consistent, in the same currency, and credible in explaining the interdependence between the Soviet and U.S. systems. The Soviets remained uninterested in limitations, however. Then despite mixed signals accompanying the later U.S. announcement that it would deploy an ABM, the Soviets moved closer to meeting U.S. demands. These two instances show that clarity and bargaining in the same currency, although obviously important, are neither necessary nor sufficient conditions for success.

2. *The Soviets receive and correctly interpret U.S. signals.* Only during the first year of the outer space case was this condition not met, and this situation hurt prospects for success. The Soviets evidently misperceived that the U.S. proposal to ban orbiting nuclear weapons also required on-site inspection and restraints on ballistic missiles. The United States never stated these requirements, however. Moreover, Gore's December 3 statement implied that ballistic missiles would not be covered. Apparently the Soviets missed

Gore's nuance and simply assumed that the requirements associated with previous disarmament proposals still held. When they finally understood the situation a year later, they reciprocated formally.

This condition obtained in the other two instances of success and in the other four instances of failure. The research suggests, therefore, that Soviet misperceptions are more significant and detrimental to success than correct perceptions are beneficial.

3. *Security is enhanced by the proposed agreement.* This condition is probably the most obvious, since states tend not to do things that they think will undermine their security. Assuming that Soviet security calculations are determined by the military doctrine prevailing at the time, this generalization was confirmed by all of the research. In seven of the eight instances, a concern for security vis-a-vis the United States was clearly manifest.

As the Soviets considered how to respond to the outer space initiative, direct security calculations led them to expect no benefits but definite long term costs if they orbited nuclear weapons. This situation moderately favored Soviet reciprocation when they formally agreed to the U.S. proposal in September 1963. For the previous year, however, they mistakenly thought the United States also wanted restrictions on ballistic missiles—which would have inhibited their plans to catch up with the United States and to accomplish retaliation and damage limitation missions. Consequently, during this year security calculations disposed them not to reciprocate formally.

Wanting to catch up to the level of U.S. strategic power or to improve their ability to carry out doctrinal missions were also key security motives behind Soviet rejections of the 1963 CTB and 1967 ABM proposals. During 1968 they realized that their ABM would have serious problems working against U.S. MIRVs, and they feared a superior U.S. ABM; this new situation disposed them to comply partially with the U.S. demands.

Security calculations also compelled them to reject U.S. proposals for both a "bomber burning" and an exchange of U.S. ERW restraint for Soviet reductions in conventional forces or SS-20s. In the bomber case, the U.S. proposal would have decreased the relative level of Soviet power and reduced their ability to carry out regional missions. In the latter case, nonreciprocation presented few if any security costs, and agreeing to the U.S. demands plausibly would have constrained their ability to carry out doctrinal missions. In the eighth instance, the LTB case, security was not at risk and other factors motivated them to reciprocate. Since this condition is highly correlated with the expected outcomes, it may be the most important condition for success. Before we make that judgement, however, we must complete our survey of relevant factors. Then, focusing on the ones most supported by the research, we will explore what happens when they come into conflict in order to determine their relative weight.

4. *Security vis-a-vis third countries is enhanced by the proposed agreement.* An obvious dimension of this factor concerns the strengthening or maintenance of barriers to entry at the level of military power of the United States and Soviet Union, a situation which favors success. The reason is that barriers would help to preserve Soviet capabilities relative to third countries that are adversaries or potential adversaries.

This factor moderately supported Soviet reciprocation in the successful LTB case, because if multilateral the agreement would serve to make it more difficult if not more expensive for third countries (such as West Germany) to develop reliable and effective nuclear weapons. Yet the Soviets did not accept the CTB proposal, even though it would have been even more effective than an LTB at constraining nuclear proliferation. This consideration was unsupportive of the U.S. ABM proposal, because superpower ABM systems would reduce the utility of ballistic missiles owned by third countries. The expected outcome occurred during the unsuccessful period of the ABM case, but not when the Soviets complied partially with U.S. demands in mid-1968.

The Soviets rejected the B-47 and ERW proposals, which would have reduced their capabilities with respect to third parties. Barriers to entry were not strictly involved, because the proposal would have had no impact on third party capabilities against the United States.

5. *Verification mechanisms are acceptable.* For the period of our case studies, all the research suggests that this meant on-site inspection was not involved. Intrusive inspection was not required in the three instances of success: the LTB case, the outer space case in September 1963, and the ABM case when the Soviets indicated interest in limitations. It was required in all of the remaining instances, and the tactic failed each time. When the Soviets discussed intrusive verification, they usually said it was unnecessary or would amount to espionage.

Gorbachev was willing to accept on-site inspection to verify compliance with the 1987 INF Treaty, which calls into question the contemporary relevance of their on-site inspection concern. At the least, however, this factor seems useful for understanding Soviet behavior in the pre-Gorbachev era.

6. *Prestige is affirmed by the proposed agreement.* This condition obtained in the three successful instances. Because the Soviets had to give up no more than the United States, the proposals upheld the norm of reciprocity. Likewise, since the proposals did nothing to constrain the Soviet ability to attain strategic parity, they affirmed the norm of equal status.

Neither supportive condition obtained in the bomber case. Since the United States considered its B-47s obsolete at the same time the Soviets viewed their TU-16s as vital, the exchange would not have been reciprocal. Moreover, because of overall Soviet nuclear inferiority, the proposal would have made the Soviets even more inferior—hardly an affirmation of equal status.

The U.S. proposal to forgo plans to deploy ERWs in exchange for the Soviets giving up their SS-20 arsenal did not meet this condition. The exchange was clearly nonreciprocal. Moreover, because it involved no compensation for British and French weapons, it did not affirm equal status between the alliances. The exchange for Soviet conventional forces would have had ambiguous results. Although reciprocity was not involved, it would not have left the Soviets at a disadvantage.

Prestige consequences were also ambiguous in the CTB and 1967 ABM cases. Although reciprocity was involved, the Soviets thought that the proposals would have hurt their ability to catch up with the United States. When they partially met U.S. demands in mid-1968, prestige calculations favored reciprocation because the proposal no longer constrained the Soviet ability to attain parity. The Soviet ABM system was unlikely to work and cause a favorable shift in the balance of power, and they were very close to attaining parity.

The first year of the outer space case is difficult to evaluate. Objectively, because the proposal involved tacit reciprocation and put no constraints on the Soviet ability to attain strategic parity, it affirmed Soviet prestige just as it did in September 1963. During the first year the Soviets mistakenly thought the agreement covered ballistic missiles, which they were planning to use to achieve strategic parity and hence equal status. Their subjective calculation, therefore, was that it would have had mixed effects on their prestige: although it would have been a reciprocal exchange, it would not affirm equal status.

7. *The relative power of the Soviet alliance network is strengthened by the proposed agreement.* Soviet security, influence, and ideological objectives are affected by political relations with and among third countries as well as by the United States. Thus the Soviet Union has an interest in minimizing hostile actions by third countries, as well as in minimizing the cohesion of political-military relations among its adversaries and in maximizing the cohesion of its own alliance network. As might be expected, it tends to be most concerned about China and West European members of NATO and least concerned about the opinion of Non-Aligned countries.

Calculations about China disposed the Soviets not to meet U.S. demands during the first year of the outer space case. China was advocating militancy toward the West, and a Soviet desire to maintain an appearance of Sino-Soviet unity disposed them to avoid accommodation with the United States. In addition, a few months after the ERW initiative, Soviet calculations about China became unfavorable for the initiative's success. The Soviets feared that Sino-U.S. ties might shift from a detente to an entente or an alliance directed against them. Worried about the security threat from such a development, they threatened to end progress in arms talks.

Since the Sino-Soviet split was obvious by the end of October 1962, the Soviets no longer felt compelled to accommodate Chinese militance in order to maintain a facade of unity. Cooperation with the United States then served to help isolate China as a dangerous and reckless state. This condition fully supported successful initiatives in the successful outer space and LTB instances. Prior to the spring of 1968, when the outcome of the Vietnam War was in doubt, it had an ambiguous impact on Soviet ABM calculations. Beginning that spring, when a communist victory seemed more likely, this condition became moderately favorable and the initiative succeeded partially.

The expected outcome of success did not occur during the first month or two of Carter's ERW initiative. As mentioned above, however, this condition soon became unfavorable. Likewise, for more than a year after the U.S. B-47 initiative, the Soviets failed to reciprocate despite the advantage that accommodation with the United States would have helped to isolate China. Finally, the favorableness of this condition was insufficient to convince the Soviets to accept the U.S. CTB proposal.

Accommodating with the United States serves to reduce fears among West European countries that the Soviet Union is a serious threat to their interests. Consequently, reciprocation can help to reduce NATO's cohesion. This condition obtained in the three instances of success. It also was moderately unfavorable in the unsuccessful ERW case. In this instance, the issue was so divisive within NATO that Soviet nonreciprocation would have had no political costs and, compared to reciprocation, even some benefits. It was ambiguous in the 1967 ABM case, because at that time the Soviet effort to weaken NATO focused on improving relations with Western Europe instead of the United States.

The Soviet concerns for improving relations with Non-Aligned countries turned out to be unimportant. In every instance, this calculation favored success—even in the five instances of failure.

8. *Money should be saved, or at least the military burden on the economy should not increase, as a result of the proposed agreement.* This factor was irrelevant in half of the instances, but the expected outcome occurred in three of the other four. In the unsuccessful CTB and bomber cases, complying with the U.S. demands would have forced the Soviets to increase defense spending if they were to reach overall strategic parity with the United States. A CTB would have curtailed qualitative improvements in nuclear firepower and forced them to rely on more expensive quantitative increases. The bomber proposal would have compelled them to procure additional, more expensive long-range bombers to carry out regional missions. In the successful

ABM instance in 1968, the U.S. proposal presented them with an opportunity to avoid wasting money on a system that probably would not work.

This condition moderately favored the unsuccessful ERW initiative. If the Soviets agreed to limit their conventional forces or SS-20s, they could have reduced their defense budget at a time when restraining the growth of military spending was important. Nonreciprocation would not have forced them to increase military spending, however. If ERWs were deployed, which was unlikely, they would have increased NATO's military capabilities only marginally.

9. *International economic benefits are likely to result from the proposed agreement.* This factor is relevant when the Soviets need and want to purchase U.S. products, and when they perceive that the purchases will be less expensive or more reliable if they collaborate on arms control.

The Soviets may be interested in purchasing U.S. grain when they have harvest shortfalls. From an economic perspective, they are fully interested in U.S. grain when the United States dominates a large share of the global grain market and offers a trade-stimulating environment. They are moderately interested when only one of these conditions applies. During 1972–74, when the United States seemed about to offer the Soviets MFN status and substantial credits, they were also moderately interested in purchasing U.S. industrial products. None of our case studies occurred during this period, however.

This condition may have been relevant in the successful September 1963 outer space instance. The Soviets had a poor harvest and needed to import wheat from the West. Since the United States did not dominate the market, however, they were only moderately interested in U.S. grain. I was unable to learn if the Soviets perceived a linkage between this economic condition and their arms control behavior. This factor may also have been relevant in the successful LTB case, if the Soviets knew by mid-1963 that they were going to have a shortfall. It was irrelevant in the remaining instances except, perhaps, for a month or so in the unsuccessful ERW case; that time was toward the end of the 1977/78 crop year, during which the Soviets suffered a poor harvest.

10. *The organizational interests of Soviet military services are not threatened by the proposed agreement.* Opposition from the military bureaucracy arises when an agreement would threaten the budgets or traditional missions of the services. If they then attempt to influence Soviet policy making, it constitutes a factor in the domestic environment of bargaining that may affect the apparent rationality of the Soviet response.

The importance of this condition is highly corroborated by the research, at least for the Khrushchev and Brezhnev eras of our case studies. The military seemed to get its way in seven of the eight instances. In all instances of failure, the Soviet military evidently worked against the proposed agreements. During the first year of the outer space case, they would have opposed both on-site inspection and restraints on missiles. Intrusive inspection would have revealed the poor quality of Soviet ICBMs and perhaps additional locations of their launch sites, and the powerful SRF opposed limits on missiles.

The Soviet military also opposed reciprocation of the CTB, B-47, and 1967 ABM instances. These proposals threatened the ability of the SRF, bomber force, and PVO (respectively) to carry out retaliation or damage limitation missions. Likewise, the ERW initiative threatened both the services' budgets and traditional missions.

The only instance in which they seemed not to prevail was when the Soviets indicated interest in offensive and defensive arms limitations in 1968. The military continued to oppose arms limitation talks—the PVO because of its missions to defend against bombers and missiles, and the SRF because it feared constraints on matching or surpassing U.S. strategic power. Despite these objections, the Soviet leadership agreed to discuss arms limitations and to halt construction of the Moscow ABM site. From the military's perspective, however, at least Soviet reciprocation was not complete. The leadership did not commit themselves formally to signing a treaty or to continue the construction moratorium.

11. *The general-secretary is secure in his authority if the proposed agreement involves a controversial concession.* This is an hypothesis supported by the research. It appears to have been relevant in only two instances, both involving ABMs, and each time the expected outcome occurred.

We know about serious controversy within the Soviet leadership during 1968 as they considered how to respond to the U.S. ABM initiative. On the one hand, the military continued to oppose arms limitation talks, and an ABM ban would have weakened Soviet capabilities vis-a-vis China, France, and Britain. On the other hand, reciprocation was favored as they calculated the impact of reciprocation on the Soviet-U.S. strategic relationship, on political relations with NATO and between China and the United States, on their prestige, and on their economy. When in mid-1968 they first said they would consider ABM limitations, Brezhnev had only recently gained ascendancy over Kosygin. This factor may be particularly important, since this is the only instance where the military failed to prevail.

Brezhnev did not become ascendant over Kosygin until the spring of 1968, and before that time the Soviets did not meet U.S. demands even partially despite a controversy surrounding the ABM issue. Working against reciprocation were negative consequences to Soviet security and to the military services, and in support of it was political relations with Non-Aligned countries. Ambiguous and hence probably controversial were calculations about the impact of their response on their military budget, on political relations involving China and NATO, and on their prestige. This factor was probably irrelevant in the remaining instances, where the obvious dominance of advantages or disadvantages most likely precluded serious controversy.

The research supports the contention that until a general-secretary gains ascendancy over his rivals, in controversial situations he tends to bolster his authority by appealing to the traditional interests of the military, heavy industry, and party bureaucracy. This situation is unfavorable for the Soviets making serious arms control concessions. After becoming ascendant, which seems to take at least several years, he is less constrained by these vested interests and an initiative is more likely to succeed than otherwise.

12. *The Soviets perceive a low level of international tension.* This was an hypothesis moderately corroborated by the research. With some qualifications involving timing, the generalization was supported in four instances, was irrelevant in two, and was unsupported in two.

In all three instances of success, the Soviets apparently perceived tensions to be at a low level (the LTB and the September 1963 outer space instances) or at a low-moderate level (the 1968 ABM instance). Moreover, in these instances they wanted to reduce tensions further or at least keep them from rising. Reciprocation thus served as a means to advance their policy objective of a detente with the United States.

When they first failed to reciprocate the outer space initiative in September 1962, tensions probably seemed high. From November 1962 until June 1963, the Soviets apparently saw an intermediate, moderate level of tension—which allegedly would have had an indeterminant impact on them. They also probably perceived a moderate level of tension during the unsuccessful CTB and 1967 ABM instances.

For the bomber and ERW cases they perceived a low-moderate level of tension. Although this situation was supposed to favor reciprocation moderately, the Soviets did not agree to the U.S. proposals. These two cases, along with the outer space case during the summer of 1963, suggest that proposals that are not balanced and clearly stated are unlikely to succeed even if tensions are low. Although the Soviets may hold an exaggerated image of the U.S. threat during periods of high tension, they do not stop looking out for their security interests when tensions are low.

RELATIVE WEIGHT OF THE FACTORS

Soviet calculations about direct security consequences and verification requirements, as well as the interests of the military, seem to be particularly important in accounting for Soviet bargaining behavior. Each factor was almost always relevant, and the expected outcomes are highly correlated with the actual outcomes. The score for security calculations is seven expected outcomes, no unexpected ones, and not relevant in the other instance. The Soviet dislike for on-site inspection was relevant in all instances, and the expected outcomes occurred every time. Finally, the Soviet military seemed to get its way in seven of the eight instances.

We can judge the relative importance of these factors by examining the instances in which they compete and then observe which seems to prevail. Unfortunately, the factors competed only in the ABM case after the United States announced deployment of its own ABM system. During 1968, as Soviet leaders confronted the weaknesses of their own system and began to see the disadvantages to them of a U.S. ABM system, security calculations disposed them to accept the U.S. demand for ABM limitations. By this time the Soviets also probably knew that on-site inspection might not be required. Working against Soviet reciprocation, however, was continuing military opposition to both offensive and defensive arms limitations.

The Soviets offered to begin negotiations and, perhaps unrelated to their bargaining, halted construction of their Moscow ABM site. At least concerning SALT, security concerns prevailed over the wishes of the military.

We cannot say that verification concerns predominated, because acceptable verification mechanisms seem to be merely a permissive condition for success, not a motivating factor. In none of our cases was on-site inspection required at the same time that security or bureaucratic factors favored reciprocation. Consequently, from our research we cannot know how important verification is relative to the other two factors.

The 1968 case suggests two additional observations. First, this is the only instance where the issue was controversial and where the general-secretary was secure in his authority. This situation may have enabled Brezhnev to make concessions to the United States despite objections from the military. Second, although the military could not convince the Politburo to reject all arms talks, it may have persuaded them to make only the minimum concessions necessary to restrain the threat that might develop from the U.S. ABM system. Consistent with this speculation, the Soviets complied only partially in that they did not commit themselves to any specific limitations. The military could then continue to hope that negotiations would fail.

The ABM case during 1968 is as close as we come to a crucial test case, and it confirms hypothesis 13. The hypothesis says that when security concerns are salient, these calculations tend to determine the general outcome of bargaining despite the presence of contrary factors. Thus the security concern is our only sufficient condition for understanding Soviet behavior. It is not a necessary condition, however, because the LTB case illustrates that sometimes security concerns are unimportant. Moreover, the observations in the preceding paragraph demonstrate that nonsecurity factors can influence the details of Soviet policy, such as its timing and scope.

The ABM case prior to the spring of 1968 is the other instance the authority of the general-secretary may have been relevant. Some controversy apparently surrounded the issue, Brezhnev was not yet secure in his authority, and the Soviets made no concessions. Detracting from the significance of the general-secretary's authority, however, was that security calculations were unfavorable for the initiative's success. The factor was irrelevant in the six remaining instances where the issue was uncontroversial.

Our research suggests that a number of additional factors are relevant, although less important than the ones we just discussed. These include U.S. signals and Soviet perceptions of them; Soviet calculations about the consequences of a proposed agreement on their prestige, on military threats from third countries, on alliance cohesion, and on their economic interests; and their perception of the level of international tension. Obviously these factors are less important than security calculations. The way to judge their relative importance, therefore, is to see what happens in circumstances where security was not at risk and where these other factors suggested opposite outcomes. Unfortunately security was not at risk only in the LTB case, and the remaining factors did not compete. Since they all favored the initiative's success or were irrelevant, we cannot determine their relative importance.

THE REMAINING HYPOTHESES: OBSERVATIONS AND SPECULATIONS

Our research supported only three of the thirteen hypotheses, and we discussed them above. It could shed no light on the hypothesis about polarity, because all of our case studies occurred during the postwar bipolar world. Of the remaining nine hypotheses, the research provides some qualified support for one, suggests another may be invalid, and indicates little about the rest.

At first glance the research seems relatively inconclusive about the strategic environment hypothesis, because the expected outcome occurred five times and the opposite outcome occurred three times. When we qualify our analysis, however, we find some support for the hypothesis: for both instances this factor was obviously more than moderately relevant, the expected outcome occurred.

The Soviets evidently perceived an unstable environment late in 1962 when the United States announced the outer space initiative and the Soviets did not reciprocate formally. The environment was unacceptable and, secondarily, U.S. intentions seemed offensive. Only in the 1968 ABM instance, when the Soviets partially reciprocated the U.S. initiative, did they probably perceive a stable strategic environment. The primary criterion obtained fully and the secondary one was ambiguous.

In the instances this factor was moderately relevant, the record is poor. The expected outcome happened only in the unsuccessful B-47 and ABM instances, where the Soviets probably perceived a moderately unstable environment. The first criterion was ambiguous, but U.S. intentions still seemed offensive. In the successful outer space instance, however, the same moderately unstable situation obtained.

Uncertainty surrounds the 1963 test ban initiatives, because they occurred in a time of transition between the early 1960s (when the environment was unacceptable) and the mid-1960s (when its nature was ambiguous). The secondary criterion did not obtain, as U.S. intentions seemed offensive through the mid-1960s. Overall, therefore, between January and June 1963 the environment could have seemed either unstable or moderately unstable. Since it was in January 1963, the CTB case may have been closer to unstable than to moderately unstable. The June 1963 LTB case, being nearer to the mid-1960s, may have been closer to moderately unstable. In this light, the factor may have been fully relevant in the CTB case (thus confirming the hypothesis) and only moderately relevant in the LTB case (where the hypothesis is unconfirmed).

The ERW case is also ambiguous, where the Soviets perceived either a stable or a moderately stable environment. The strategic environment was acceptable. The problem, however, is the difficulty of determining the transition date from when the Soviets perceived U.S. intentions to be ambiguous to when they seemed offensive. If they seemed offensive in April 1978, then overall the environment would have seemed moderately stable. If they still seemed ambiguous, the environment would have been stable and this case would work against even the qualified hypothesis.

If we have more than a spurious correlation for the nonambiguous instances, this factor may be important when the factor has more than a moderate value. Unfortunately, from our case studies we cannot infer that this correlation is not spurious. In the two or three relevant instances, the key factor of Soviet security calculations suggested parallel outcomes. Likewise, in the unsuccessful B-47 and ABM instances, Soviet security calculations worked against reciprocation at the same time that they probably perceived a moderately unstable environment. In two of the three instances where the expected outcome did not occur (i.e., in the successful outer space and unsuccessful ERW instances), the security factor worked in the opposite direction. The environment may have been moderately unstable in the remaining LTB case, but security was not at risk and the other factors favored or at least did not oppose reciprocation.

The overall situation is too inconclusive to justify giving the strategic environment prominence as a corroborated factor. If subsequent research corroborates the hypothesis, however, the following speculations and observations would gain in credibility and importance.[1]

First, in situations where a U.S. proposal offers the Soviets a way to reduce their vulnerability, their perception of the strategic environment influences whether or not they believe that the arms control path is available. The 1968 ABM instance is consistent with this speculation, because Soviets pessimistic about the U.S. ABM potential may have begun to see the U.S. proposal as a way to avoid a return to a vulnerable situation. The unsuccessful CTB instance is not particularly illustrative, however, because the Soviets correctly predicted that the U.S. proposal would constrain their ability to work out of a vulnerable situation. The unsuccessful outer space instance is not helpful either, because objectively the status quo offered no less vulnerability than the U.S. proposal. Subjectively, of course, they misperceived the scope of the U.S. proposal so that it too seemed to be an obstacle to safety. Perhaps the unstable strategic environment fueled their misperceptions. Then again, high international tensions may also have been important.

Second, the argument points to a paradox: We want arms control agreements to help create crisis stability, but efforts to reach agreements are more likely to succeed when this situation already exists. In other words, agreements may be least likely when they are most needed, and most likely when least needed. Even if this situation obtains, however, the 1968 ABM instance suggests that arms control can still serve to avoid a return to vulnerability, to avoid wasting money, and to serve political objectives such as reducing tensions.

The unsupported hypothesis is that success is favored when bargaining involves only informal verbal communication. The expected outcome occurred twice, when no formal negotiations accompanied the successful outer space and ABM instances. It did not occur six times, however, because communication was formal in the successful LTB case and informal during five failures (the unsuccessful stages of the outer space and ABM cases, as well as in the CTB, B-47, and ERW cases).

A deeper examination of the outer space case presents a mixed picture. On the one hand, influential political forces in the United States opposed a treaty banning orbiting nuclear weapons.[2] Formal negotiations would have given them an opportunity to disrupt progress toward a ban; the same situation may have applied in the Soviet Union. On the other hand, because a Soviet misperception of the scope of the U.S. proposal may have been the major obstacle to their official reciprocation, formal negotiations would have helped to clarify the U.S. position much earlier. For the remaining instances, no causal evidence emerged suggesting that this factor made much difference in Soviet decision making.

The poor showing for this hypothesis does not necessarily mean that the opposite is true, that only formal communication should be involved. Which approach is best may depend on circumstances that are not obvious from our case studies. At the least, our research suggests that to minimize the prospect of misperceptions, U.S. negotiators should diligently seek feedback from their Soviet counterparts on their specific objections to a U.S. proposal—even if the communication is only informal.

Whether or not a series or a campaign of initiatives was under way seemed to have made no difference. A series was in progress both when the outer space initiative succeeded and the B-47 initiative failed, and one was not under way during the remaining instances. A campaign of initiatives was operating when the LTB initiative succeeded and when the B-47 initiative failed, and less-extensive campaigns accompanied the successful outer space instance and unsuccessful CTB and ERW cases. No campaign was under way during either ABM instance or in the outer space case prior to Kennedy's June 1963 LTB initiative. Perhaps these approaches were not properly tested because too few initiatives were involved, or maybe the importance of these factors was overwhelmed by other factors. The latter guess is plausible, because security was an issue in all but the LTB case. The least we can say is that these approaches are unpromising when proposals would harm Soviet interests.

Obviously, accompanying an initiative with an objective history of previous bargaining interactions should not harm and may even help an initiative's prospect of success. Steve van Evera was right in saying that states rarely do this. In none of our instances did an official history clearly accompany an initiative. For three instances, it is ambiguous whether or not this condition obtained. Kennedy's American University speech provided a hint of an objective history to the outer space and LTB cases. This may have aided Soviet reciprocation of the LTB initiative, but they did not formally reciprocate the outer space initiative until after the United States clarified the limited scope of the proposal. In the unsuccessful B-47 case, the United States discussed several additional initiatives but only in a fragmented and incomplete manner. In the remaining five instances, this condition clearly did not obtain.

Three hypotheses speculate that success is favored when state A responds to B's nonreciprocation quickly, moderately, and defensively. None receives support. The United States responded quickly to Soviet nonreciprocation in the CTB case, but this behavior failed to stimulate Soviet interest in the proposal. The United States did not respond quickly to Soviet disinterest in the B-47, ABM, and ERW cases. As expected, they did not reciprocate in the B-47 or ERW cases. They eventually did in the ABM case, months after the United States responded by announcing deployment of its own ABM. The issue was irrelevant in the outer space case, because the Soviets reciprocated tacitly all along, as well as in the LTB case, when they reciprocated quickly.

The United States clearly responded moderately and defensively only in the unsuccessful B-47 case, when Soviet nonreciprocation led it to slow its rate of B-47 deactivation and to store planes instead of destroy them. The opposite situation obtained in the CTB case, where the United States responded to continued Soviet disinterest in more elaborate verification mechanisms by resuming testing at a time the Soviets were not testing; this evident overreaction did not seem to help either. These two factors were irrelevant in the outer space and LTB cases because the Soviets never really defected, in the ERW case because the United States did not respond at all to Soviet defection, and in the ABM case for most of 1967.

When the United States finally announced deployment of its own ABM, its communication on these two factors became ambiguous. McNamara signaled a moderate and defensive response to continued Soviet disinterest, but others and the deployment plans suggested an immoderate response. Interestingly enough, during 1968 the stronger U.S. response seemed to enhance Soviet interest in arms talks more than the moderate, defensive signals. But then again, Soviet security calculations "kicked in" at that time and may have overwhelmed any other factors.

I found next to no evidence on the impact of initiatives on the balance of political forces within the Soviet Union. If we accept the image of some "crypto-politics," then deductively we can assume that this factor has some relevance. For example, a U.S. initiative that is unfavorable to Soviet interests would strengthen the position of Soviet militarists and undermine arguments for arms control. A balanced proposal, in contrast, should have the opposite impact. I suspect that this factor is most important when the United States offers a fair proposal, the general-secretary wants arms control, and he is healthy and secure in his authority.

ADVANTAGES AND DISADVANTAGES OF USING UNILATERAL INITIATIVES

Our cases revealed some advantages. In the outer space, LTB, and ABM cases, the tactic apparently helped to reach agreements, and in the LTB case it helped to reduce tensions. In the CTB case it served domestic and international propaganda purposes, making it marginally easier for the United States to do what it planned to do anyway (i.e., resume underground testing). Carter's ERW initiative also had the propaganda advantage of making it easier for him to cancel the project.

Carter's initiative was not without a disadvantage. In the face of Soviet nonreciprocation, he failed to implement the conditional part of the initiative as he said he would. Since this made him look indecisive, it marginally harmed the U.S. position as the leader of NATO as well as U.S. credibility in bargaining with the Soviets. He could have avoided these problems by implementing the tactic properly.

Ending conditional restraint may sometimes have disadvantages, however. Although producing the ERW would have reduced West Germany's resentment toward Carter, the Soviets would have renewed a propaganda barrage that would have caused more political turmoil in NATO. A "net assessment" of the likely advantages and disadvantages is therefore appropriate. Finally, the United States responded to a lack of Soviet interest in its "bomber burning" proposal by storing some of the B-47 bombers taken out of service instead of destroying them. This cost money, and it brought the Soviets no closer to reciprocation. Furthermore, because the U.S. proposal was so one-sided, it may have unnecessarily increased Soviet suspicions of U.S. intentions, as well as harmed the reputation of initiatives.

In sum, initiatives can help to reach agreements and to reduce international tension. Even unsuccessful ones may serve international and domestic propaganda purposes. Improperly implemented initiatives, however, may harm U.S. credibility with its allies and adversaries alike. But even properly implemented initiatives do not always work, and they may have unnecessary or undesirable costs. Such costs could be avoided by not using the tactic when success is unlikely. In chapter 10 we will explore how to make this prediction.

THE UNILATERAL INITIATIVE-BARGAINING CHIP CONNECTION

A bargaining chip is another tool used in arms control bargaining, and its stated purpose is also to facilitate mutual arms limitations by putting pressures on state B. Instead of A's initial act being restraint, however, state A begins to test, produce, or deploy the weapon. The signal to B combines a threat to continue the action so long as B does not make an appropriate concession, with a promise to stop or reverse its action only if B makes the concession. It is different from a weapon acquired to "negotiate from strength." This latter purpose involves the development and deployment of new weapons that are not intended to be traded away during negotiations, but that are to be retained in order to strengthen the country's military capabilities so that the opposing country will not see it as weak.[3]

Most proponents of the unilateral initiative tactic view initiatives as an antithetical alternative to bargaining chips that is much more likely to control the arms race. They may be right if the emphasis is on "*more likely* to control the arms race," but they tend to discount any role for bargaining chips. Hence Robert Bresler and Robert Gray call for "transforming the bargaining chip into a peace initiative."[4] Herbert Scoville warned that "promoting weapons as arms control bargaining chips is like playing a dangerous game of Russian roulette, with world survival at stake."[5]

These writers downplay the mixed record of bargaining chips, which, like unilateral initiatives, succeed only sometimes. For instance, U.S. testing and deployment of MIRVs failed in one of its alleged purposes—to compel the Soviets to agree to ban multiple warheads.[6] In contrast, the U.S. decision to produce and deploy an ABM system contributed to Soviet concessions on offensive and defensive weapons.[7]

Our purpose is not to explore the usefulness of bargaining chips. That task has been done adequately elsewhere, and the analysis closely resembles what we have developed here.[8] The point is that the unilateral initiative tactic, although perhaps more promising than the bargaining chip approach, is not necessarily a substitute for it. The historical record may show that the utility of each tactic varies with circumstances.

Furthermore, and what few realize, is that one of the sources of a bargaining chip is a failed conditional unilateral initiative! This happened in our ABM case. President Johnson's unilateral restraint in producing and deploying an ABM system failed to interest the Soviets in ABM limitations. Not until the United States began to implement the threat aspect of the initiative did the Soviets change their tune. Despite mixed signals from the United States, from the viewpoint of Soviets engaging in "worst-case analysis," this U.S. action seemed to begin the implementation of a bargaining chip—even though the United States was not yet using the term. Evidently they expected U.S. ABM deployment to continue until they made concessions in SALT. As is the case with the mixed record of bargaining chips, implementing the threat aspect of a unilateral initiative does not guarantee success. The United States did this in the CTB and B-47 cases, and the Soviets moved no closer to reciprocation.

SUGGESTIONS FOR ADDITIONAL RESEARCH

Our research has furthered our understanding of the identity and relative importance of a number of factors that influence the success of unilateral initiatives. With our small number of case studies and limited evidence, however, the degree of certainty of our principal findings could stand improvement. Moreover, since the research reveals little about the validity of many hypotheses, we still have gaps in our knowledge about the conditions favoring successful initiatives. Finally, there are related questions that we have made no attempt to answer.

To begin our survey, parts of the research in this book may need improvement. For example, my analysis of how the Soviets perceive the level of international tension or the stability of the strategic environment might need refinement. Additional or new types of evidence could also help.

Our understanding of the conditions favoring successful initiatives would be enriched with additional case studies. Still focusing on Soviet responses to U.S. initiatives, we could loosen some of our criteria for choosing case studies. First, we could examine U.S. initiatives not directly related to the U.S.-Soviet balance of power.[9] Second, we could study the instances of purely tacit American restraint and see how they affected Soviet behavior.[10] Some of these cases probably did not obviously affect Soviet security calculations. Such cases would be especially interesting, because they might highlight the relative importance of nonsecurity factors. In only our LTB case was security unimportant, but unfortunately none of the corroborated factors competed.

As of the time this book went to press, the United States had implemented no unilateral initiatives since Gorbachev became general-secretary. For more accurate predictions of how he might respond to possible future U.S. initiatives, studies of Soviet foreign and defense policies since he consolidated his authority would be useful.[11]

Countries other than the United States are interested in controlling arms competitions with their adversaries. The Soviet Union is obviously interested in understanding the conditions under which its unilateral initiatives lead to U.S. reciprocation—either formally as a U.S. policy or informally through congressional constraints on the president's policy. Smaller countries as well may want to know about the tactic's utility. Those in a primarily bilateral adversary relationship could probably benefit from understanding U.S.-Soviet interactions. Others may be in a regional situation that resembles a multipolar world. They would profit from a study of cases that occurred in the multipolar structure preceding World War II.[12] Findings from cases in multipolar and bipolar situations could then be compared to evaluate our untested hypothesis on polarity.

All of the cases mentioned so far took place during peacetime. If some other instances occurred during wartime, a study of them would shed some light on the difference that this situation makes.

Our understanding of the advantages and disadvantages of using the tactic would be furthered with research into cases where the tactic obviously harmed the state using it. We can imagine a case, for instance, where an initiative led to some unilateral disarmament that harmed state A's security.

Additional research could also help us to answer two questions that we have not yet asked. First, under what conditions do unilateral initiatives arise? Understanding how this works in the United States might help to avoid missing promising opportunities to control the U.S.-Soviet arms competition. We could contrast cases where the government did not use the tactic—even though success would have been possible—with cases where it did. One example of a missed opportunity concerns MIRVs, where the United States failed to restrain MIRV testing as a conditional unilateral initiative designed to encourage Soviet concessions on BMD and on multiple warheads.[13] If the research highlights key factors that can be manipulated by domestic political actors, then it would have a useful policy function.

The United States would benefit from being able to predict when the Soviets are likely to use the tactic. A study of their 1958 test ban initiative, others during 1963–65, and their recent ASAT and CTB initiatives would be illustrative. With this knowledge, especially if some of the constraints on reliable evidence can be overcome, the United States would be better able to predict Soviet behavior and thus seem less surprised. It might even be able to act in ways to encourage Soviet initiatives.

Second, when are successful unilateral initiatives sustained? The outer space and LTB initiatives meet this condition. The ABM initiative may not, if questionable Soviet compliance behavior combines with a resurgent U.S. interest in BMD to lead to abrogation of the ABM Treaty. The moratorium the Soviets started in 1958 did break down in 1961. Research into these and other such cases may suggest some additional advice and cautions about the tactic.

10

Applications of Knowledge

Assuming that additional evidence and analysis will corroborate our principal findings, this chapter illustrates how this basic knowledge can be applied to make some policy-relevant predictions and prescriptions.

PREDICTIONS

The 1984 Republican Platform accused Jimmy Carter of naivete in hoping that U.S. unilateral restraint would compel the Soviet Union to exercise parallel restraint, and it charged that such delays in modernization harmed U.S. security interests.[1] Here we will focus on a narrow dimension of this controversy: If Carter had been more decisive in implementing the ERW initiative, would the Soviets have agreed to make significant concessions in conventional forces or in INF in exchange for U.S. restraint in producing and deploying ERWs?

Let us assume that the United States clearly and consistently signaled its demands and especially its commitment to make the initiative conditional. Like President Johnson when he announced his ABM initiative in January 1967, Carter could have allocated but set aside funds to begin ERW production and committed himself to spend them early in the next fiscal year if the Soviets did not meet the conditions of the initiative.

A NATO endorsement of Carter's decision would have added credibility to his threat to produce ERWs. For the sake of argument, let us assume that West European members of NATO agreed with Carter's policy and publicly said so. In obtaining this endorsement, let us further assume that Carter met Helmut Schmidt's demand that the United States be prepared to produce the weapon in the absence of a precommitment by West Germany to deploy it. Then, if the Soviets did not meet U.S. demands, the United States would have begun to produce the weapon, would have asked West Germany for permission to deploy the ERW on its territory, and would have begun deployment.

NATO's endorsement would have signaled a different alliance situation to the Soviet Union. In the actual ERW case, Soviet calculations about NATO moderately opposed reciprocation for two reasons. First, the issue was so divisive within NATO that not meeting U.S. demands presented no political costs and perhaps offered some benefits. The new scenario assumes that the issue had become much less divisive. Consequently, since nonreciprocation would have detracted from the Soviet image of reasonableness, in some small amount it would have strengthened NATO's cohesion. Moreover, carrying out the threat to produce and deploy the weapon would not have harmed NATO's cohesion significantly. Second, because of Carter's apparent vacillation in the original case, meeting his demands would have exonerated his policy and thus would have affirmed sound U.S. leadership of NATO. In the new scenario, Carter's policy was accepted by NATO and thus U.S. leadership already was assured. Consequently, reciprocation would not have strengthened NATO's cohesion. Overall, therefore, in this new scenario Soviet calculations about NATO's cohesion probably would have favored reciprocation.

Five other conditions continued to favor the initiative's success: accurate Soviet perceptions of U.S. signals; Soviet calculations about China, saving money (which was moderately favorable), and importing U.S. grain; and Soviet perceptions of a low-moderate level of international tension.

In this new scenario, another factor may have shifted from irrelevant to favorable: Brezhnev was ascendant in his authority. This situation was not relevant in the original case, because the proposal had so many disadvantages that it probably was not controversial within the Soviet leadership. For the sake of argument, let us assume that the new advantages developed above introduced some controversy.

Additional factors still worked against reciprocation, however. First and foremost, Soviet security calculations opposed meeting U.S. demands. Since ERWs probably would not have increased NATO capabilities significantly, non-reciprocation would not have had net military costs. Moreover, reciprocation would have reduced Soviet military capabilities vis-a-vis both the United States and West European members of NATO. Second, verifying compliance with an agreement would have required on-site inspection at a time the Soviets opposed it. Third, the military services obviously opposed an agreement because it would have reduced their budgets and their ability to carry out traditional missions. Fourth, U.S. demands were not in the same currency as the initiative. Soviet calculations about prestige would have continued to be irrelevant for the linkage to conventional forces and unfavorable for the linkage to INF.

Overall, seven conditions could have been moderately or fully favorable for the initiative's success: clear U.S. signals and Soviet perceptions of them, Soviet calculations about political relations among its adversaries and about domestic and international economic advantages, a strong general-secretary, and perceptions of tensions. Fewer factors worked against success: U.S. demands were not in the same currency as the initiative; unfavorable Soviet calculations about its military relationships with both the United States and third parties, on-site verification requirements, and prestige (for the INF linkage); and the interests of the military services. Because we know that security calculations dominate Soviet decisions, however, the initiative probably still would have failed. Since proper implementation of the initiative would not have produced the desired Soviet concessions, criticism of Carter's conduct is unjustified as far as the outcome of bargaining with the Soviet Union is concerned.

When we try to predict the future under the usual circumstance where we cannot be sure about the impact of some key factors, a sound analysis should speculate about probable outcomes under the range of plausible contingencies. To both illustrate this process and explore what I call a "counterfeit" unilateral initiative, let us speculate about what would happen if the United States used its deployment plans for the MX missile as part of a unilateral initiative.[2]

A counterfeit initiative is an abuse of the initiative tactic, and it could be used when a country wants to manipulate its own domestic political actors. The initiative would be doomed to fail in its stated purpose of compelling another country to reciprocate, but it would serve as a trick to help secure funds for a weapon that otherwise would be unobtainable. This motive alone does not mean that its use is necessarily bad. That judgment depends on the national security requirements of a particular situation, the availability of other options to fulfill arms control objectives, and domestic constraints on meeting the security requirements.[3]

For two weeks in 1984, the MX was part of a counterfeit unilateral initiative. It may become one again if the MX debate is not over.

One of President Reagan's objectives was to end the Soviet advantage in large ICBMs, which threaten U.S. missile silos to a greater extent than U.S. ICBMs threaten Soviet silos. His preferred solution was a mutual ban on large ICBMs; this would require the Soviets to give up over 600 ICBMs of a size comparable to or larger than the MX. If an agreement could not be reached, he wanted to deploy 100 MX missiles to match at least partially these Soviet capabilities.[4] The House of Representatives was unhappy with his policy. For a short time it formulated an alternative approach that resembled—in effect though perhaps not in intention—a counterfeit unilateral initiative.

In May 1984 support for the MX was weak in the House. To avoid total defeat, Les Aspin (D-Col.) and Melvin Price (D-Ill.) offered a complex amendment to the FY 1985 military authorization bill. It called for production and deployment of 15 MX missiles, but fenced in the necessary funds for at least six months. The restraint was conditional in order to give the Soviets an incentive to make concessions. If they returned to the bargaining table within six months of the beginning of FY 1985, the United States would delay spending the funds for another six months. If the Soviets then made no significant concession during that time (i.e., did not agree to forgo their large ICBMs), then the government would spend the funds.

The House passed the amendment on May 16, 1984. Two weeks later, however, it dropped the automatic six-month delay that was supposed to begin on April 1, 1985, if the Soviets had by then resumed negotiations. A later House-Senate compromise raised the number of MX missiles to twenty-one. Several weeks before the April deadline, Congress unfenced these funds. This raised the total authorized for production to forty-two. Congress turned to the FY 1986 military authorization bill in the summer of 1985. The Pentagon wanted to deploy a total of 100 MXs in Minuteman silos, but Congress limited to 50 the number that could be housed in these silos.[5]

Is the MX debate finished? Representative Aspin thought so: "In my view, there is no way we are ever going to build more than 50 MX missiles. The issue is over."[6] Senator Dan Quayle (R-Ind.) disagreed: "I personally do not think it is over for good."[7] By late 1985, reports began to surface about new and politically feasible methods for deploying MX in a mobile mode."[8] Early in 1988, Defense Secretary Frank Carlucci said he wants to deploy a total of 100 MX missiles, all of them on a rail-garrison system.[9] Representative Nicholas Mavroules (D-Mass.) denounced Carlucci's plan, calling it "an insult to both Congress and the nation."[10]

If another administration seeks to deply more than 50 MXs, we may see the revival of the Aspin-Price approach. If we do, and if its intention is to generate congressional support for the MX under circumstances where the sponsors expect or want the bargaining tactic to fail, then it would be a true counterfeit unilateral initiative. Such an approach has a special appeal, since the U.S. is under pressure to respond to Soviet unilateral initiatives. Since August 1983, they have announced conditional moratoriums on tests of ASAT weapons and on underground nuclear tests.[11] Some might think that a U.S. unilateral initiative, albeit a counterfeit one, would serve to decrease pressures to reciprocate or to make comparable concessions.

The analysis below shows that neither the promise of forgoing MX deployment, nor the threat to deploy 100 of them in the absence of the Soviet concession, will compel them to give up their large ICBMs.

Before proceeding with our contingent analysis, we should note that in negotiations leading to the 1979 SALT II Treaty, the Soviets had no problem with President Carter's plan to deploy 200 MX missiles in a mobile mode.[12] Have circumstances changed so much that if Congress goes along with a revived Aspin-Price approach, the Soviets would now give up their large ICBMs in exchange for no U.S. MX missiles? The answer is probably no, because more important conditions work against Soviet reciprocation than for it.

U.S. signals probably would not be clear and consistent. They certainly were not when the United States previously discussed bargaining over large ICBMs. While Aspin said the U.S. would make the proposed trade, Defense Secretary Caspar Weinberger said the MX was a vital part of strategic modernization that would be deployed no matter what the Soviets did.[13] It is also likely that the media would cast doubt on U.S. intentions, just as it did with Kennedy's January 1963 CTB initiative.[14]

Let us assume that the Soviets receive the American signals. Given the likely mixed nature of these signals, however, interpretation is inherently problematic. As in the CTB case, they would probably perceive an MX initiative as a propaganda ploy and not as a cooperative gesture.

The analysis of Soviet calculations is complicated by two unknowns. First, will Soviet doctrine stay as it has been for most of the 1980s, or will it move farther away from damage limitation and toward mutual deterrence? For the sake of brevity, our analysis examines only the contingency where the former doctrine obtains. Second, will the Soviets have to worry about U.S. BMD? We will examine the possibility of no U.S. BMD, as well as extensive U.S. BMD deployment. We will not examine other contingencies, such as trading adherence to the ABM Treaty for deep cuts in Soviet offensive capabilities.

Taking first the scenario of both sides adhering to the ABM Treaty, the Soviet desire for a counterforce capability second to none would work against reciprocation. If they do not reciprocate and the United States deploys 100 MX missiles, they would still retain a land-based counterforce advantage (although a reduced one) because they have so many more large ICBMs. In contrast, if they accept the U.S. proposal, they would forgo this advantage and accept equality. This conclusion assumes Soviet advantages in numbers of ICBMs and their payloads, and U.S. advantages in accuracy and reliability of missiles. The United States is ahead in other counterforce areas, however, particularly in cruise missiles and antisubmarine warfare. In 1989, when the United States begins to deploy the D-5, the Soviets would be at an even greater disadvantage. In terms of relative counterforce capabilities, therefore, reciprocation would leave the Soviets worse off than nonreciprocation.

The Soviets must also consider the impact of U.S. behavior on their ability to retaliate after a U.S. attack. This aspect of doctrine would range from moderately favorable for an agreement if the United States does not deploy the D-5 to irrelevant if it does.

Calculations that consider only land-based ICBMs in fixed silos would favor reciprocation, because reciprocation would leave the Soviets with more survivable missiles and warheads than otherwise.[15] As of late 1987, their arsenal consisted of about 1300 ICBMs in fixed silos and 130 mobile. It is the missiles in fixed silos that are most vulnerable to attack by the MX. Of these, about 500 have one warhead. The remaining 800 carry from three to ten MIRVs each. Assuming perfect reliability, with as few as 100 MX missiles, targeting two of the missile's ten warheads at each Soviet silo would probably destroy about 500 silos. The United States would retain 450 Minuteman II missiles (each with one warhead) and 450 Minuteman III missiles (each with three MIRVs). These 1800 warheads could probably destroy almost all the remaining 800 Soviet missiles in fixed silos. In contrast, without the MXs' advantages of large warheads, high accuracy, and large number of MIRVs, the U.S. arsenal of 450 Minuteman II and 550 Minuteman III would carry only 2100 warheads—too few to target two at each of the Soviets' 1300 fixed silos.

Detracting from the importance of this calculation, however, is that the Soviets have other options to reduce the vulnerability of their land-based arsenal than meeting U.S. demands. In particular, they are likely to continue to deploy more mobile missiles.[16] As of late 1987, they were constructing at least twenty sites for the single-warhead SS-25 missile. With nine missiles per site, they are already planning to deploy at least 180 of these missiles. They have also begun to deploy the rail-mobile, MX-sized SS-24, each of which carries ten MIRVs. This situation plausibly reduces the impact of a need for an assured retaliation capability to moderately favorable for Soviet reciprocation. If the United States deploys the D-5, all Soviet silos will become vulnerable whether or not the U.S. deploys the MX.[17] Under this condition, their concern for an assured retaliation capability would become irrelevant in this caluculation.

In sum, the damage limitation aspect of doctrine would be unfavorable for reciprocation whether or not the United States deploys the D-5. The assured retaliation aspect would be moderately favorable without the D-5 and irrelevant with it. Assuming that the assured retaliation aspect is more important than the damage limitation mission, overall doctrine suggests that Soviet security calculations would be ambiguous if the United States does not deploy the D-5 and moderately unfavorable if it does.

In the event that the Soviets make their calculations in a strategic environment where they know the United States will deploy an extensive BMD, their security calculations would be unfavorable for reciprocation. They would probably respond to the U.S. BMD with offensive counters designed to saturate the system.[18] A simple and inexpensive means to accomplish this is to increase the number of warheads on their ICBMs. The SS-18, for example, is sufficiently large to carry at least thirty MIRVs. In this strategic contest, therefore, the Soviets would probably consider their large missiles vital for assured retaliation and damage limitation missions. The U.S. proposal would reduce their capabilities for both missions.

The U.S. proposal would have no impact on barriers to entry at the two countries' level of power, but it would reduce Soviet capabilities with respect to nuclear-armed countries such as China, Britain, and France. In the environment following the 1987 INF Treaty, where the Soviets must give up all of their SS-20 missiles, the Soviets will have to allocate some of their strategic systems for prompt counterforce missions against the nuclear forces of these countries. Since the U.S. proposal would reduce their ability to do that, this factor works against reciprocation.

Since a ban on large ICBMs could be verified by national means, the U.S. proposal would meet this condition. Alliance calculations would also favor the initiative's success. Since reciprocation would make the Soviets appear conciliatory in the eyes of West Europeans, by some small amount it would tend to weaken NATO's cohesion. Likewise, the concession would help to fulfill the Soviet objective of decreasing U.S. interest in improving relations with China. Moreover, because Sino-U.S. ties have not evolved to an entente or an alliance and are unlikely to do so in the near term, the Soviets will likely continue to be interested in collaboration with the United States.[19]

Calculations about prestige would be unfavorable. A U.S. offer to forgo a plan to deploy 100 MX missiles in exchange for over 600 of the Soviets' largest missiles hardly affirms the norm of reciprocity. Given that the agreement would leave the Soviets inferior in overall counterforce capabilities, it would not affirm equal status. Since a ban on large ICBMs would leave the Soviets behind in overall counterforce capabilities, the U.S. proposal would also dispose the Soviets to increase defense expenditures in areas of U.S. advantage at a time they can hardly afford it. Moreover, if the United States deploys BMD, the Soviets would have to rely on more expensive means to retain an assured retaliation capability. With or without a U.S. BMD, however, domestic economic calculation would be unfavorable for reciprocation.

Soviet calculations about the international economic consequences of their bargaining behavior are impossible to predict, because at this writing we cannot know their grain requirements. Given that both security and bureaucratic factors would likely work against reciprocation, anything short of a catastrophic, unprecedented harvest failure probably would not sway the leadership to reciprocate.

The Soviet military, particularly the SRF would strongly resist a ban on large ICBMs. Over 600 of these missiles are deployed, and their effectiveness would be in doubt only if they were hit in a first strike. This situation works against reciprocation, because the SRF would want to retain the ability to carry out traditional counterforce missions.

When this book went to press, the Soviets apparently perceived a low-moderate level of international tension. The deductive approach suggests that in mid-1988, tensions probably seemed to be at a low-moderate or moderate level. On the threatening side, President Reagan continued to push for the D-5 SLBM, the MX ICBM, and for BMD. He also wanted to continue his foreign policy to "roll back" communism in Angola and Nicaragua. On the reassuring side, the 1987 INF Treaty will reduce the military threat posed by quick and accurate U.S. missiles. Congress also constrained Reagan's plans for ASAT weapons, BMD, military spending in general, and the Contras in Central America. Finally, at the June 1988 Moscow Summit, President Reagan said he no longer thinks the Soviet Union is an "evil empire."

Soviet rhetoric indicated an even lower level of tension, perhaps a low or a low-moderate level.[20] Apparently Gorbachev thinks that a necessary condition for the success of his major domestic reforms is a less threatening international environment.[21] According to Soviet academician Georgi Arbatov, a part of the Soviet strategy is to improve relations with a "secret weapon"—"we would deprive America of the Enemy."[22]

Since Gorbachev is apparently ascendant over his rivals, we can give equal weight to the deductive and inductive indicators of Soviet perceptions. Overall, therefore, early in 1988 they probably saw a low-moderate level of tensions and wanted to keep them low. Assuming this situation continues, this factor would be moderately favorable for Soviet reciprocation.

If Gorbachev retains his position as general-secretary, we can assume that he will remain ascendant in his authority. This factor would be favorable if the issue were controversial. A review of the situation suggests, however, that it would not be especially controversial because the proposal has many more disadvantages than advantages. In particular, Soviet security calculations would work against reciprocation in the likely event that the United States deploys the D-5. Security concerns would also be unfavorable if the United States deploys an extensive BMD system. Even without BMD and the D-5, when security calculations about the United States would be ambiguous, their calculations about military relations with other nuclear powers would be unfavorable, as would their calculations about prestige and the domestic economy. Moreover, the SRF would resist reciprocation.

Favoring the initiative's success is the likelihood that the Soviets would receive and correctly interpret U.S. signals. Given the probable unfavorable situation of mixed U.S. signals, however, the favorableness of this factor may be only apparent and not real. Fully favoring reciprocation are acceptable verification requirements and calculations about NATO's and China's political relations with the United States. Their perception of the level of tension is likely to be moderately favorable.

Overall, unfavorable circumstances would be more numerous and more important than the favorable ones. In this situation, since Gorbachev would not face much controversy, his ascendance probably would be irrelevant. Since neither the promise of no MX deployment nor the threat of MX deployment are likely to compel the Soviets to give up their large missiles, the MX should be evaluated solely on its strategic merits.[23]

PRESCRIPTIONS FOR UNILATERAL INITIATIVES

General Recommendations

An opportune time to use the unilateral initiative tactic is when the Soviets perceive a low or low-moderate level of international tension and when they want tensions to be low. This circumstance corresponds to all three instances of success that we examined.

As of mid-1988, when this book went to press, only the Soviets used the tactic during the 1980s. As we mentioned in chapter 1, their ASAT initiative worked at least partially.[24] If the United States wants to be more than reactive in bargaining and wants to help ensure that the momentum of arms control serves U.S. interests, it could use the tactic again in order to regain the initiative or at least to be an equal player. A thoughtful U.S. policy might even help deepen the apparent Soviet doctrinal shift toward mutual security.[25]

As evidence that the time is ripe for U.S. initiatives, in 1985 Gorbachev replied to a concern that Soviet initiatives might not be sincere:

If all that we are doing is indeed viewed as mere propaganda, why not respond to it according to the principle of "an eye for an eye, a tooth for a tooth"? We have stopped nuclear explosions. Then you Americans could take revenge by doing likewise. You could deal us yet another propaganda blow, say, by suspending the development of one of your new strategic missiles. And we would respond with the same kind of "propaganda." And so on and so forth. Would anyone be harmed by competition in such a "propaganda"? Of course, it could not be a substitute for a comprehensive arms-limitation agreement, but it would be a significant step leading to such an agreement.[26]

Sometimes unilateral initiatives may be essential. In particular, when U.S. interests would be better served in an environment where neither party has a weapon compared to one in which both do, and where the weapon is nearing the "point of no return" in its procurement process, then conditional unilateral restraint may be the only way to prevent the unfavorable environment from developing. Our research provides no illustrations of this situation, but the history of MIRVs does.

In 1968 neither country had MIRVs, but the United States had deployed MRVs and the Soviets had tested MRVs. Partly to compel the Soviets to agree to a ban on multiple warheads and to agree to ABM limitations, the

United States began to test MIRVs in August 1968 and to deploy them in 1970. During the SALT negotiations neither party was serious about MIRV limitations. The Soviets tested their own in 1973 and later deployed MIRVs that began to threaten the U.S. Minuteman force.[27]

Testing was the "point of no return" in the MIRV procurement cycle. Once tested, a MIRV ban could not be verified without continuous on-site inspection—which at the time the Soviets opposed. A test ban could have been verified without intrusive inspection. Even if an inspection arrangement could have been reached, however, the Soviets would not have accepted the military and prestige disadvantages of a situation where the United States had perfected the system and they had not. If the ban broke down, the United States could easily have won the race to deploy an effective system.

If the U.S. purposes had been only to maintain an ability to penetrate Soviet antimissile defenses and to prevent the Soviets from acquiring MIRVs, then testing MIRVs was unnecessary for the first objective and counterproductive for the second. As was known in the mid-1960s, the lead time for extensive Soviet ABM deployment was longer than the lead time for MIRV testing and deployment. The Soviet ABM capability was not significant, they had recently halted construction of their Moscow site, and the United States could have quickly detected a significant increase in Soviet deployments and responded to widespread Soviet ABM deployment in plenty of time to maintain its assured retaliation capability. The United States unfortunately foreclosed the opportunity to use conditional restraint in MIRV testing as a unilateral initiative. This tactic would have made it possible (although not necessarily certain) that the Soviets would have agreed to ban MIRVs.[28] At the time, however, too many other arguments and bureaucratic interests favored MIRVs, and U.S. leaders did not sufficiently appreciate the consequences of a MIRV-dominated world.[29]

Despite the tactic's advantages, it is no panacea. Not only does it sometimes fail, but occasionally its use can be counterproductive to prudent defense management. We have already discussed the problem of a counterfeit unilateral initiative, which may stick the country using it with a weapon that is expensive and strategically unnecessary or unwise. We also saw the United States retain some B-47s beyond their useful lives for bargaining purposes.[30] The Soviets made no concessions, and the United States spent extra funds to store (for a while) the bombers it removed from service. This initiative also probably created some unnecessary Soviet suspicions of U.S. intentions. Such initiatives give the tactic a negative reputation. Unless using a weapon as part of a bargaining tactic is very likely to compel the Soviet Union to make important concessions that otherwise would be unobtainable, the United States should judge the value of weapons solely on their own merits.

When using a unilateral initiative, the United States may be able to affect the value of up to ten factors that influence Soviet behavior. It has little or no control over the remaining two, which involve Soviet perceptions of U.S. signals and the general-secretary's authority. With the understanding that the United States might not be able to or even want to follow all these prescriptions, let us explore what the United States could do to maximize the probability that an initiative will succeed.

1. *U.S. signals about its demands and its commitments should be clear, complete, and consistent. When possible, bargaining should also be in the same currency.* This condition would minimize the prospect that the Soviets would misperceive the nature and scope of U.S. demands or even miss the signals. Moreover, to make the interdependence between the behaviors of the two sides obvious, the concession demanded by the United States should where possible be in the same currency as the terms of its initiative. To enhance its credibility to carry out its commitments to continue restraint if the Soviets reciprocate or to end conditional restraint if they do not, the administration should build a bipartisan consensus behind the policy to minimize the prospect of mixed signals that cause doubt of U.S. commitments. Public support from our NATO allies would also help. The administration could facilitate this consensus if it clearly explained its rationale to key congressional and NATO leaders. It should explain why using the tactic is appropriate, how it fits into the country's view of the national interest and U.S.-Soviet relations, why it stands at least a fair chance of working, and what the United States will do it if fails. As Steven Van Evera suggested, if the United States also elaborates this rationale to the Soviets, the parties would be more likely to have the same understanding of the past, present, and likely future situations. This circumstance would make Soviet reciprocation more likely than otherwise.[31]

2. *The United States should never make demands that would cause a net decline in Soviet military security. When possible, the proposal should promise to enhance Soviet security.* Since the Soviet security calculation is the most important factor influencing their behavior, analysts should pay sufficient attention to it. Moreover, because Soviet perceptions of military security are largely determined by the military doctrine prevailing at the time, analysts should take special care to determine the nature of contemporary Soviet doctrine. When aspects of doctrine are uncertain, separate analyses should be conducted for each plausible contingency. The evidence tentatively suggests, for example, that for Soviet strategic doctrine an assured retaliation capability is more important than a war-fighting, war-winning damage limitation capability.[32] Doctrine *may* be moving even farther away from damage limitation and toward "mutual security" and "stability" as commonly understood by deterrence theorists.[33] An initiative that satisfies the security condition for both interpretations of doctrine is more likely to suc-

ceed than one that satisfies only the "mutual security" emphasis.

3. *The United States should avoid initiatives that if reciprocated would increase the military threat to the Soviet Union from third countries.* Also, if a U.S. proposal would strengthen barriers to entry at the level of power of the U.S. and the Soviet Union, the United States could privately promote this advantage.

4. *Compliance with the U.S. initiative should be readily verifiable.* The Soviets are less concerned about on-site inspection than they were in the past, but they still have their limits. Initiatives that result in agreements that could be verified by national technical means or with an acceptable degree of intrusiveness would be more likely to succeed than otherwise. They would also help to avoid increasing Soviet suspicions of U.S. intentions unnecessarily, a situation that is unfavorable for successful initiatives.

5. *The U.S. proposal should, when possible, affirm norms of reciprocity and equal status.* This Soviet concern for prestige, like the remaining factors, is especially important when Soviet security calculations are irrelevant, ambiguous, or unknown. Reciprocity is affirmed when a proposal would require the Soviets to give up no more than the United States. In circumstances where asymmetrical concessions are required, such as when the United States wants the Soviets to dismantle an effective system that we have only on the drawing board, the United States should make every effort to compensate the Soviets in another area by making an additionl concession. A campaign of several simultaneous initiatives could, if properly designed, accomplish this objective. Such a campaign could also be used to make more favorable other Soviet calculations, such as those concerning their security and military budget.

Equal status is affirmed when the proposal would not lock the Soviets into overall military inferiority or reduce their position to inferiority, as well as when it contains no linkages that constitute interference in their domestic affairs or that constrain their role as a global power.

6. *The United States should be cautious about forming an anti-Soviet entente or alliance with China.* The United States might want to create such a relationship with China for other reasons, but U.S. policy makers should understand that it would pose an increased military threat to the Soviet Union. Under this condition, the Soviet demand for "equal security" would work against their accepting parity with the United States and thus against the type of initiatives the United States is likely to forward.

7. *When the general U.S. foreign policy permits it, the United States could present the Soviets with a trade-stimulating environment.* Under this condition, and when the Soviets need to import from the United States, the Soviets would have at least an indirect international economic incentive to be cooperative in arms control negotiations.

This condition is likely to be most relevant when the Soviets have poor harvests and a need to import coarse grains—the one area where the United States dominates a large share of the global market (about 50 percent in FY 1987).[34] Continuing to sign long-term grain agreements with the Soviet Union would make the United States seem like a reliable source, an image that was harmed when it imposed economic sanctions after the Soviets invaded Afghanistan. These agreements would somewhat insulate Soviet buying patterns from political issues including arms control, but they would make U.S. grain more important to them than otherwise.

The Soviets are interested in more than simply purchasing U.S. grain. They have a chronic shortage of foreign exchange that constrains their ability to import both agricultural and industrial products. If the United States were to present an economic environment more trade-stimulating than it has been, the Soviets would have added reasons to restrain their military and political competition with the United States. The United States could, for instance, drop the Jackson-Vanik and Stevenson amendments to the U.S.-Soviet Trade Agreement. These amendments link granting the Soviets substantial credits and MFN status to human rights changes in the Soviet Union. Because the Soviets find interference in their domestic affairs unacceptable, the denial of credits makes it more difficult to purchase U.S. goods. Denial of MFN status also restricts their ability to export to the United States and thus to earn more foreign exchange. In effect, the amendments deny the United States some carrots and sticks that could be used to influence Soviet foreign and defense policies.[35] Consequently, nullifying the amendments would increase the Soviet interest in purchasing U.S. industrial products from unimportant to moderately important. It would not be fully important because the United States does not dominate the global market in industrial products.

8. *The U.S. proposal should, when possible, not force the Soviets to increase their military budget, and preferably it should enable them to decrease the burden of military spending on their economy.*

9. *The U.S. proposal could avoid threatening the Soviet military's budgets and traditional missions.* When this is impossible or undesirable, the United States could permit a rechanneling of the military budget into less threatening areas. This prescription could help to minimize the military's opposition to proposed agreements, a concern that would be particularly important when the issue is controversial and when the general-secretary is not ascendant in his authority or is seriously ill. If Gorbachev succeeds with his reforms, however, this condition may be less important than otherwise.[36]

This prescription may sometimes conflict with the previous concern for the economy. For example, if the United States wanted to minimize the SRF's opposition to deep cuts in large ICBMs, its proposal could permit both countries to increase deployments of land-mobile ICBMs, which are very expensive.

10. *The United States should avoid increasing international tensions unnecessarily, and it could act in ways that would dispose the Soviets to perceive a low level of tension.* The Soviets are likely to see low tensions when U.S. actions do not challenge their vital interests or involve means with a high potential for escalation, and when U.S. rhetoric does not threaten the legitimacy of either their domestic regime or roles of a superpower or global power. Most obviously, the United States should continue to avoid military and political behavior that threatens Soviet influence in East Europe.[37] Particularly helpful would be political statements that affirm the right of the Soviet Union to exist, that acknowledge common as well as conflicting interests, and that advocate collaborative steps that would serve the interests of both countries.

Particular Recommendations

Shifting from general prescriptions to ideas for specific proposals, the United States could implement a number of unilateral initiatives. Because of space limitations, however, in this last section I shall simply describe several of them briefly and offer sources that can aid complete analyses. Such analyses should include rationales for why an intiative would serve U.S. national interests, suggestions on how best to implement it, and predictions of the short- and long-term outcomes of bargaining. I leave it up to the reader to reach his or her own conclusions about the desirability and feasibility of the ideas.

One proposal is to minimize emerging dangers caused by fast and accurate SLBMs. It derives from the D-5 debate.[38] As was discussed in chapter 8, the D-5's improved guidance system will for the first time give an SLBM the ability to destroy hardened targets. Furthermore, the scope of the planned deployment will enable the United States to destroy all Soviet ICBMs in fixed silos. Finally, under certain conditions the D-5 could destroy its targets in under fifteen minutes: close patrolling near the adversary's shores, an ability to launch in the so-called depressed trajectory flight path (in contrast to the traditional parabolic path that goes outside the atmosphere and takes longer), and terminal guidance on the warheads to overcome sources of error introduced by passing through the atmosphere. Fifteen minutes is significant, because that is a standard time for bombers on "runway alert" to take off and escape after warning of an attack. If SLBMs could hit all their targets accurately in under 15 minutes, then both ICBMs in fixed silos and bombers on runway alert would be vulnerable to preemption—a situation hardly conducive to "crisis stability." Moreover, with reduced warning time, political leaders might have to delegate authority to launch ICBMs to a computer or to military personnel—a situation making it more likely that a technical malfunction will lead to a false warning of attack and, especially if this occurred during a superpower crisis, an "accidental" nuclear war. It might also lead to an unauthorized launch. Recall that unlike bombers, ICBMs cannot be recalled once launched.

As in the MIRV case, if the United States acquires this new counterforce capability the Soviets will follow. The "window of vulnerability" would then extend to both fixed ICBMs and to bombers. In addition, because D-5 testing began in January 1987, it may have passed the point of no return in its procurement cycle (a controversy beyond the scope of this short discussion, as is the desirability of the D-5 itself).[39] In order to constrain the development of unnecessarily dangerous SLBM capabilities, the simplest and least controversial objective is a mutual ban on testing SLBMs in the depressed trajectory mode. Since neither side has conducted such tests, it is not too late for an easily verifiable agreement. To facilitate agreement, the United States could declare its intention not to conduct such tests as long as the Soviets similarly refrain.

Somewhat more controversial and difficult to implement—but still perhaps desirable—would be agreements not to conduct SLBM patrols near each other's shores, and to deploy only a small number of submarines carrying the missiles so that the system would not threaten a large percentage of ICBM silos. The United States could exercise restraint in these areas, continuation of which would be conditional on reciprocal Soviet restraint.

Another proposal is to end the production of fissionable materials for nuclear weapons, which could help to constrain the amount of nuclear weaponry.[40] U.S. initiatives to reduce the production of enriched uranium and plutonium, and to permit international inspection to verify the cutoffs, would encourage (though not necessarily guarantee) Soviet reciprocation. The place to begin, I think, is with a thorough study of the past history of such efforts. Particularly important is to resolve the controversy over whether or not the Soviets reciprocated Johnson's 1964 initiative as Khrushchev claimed.[41] It is hoped that this study will suggest advice and cautions for formulating initiatives appropriate to contemporary circumstances.

A final proposal is to agree on a system for the uniform reporting of military expenditures.[42] If implemented, it would facilitate comparison of military budgets and their percentage of GNPs, would help to create a comprehensive picture of each country's armaments and thus aid equivalent across-the-board or comparable reductions, would assist verification of arms control agreements, would help to determine whether those forces not limited by agreement grow when other forces are limited, would establish a possible basis for increasing or decreasing aid to a country based on whether or not its military spending is excessive, and would put into place a mechanism through which each country's rhetorical commitment to peace and disarmament can be compared with actual behavior.

The proposal was first introduced into the UN system in 1974. Negotiations have continued, but a major impasse remains over the issue of verification. As of the time this book went to press, the Soviet Union has not agreed to measures that would guarantee the accuracy of their reported figures. The United States could undertake initiatives including the following to break the impasse:

- Report U.S. figures for expenditures on all types of strategic bomber aircraft during the present fiscal year. If the Soviets reciprocate by reporting their own bomber figures, the United States would continue to report; if it does not, we would stop. A possible variation is to continue reporting on bombers even without Soviet reciprocation, but say when the initiative is first announced that reciprocation would lead the United States to report additional figures for another type of weapon.

- Permit verification of the figures for bombers by a Group of Experts working with the UN's Department of Disarmament Affairs. If the first variation above is selected, require Soviet reciprocation to continue.

- Inform the UN secretary-general that the United States will submit its report at the beginning of each fiscal year and ask the secretary-general to report publicly in a speech or press release which countries have participated in the system.[43]

Notes

Chapter 1

1. Paul C. Warnke, "Apes on a Treadmill," *Foreign Policy*, no. 18 (Spring 1975): 28.

2. Robert Bresler and Robert Gray, "The Bargaining Chip and SALT," *Political Science Quarterly* 92 (Spring 1977): 88.

3. Jerome B. Wiesner, "Unilateral Confidence Building," *Bulletin of the Atomic Scientists* 40 (January 1984): 45.

4. Herbert Scoville, Jr., "Reciprocal National Restraint: An Alternative Path," *Arms Control Today* 15 (June 1985): 1.

5. *Congressional Quarterly Weekly Report* 42 (July 21, 1984): 1774.

6. Albert Carnesale and Richard N. Haass, eds., *Superpower Arms Control: Setting the Record Straight* (Cambridge, MA: Ballinger, 1987), 336.

7. Patrick Glynn, "The Moral Case for the Arms Buildup," in *Nuclear Arms: Ethics, Strategy, Politics,* ed. James R. Woolsey (San Francisco: Institute for Contemporary Studies, 1984), 39.

8. *Congressional Quarterly Weekly Report* 42 (August 25, 1984): 2116.

9. Authors noted here claim that the tactic works or does not work. None of the proponents mention failures, and none of the opponents acknowledge any successes. The extreme proponents advocate unilateral disarmament unconditionally or as an acceptable outcome of a series of smaller initiatives. See Erich Fromm, "The Case for Unilateral Disarmament," in *Arms Control, Disarmament, and National Security,* ed. Donald G. Brennan (New York: Braziller, 1961); and April Carter, ed., *Unilateral Disarmament* (London: Housemans, 1966). Others prescribe the tactic but advise proceeding with subsequent initiatives only if the Soviets reciprocate the first. Warnke and Bresler and Gray are examples (see notes 1 and 2 above). See also Harold Willens, *The Trimtab Factor* (New York: William Morrow, 1984), 108. Those who say only that the tactic fails include Glynn and the 1984 Republican Platform (see notes 7 and 8 above).

10. Some authors using a contingent approach do not mention cases of failure but offer criteria for implementing the tactic. This suggests they recognize, at least implicitly, that an improperly implemented tactic may fail. See Scoville, "Reciprocal National Restraint," 7; Robert Woito, *To End War* (New York: Pilgrim Press, 1982),

493-504; Jane M. O. Sharp, "Isaiah Revisited," *Bulletin of the Atomic Scientists* 34 (April 1978); and Russel Hardin, "Contracts, Promises, and Arms Control," *Bulletin of the Atomic Scientists* 40 (October 1984).

The remaining authors explicitly acknowledge that failures occur. Some use a theory or conceptual framework to suggest what factors are most important. Two write in the tradition of bargaining and game theory. First, see three works by Thomas C. Schelling: "Reciprocal Measures for Arms Stabilization," in Brennan, *Arms Control; The Strategy of Conflict* (New York: Oxford University Press, 1963); and *Arms and Influence* (New Haven, CT: Yale University Press, 1966). Second, see Robert Axelrod, *The Evolution of Cooperation* (New York: Basic Books, 1984). Charles E. Osgood uses a social-psychology theory: *An Alternative to War or Surrender* (Urbana: University of Illinois Press, 1962). For particular page numbers, see citations for these works in chapter 2.

Gerald M. Steinberg uses a collection of theories and weighs the conditions. See *Satellite Reconnaissance: The Role of Informal Bargaining* (New York: Praeger, 1983), 103-124. See also Alexander L. George, "Strategies for Facilitating Cooperation," in *U.S.-Soviet Security Cooperation: Achievements, Failures, Lessons,* ed. Alexander George, Philip J. Farley, and Alexander Dallin (New York: Oxford University Press, 1988), 702-7.

Others use an ad hoc collection of theories and do not say which factors are most important. See Walter C. Clemens, *The Superpowers and Arms Control* (Lexington, MA: Lexington Books, 1973), 55-58, 69, 87, 96-100, 121; Gordon L. Shull, "Unilateral Initiatives in Arms Control: Promise, Problems, Prospects" (Wooster: Ohio Arms Control Study Group, 1976); Franklin A. Long, "Unilateral Initiatives," *Bulletin of the Atomic Scientists* 40 (May 1984): 50-54; and Amitai Etzioni, "The Kennedy Experiment," *Western Political Science Quarterly* 20 (1967), and *The Hard Way to Peace: A New Strategy* (New York: Collier Books, 1962), ch. 4. A more recent analysis is by George W. Downs, David M. Rocke, and Randolph M. Siverson, "Arms Races and Cooperation," *World Politics* 38 (October 1985), who emphasize game theory but bring in other factors. See also George Downs and David Rocke, "Tacit Bargaining and Arms Control," *World Politics* 39 (April 1987).

Some use no formal theory. See George Rathjens, "Unilateral Initiatives for Limiting and Reducing Arms," in *New Directions in Disarmament,* ed. William Epstein and Bernard T. Feld (New York: Praeger, 1981), 173-83; and Philip Towle, "Unilateralism; or Disarmament by Example," *Arms Control: The Journal of Arms Control and Disarmament* 2 (London, May 1981). Unlike the above authors who favor the tactic, Towle thinks it rarely works and hence is undesirable.

A final author is Kenneth Adelman, who says that unilateral restraint sometimes results in mutual restraint. He does not offer a contingent analysis of the factors favoring success, however. See "Arms Control With and Without Agreements," *Foreign Affairs* 63 (Winter 1984/85): 250-60.

11. Paul B. Stares, "Deja vu: The ASAT Debate in Historical Context," *Arms Control Today* 13 (December 1983): 6.

12. John H. Cushman Jr., "299 Billion Budget Presented, With Deep Cuts," *New York Times,* February 19, 1988.

13. See Jack Snyder, "The Gorbachev Revolution: A Waning of Soviet Expansionism?" *International Security* 12 (Winter 1987/88): 119-20.

14. Michael R. Gordon, "U.S. Again Says It Won't Join Soviet Moratorium," *New York Times*, August 19, 1986; U.S. Department of State, Bureau of Public Affairs, "Requirements for US Nuclear Testing," *GIST*, June 1987.

15. "Legislature asks US to end nuclear tests," *Boston Globe*, July 1, 1987.

16. Y. Primakov, "A New Philosophy of Foreign Policy," *Pravda*, July 10, 1987, in the *Current Digest of the Soviet Press* 39 (August 12, 1987), 4.

17. Woito, *To End War*, 494-502.

Chapter 2

1. Schelling, *Strategy of Conflict*, 3-6, 15-16, 22, 43-50, 108, 121, 132-34, 160-72, 195-96; and, *Arms and Influence*, 3, 69-89, 270, 280-82.

2. Schelling's model is more suggestive than economic models of bargaining, which do not help us to understand situations of interest (i.e., circumstances where bargaining skills play a role and where the issue in contention is not continuously divisible). See Oran R. Young, ed., *Bargaining: Formal Theories of Negotiation* (Chicago: University of Illinois Press, 1975), 131-34, 141, 303.

3. Axelrod, *Evolution of Cooperation*.

4. Ibid., 36, 124-39, 173-74.

5. Ibid., 13, 124-32.

6. This analysis and resulting hypothesis profited greatly from a phone conversation with Steven Van Evera during the summer of 1987. See also Van Evera, "Why Cooperation Failed in 1914," *World Politics* 38 (October 1985): 81-83, 112-17.

7. Axelrod, *Evolution of Cooperation*, 184-86.

8. See Downs, Rocke, and Siverson, "Arms Races and Cooperation," 141; Scoville, "Reciprocal National Restraint," 7; and Osgood, *Alternative to War or Surrender*, 103-4.

9. Axelrod, *Evolution of Cooperation*, 138, 176, 187.

10. Robert Jervis, "Cooperation Under the Security Dilemma," *World Politics* 30 (January 1978): 169-70, 188, 214.

11. See Downs, Rocke, and Siverson, "Arms Races and Cooperation," 145.

12. Ibid., 143.

13. Schelling, *Arms and Influence*, 146-47.

14. Schelling himself admits that states do not always act like unitary, rational actors (*Strategy of Conflict*, 16). Axelrod adds that his own formulation leaves out factors in the environment of bargaining (*Evolution of Cooperation*, 19, 190).

15. Authors who criticize game-theoretic models for omitting domestic factors include Joanne Gowa, "Anarchy, Egoism, and Third Images," *International Organization* 40 (Winter 1986); Downs, Rocke, and Siverson, "Arms Races and Cooperation," 122, 136; Graham Allison and Frederic Morris, "Armaments and Arms Control: Exploring the Determinants of Military Weapons," *Daedalus* 104 (Summer 1975). Van Evera adds that a common interpretation of the history of previous interactions is rare, in large part because militaries tend to take credit for concessions granted by the other side (phone conversation, summer 1987).

16. Both Young (*Bargaining*, 398, 406) and William Zartman ("Negotiation as a

Joint Decision Making Process," *Journal of Conflict Resolution* 21 [December 1977]: 637) lament that power has not been incorporated into a theory of bargaining.

17. See Leon Sloss and Helmut Sonnenfeld, in *A Game for High Stakes: Lessons Learned in Negotiating with the Soviet Union*, ed. Leon Sloss and M. Scott Davis (Cambridge, MA: Ballinger, 1986), 6-7, 24.

18. See Sloss, *Game for High Stakes*, 7; Gerard C. Smith, cited in *The Soviet Calculus of Nuclear War*, ed. Roman Kolkowicz and Ellen P. Mickiewicz (Lexington, MA: Lexington Books, 1986), 144; and George W. Breslauer, "Why Detente Failed," in *Managing the United States-Soviet Rivalry*, ed. Alexander George (Boulder, CO: Westview Press, 1983), 331.

19. Joseph de Rivera, *The Psychological Dimensions of Foreign Policy* (Columbus, OH: C. E. Merrill, 1965), chs. 2-3; and John Steinbruner, *Cybernetic Theory of Decision* (Princeton, NJ: Princeton University Press, 1974), ch. 4. See also Robert Jervis, *Perception and Misperception in International Politics* (Princeton, NJ: Princeton University Press, 1976).

20. Deborah W. Larson, "Crisis Prevention and the Austrian Treaty," *International Organization* 41 (Winter 1987): 29-34, 57-58.

21. Allison and Morris, "Armaments and Arms Control," 122-27.

22. Robert J. Art and Stephen Ockenden, "The Domestic Politics of Cruise Missile Development," in *Cruise Missiles: Technology, Strategy, Politics*, ed. Richard Betts (Washington, D.C.: Brookings Institution, 1981).

23. Steinberg, *Satellite Reconnaissance*, 101-111, 119-24, 182.

24. Jervis also makes this argument. See his *Logic of Images in International Relations* (Princeton, NJ: Princeton University Press, 1970), 123, 128, 181.

25. Downs, Rocke, and Siverson, "Arms Races and Cooperation," 143.

26. Robert J. Art, "Bureaucratic Politics and American Foreign Policy: A Critique," *Policy Sciences* 4 (December 1973).

27. Morton Halperin, *Bureaucratic Politics and Foreign Policy* (Washington, D.C.: Brookings Institution, 1974), 297-310.

28. Osgood, *Alternative to War or Surrender*, 21-36, 56-62.

29. See Robert A. Levine, "Unilateral Initiatives: A Cynic's View," *Bulletin of the Atomic Scientists* 19 (January 1963); I. L. Horowitz, "Unilateral Initiatives: A Strategy in Search of a Theory," *Diogenes*, no. 50 (Montreal: Mario Casalini, Ltd., Summer 1965); and Woito, *To End War*, 493-503.

30. See Jervis, "Security Dilemma," 187-91, 199-202, 214.

31. Van Evera, "Why Cooperation Failed," 81-83, 112-13.

32. See Ibid., 116; Sidney B. Fay, *The Origins of the World War*, Vol. I (New York: Macmillan, 1929), 312; A. J. P. Taylor, *Struggle for Mastery in Europe* (Oxford: Clarendon Press, 1954), 502; and E. L. Woodward, *Great Britain and the German Navy* (London: F. Cass and Co., 1935), 292-94, 306-7, 398-403.

33. See David Ignatious, "We've Learned to Stop Worrying and Love Arms Control," *Washington Post National Weekly Edition*, September 14, 1987; and Samuel P. Huntington, "Playing to Win," *The National Interest*, no. 3 (Spring 1986): 8-16.

34. Kenneth N. Waltz, *Theory of International Politics* (Reading, MA: Addison-Wesley, 1979), 40-41, 89-91.

35. For a balance of power theory, see Ibid., 117-21. Glenn Snyder and Paul Dies-

ing also use a systemic approach to examine bargaining: *Conflict Among Nations: Bargaining, Decision Making, and System Structure in International Crises* (Princeton, NJ: Princeton University Press, 1977), 471-80.

36. Allison and Morris, "Armaments and Arms Control," 126.

37. Steinberg, *Satellite Reconnaissance,* 95-101.

38. See Alexander George, "Case Studies and Theory Development: The Method of Structured, Focused Comparison," in *Diplomatic History: New Approaches in History, Theory, and Policy,* ed. Paul G. Lauren (New York: The Free Press, 1979).

39. The game experiment method of research can sometimes suggest valid insights that one might miss when simply reading the historical literature. Its utility is limited, however, because the computer simulation or the laboratory situation of the experiments is not sufficiently isomorphic with the part of the real world of interest to us. When conducted by individuals in a laboratory environment, for example, the situation introduces factors of its own that sometimes overwhelm a causal factor under study. Also, key aspects of the real world are extremely difficult to duplicate in a laboratory or a computer program, such as the stakes involved in the competition and especially the institutional setting in which decisions are made. See criticisms in Alan C. Isaak, *Scope and Methods of Political Science* (Homewood, IL: Dorsey Press, 1975), 99-100, 152; James E. Dougherty and R. L. Pfaltzgraff, Jr., *Contending Theories of International Relations* (New York: J. P. Lippincott, 1971), 329, 355, 362, 369-78. Consequently, I treat experiments as a source of potentially important factors—the beginning of research—rather than as the research itself.

40. For a listing of the instances the tactic was used in the nineteenth and twentieth centuries, see William M. Rose, *Bargaining Tactics for Arms Control: A Theoretical and Historical Analysis* (Ph.D. diss., University of California, Berkeley, 1984), 296-305.

41. The criterion that the proposed agreement must involve a weapon or component of a weapon that is directly related to the U.S.-Soviet balance of power means that we will not examine several potential cases:

a. The United States undertook initiatives in 1962-67 to facilitate international inspection of nonmilitary reactors. See U.S. Arms Control and Disarmament Agency, *Documents on Disarmament, 1964* (Washington, DC: GPO), 79-82, 214-21; U.S. Library of Congress, Environment and Natural Resources Policy Division, *The International Atomic Energy Agency: Applications of Safeguards in the United States,* prepared for the Committee on Foreign Relations, U.S. Senate (Washington, DC: GPO, 1979), 96th Cong., 1st sess., 1-4, 15-17, 32. See also Paul Lewis, "Soviets Said to Approve Inspection of Two Nuclear Reactors This Month," *New York Times,* August 6, 1985, 1.

b. The parties apparently reduced defense spending in tandem during 1963-65, but no particular weapon was involved. Moreover, third parties were exceptionally important: as the United States stepped up its involvement in Vietnam during 1965, it requested a supplemental defense budget. See Ruth Sivard, *World Military and Social Expenditures, 1978* (Leesburg, VA: WMSE, 1978), 19-20; Arnold Horelick and Myron Rush, *Strategic Power and Soviet Foreign Policy* (Chicago: University of Chicago Press, 1966), 155; Abraham S. Becker, *Military Expenditure Limitations for Arms Control* (Cambridge, MA: Ballinger, 1977), 2-5, 93-97, 117-19.

c. President Jimmy Carter undertook initiatives designed to control arms transfers to third countries, such as his promise not to be the first to introduce advanced military technology to a region. However, a particular weapon was not at issue, the U.S.-Soviet balance of power was not directly involved, and success also required restraint by additional arms suppliers such as the French. See Jane Sharp, "Swords and Plowshares in the Carter Administration," *Arms Control Today*, June 1977: 1-4; and Coit D. Blacker and Gloria Duffy, *International Arms Control: Issues and Agreements*, 2d ed. (Stanford, CA: Stanford University Press, 1984), 327.

42. One criterion for selection of case studies is that the U.S. told the Soviets what sort of reciprocation it wanted. It was not evoked in *Superpower Arms Control: Setting the Record Straight*, ed. Carnesale and Haass, 336-50. Along with a very brief discussion of several initiatives where the Soviets were asked for reciprocation, the authors included Carter's cancellation of the B-1 bomber and other instances of U.S. restraint where the United States did not tell the Soviets what it wanted. I suspect that their method of selecting examples to study accounts for their pessimism about the tactic.

This criterion leads us to reject eight cases where the United States did not tell the Soviets what to do:

a. The United States did not produce an antisatellite system in 1960–63, which contributed to tacit agreements with the Soviets not to deploy such systems or otherwise interfere with reconnaissance satellites. See Steinberg, *Satellite Reconnaissance*, 30-35, 66-67, 71-87, 143-45.

b. The United States withdrew 8000 troops from West Germany in April 1964, and evidently the Soviets subsequently removed about 14,000 troops. However, "from the available evidence, it does not appear that there was an informal American-Soviet agreement on 'mutual example' force reductions in Europe in 1963–64. The Soviets . . . evidently understood that our reduction was made for reasons of our own." See J. E. Mayer, "American-Soviet Bilateral Talks on 'Mutual Example' Force Reductions in Europe, 1963-64," prepared for U.S. ACDA (December 8, 1969), cited in Becker, *Military Expenditure Limitations*, 121 n. 13.

c. The United States did not improve ballistic missile warhead accuracy as much as was possible during the period 1964–74. See Glynn, "Moral Case," 39.

d. The United States decreased defense spending in real terms from 1965–75. See U.S. ACDA, *Arms Control Report* (Washington, DC: GPO, 1976), 8-9; and Becker, *Military Expenditure Limitations*, 5-6.

e. In 1968 the United States stopped adding ICBMs and SLBMs to its strategic inventory, and the Soviets did not reciprocate. See Carnesale and Haass, *Superpower Arms Control*, 337.

f. The United States halted chemical weapons production in 1969. Production stopped because the military's requirements at the time had been purchased and the Department of Defense was preparing to move soon into binary weapons as a replacement. Nixon's November 25 announcement, though it constrained production of only biological weapons, ended further chemical weapons production plans (see note 43 below). On November 19 Congress had also placed several constraints on further testing and production of chemical weapons; this action, however, was unrelated to any effort to get the Soviets to agree to a production ban. See *Report of the Chemical Warfare Review Commission* (Washington, DC: GPO, 1985), 17-19; Hugh

Stringer, *Deterring Chemical Warfare: U.S. Policy Options for the 1980s* (New York: Pergamon-Brassey's, 1986), 29; and Blacker and Duffy, *International Arms Control,* 142-43.

g. President Carter canceled the B-1 bomber in 1977, largely because it was not cost-effective compared to cruise missiles. See *Congressional Quarterly Almanac* 33 (June 30, 1977): 393.

h. The United States withdrew 1000 tactical nuclear weapons from Europe in 1980. This less-publicized provision of the December 1979 NATO intermediate-range nuclear force decision was not linked to any Soviet concessions. See Cyrus Vance, in U.S. ACDA, *Documents on Disarmament, 1979,* 805-6.

43. The criterion that the outcome is clear is needed so that we know if we are explaining the tactic's success or failure. It leads us to reject cases involving fissionable materials and biological weapons.

a. On January 8, 1964, President Johnson announced that "we are cutting back our production of enriched uranium by 25 percent. We are shutting down four plutonium production piles. We . . . call on our adversaries to do the same." On April 20, Khrushchev responded that the Soviet Union would stop constructing two plutonium reactors, would reduce production of enriched uranium for weapons, and would allocate more fissionable material for peaceful uses. See U.S. ACDA, *Documents on Disarmament, 1964,* 4, 7-8, 165-68; and John M. Taylor, *Restricting Production of Fissionable Material As An Arms Control Measure: An Updated Historical Overview* (Albuquerque: Sandia National Laboratories, September 1986), 4-5, 11-38, 63-64.

The United States announced a further decrease in the rate of production of enriched uranium on February 15, 1965. See U.S. ACDA, *Documents on Disarmament, 1965,* 18-19. Apparently without further public announcement, Johnson went on to end all U.S. production of enriched uranium, and Nixon shut down three more plutonium production reactors. See Frank von Hippel and Barbara G. Levi, "Controlling Nuclear Weapons at the Source: Verification of a Cutoff in the Production of Plutonium and Highly Enriched Uranium for Nuclear Weapons," in *Arms Control Verification: The Technologies Make It Possible,* ed. Kosta Tsipis, David W. Hafemeister, and Penny Janeway (New York: Pergamon-Brassey's, 1986), 355.

Did the U.S. unilateral initiatives succeed, at least the ones announced publicly? William Epstein argues that they did. See "The Time is Ripe for the Cutoff of Production of Fissionable Materials for Nuclear Weapons," in Epstein and Feld, *New Directions in Disarmament,* 52. Henry M. Jackson, when chair of the Joint Atomic Energy Committee's military applications subcommittee, disagreed. See Chalmers M. Roberts, "Jackson Says Reds Renege on Khrushchev Nuclear Cutback Pledge," *Washington Post,* November 24, 1965, 8.

Recent scientific studies cast doubt on our ability to check earlier Soviet claims of cutbacks. One says that "we have no information on the current rate of production of weapons-grade uranium in the Soviet Union." See von Hippel and Levi, "Controlling the Source," 356. The calculations also suggest that the Soviets may have actually increased production of plutonium (ibid., 353-54). At any rate, they seem to agree with Jackson: "There . . . is no clear evidence of a production cutback such as that which occurred in the United States in the late 1960s" (ibid., 356).

Sources I found were also insufficiently specific to confirm or falsify Khrushchev's claim that the Soviet Union halted construction of two plutonium production plants.

Related to the cutoff proposal was another U.S. action that at first glance appears to be a unilateral initiative. On August 11, 1966, Adrian Fisher, deputy director of ACDA, invited members of the Eighteen Nation Disarmament Committee to visit a shut-down plutonium production reactor at the Hartford plant. The purpose was to demonstrate a relatively nonintrusive method for monitoring shut-down reactors. He said, however, that the demonstration "does not in itself reflect a decision to place that reactor unilaterally under international safeguards. However, the United States is prepared to accept international verification of the shut-down of a Hartford reactor if the Soviet Union is prepared to reciprocate." If this had been such a decision, we would have had another case study because U.S.-Soviet military capabilities would have been involved. The demonstration was later scheduled for November 16. See U.S. ACDA, *Documents on Disarmament, 1966,* 554-58, 687-88, 834.

b. On November 25, 1969, President Richard Nixon unilaterally and unconditionally renounced biological warfare and ordered the destruction of U.S. stockpiles, and he called on other nations to follow suit. On February 14, 1970, he extended the ban to include toxins. See *Public Papers of the President of the United States: Richard Nixon, 1969* (Washington, DC: GPO, 1971), 968-70; Blacker and Duffy, *International Arms Control,* 142; Mark C. Storella, *Poisoning Arms Control: The Soviet Union and Chemical/Biological Weapons* (Cambridge, MA: Institute for Foreign Policy Analysis, 1984), 14; and U.S. ACDA, *Documents on Disarmament, 1969,* 743-46.

It is unclear if the Soviets reciprocated. Arkady Shevchenko claims that despite signing the Biological Weapons Convention, the Soviets have kept their weapons (*Breaking with Moscow,* [New York: Knopf, 1985], 173-79). Some also interpret the April 1979 outbreak of anthrax at Sverdlovsk as proof of Soviet retention of stockpiles, while others say the evidence is inconclusive. See Elisa D. Harris, "Sverdlovsk and Yellow Rain: Two Cases of Soviet Noncompliance?" *International Security* 11 (Spring 1987); Robert J. Einhorn, *Negotiating from Strength: Leverage in U.S.-Soviet Arms Control Negotiations* (New York: Praeger, 1985), 8.

44. Shevchenko, *Breaking with Moscow.*

Chapter 3

1. Waltz, *Theory of International Politics,* 117-18; and *Man, the State, and War* (New York: Columbia University Press, 1959), 205-218; K. J. Holsti, *International Politics: A Framework for Analysis,* 3d ed. (Englewood Cliffs, NJ: Prentice-Hall, 1977), 138-151.

2. Richard Lowenthal, "The Logic of One-Party Rule," in *The Conduct of Soviet Foreign Policy,* 2d edition, ed. Erik P. Hoffmann and Frederik Fleron, Jr. (New York: Aldine, 1980), 117-30; and George Breslauer, "Ideology and Learning in Soviet Third World Policy," *World Politics* 39 (April 1987), 430-31.

3. For discussions of the "correlation of forces," see Raymond L. Garthoff, *Soviet Military Policy: An Historical Analysis* (New York: Praeger, 1966), 65-97; P. H. Vigor, *The Soviet View of Disarmament* (New York: St. Martin's Press, 1986), 11-14; Harriet F.

Scott and William F. Scott, eds., *The Soviet Art of War: Doctrine, Strategy, and Tactics* (Boulder, CO: Westview Press, 1982), 5-6, 154, 186-87, 194; Alfred L. Monks, *Soviet Military Doctrine: 1960 to the Present* (New York: Irvington Publishers, 1984), 122, 145 n. 1, 326; and Snyder, "The Gorbachev Revolution," 95-96, 124.

4. Morton Schwartz, *The Foreign Policy of the USSR: Domestic Factors* (Encino, CA: Dickenson, 1975), 97.

5. See Samuel L. Sharp, "National Interest: Key to Soviet Politics," in *Conduct of Soviet Foreign Policy*, ed. Hoffmann and Fleron, 108-117; and Adam Ulam, *Expansion and Coexistence: The History of Soviet Foreign Policy 1917–67* (New York: Praeger, 1968), 30, 314-77.

6. The Soviets have precise definitions for doctrine, strategy, tactics, military science, and military art. To understand Soviet behavior during peacetime bargaining, in the text we need define only doctrine. For the other definitions, see Harriet F. Scott and William F. Scott, *The Armed Forces of the USSR*, 2d ed. (Boulder, CO: Westview Press, 1982), ch. 3; and Tsuyoshi Hasegawa, "Soviets on Nuclear War-Fighting," *Problems of Communism* 35 (July-August 1986): 69.

7. Scott and Scott, *Soviet Art of War*, 271.

8. Scott and Scott, *Armed Forces of the USSR*, 376.

9. Ibid., 37, 41-54, 376.

10. Scott and Scott, *Soviet Art of War*, 168-70.

11. Scott and Scott, *Armed Forces of the USSR*, 45.

12. Hasegawa, "Nuclear War-Fighting," 70.

13. Ibid.

14. Scott and Scott, *Armed Forces of the USSR*, 56-59.

15. Stephen Meyer, "Soviet Perspectives on the Paths to Nuclear War," in *Hawks, Doves, & Owls: An Agenda for Avoiding Nuclear War*, ed. Graham Allison, Albert Carnesale, and Joseph Nye, Jr. (New York: W. W. Norton, 1985), 170, 178, 183.

16. Hasegawa, "Nuclear War-Fighting," 70.

17. Ibid., 71.

18. Monks, *Soviet Military Doctrine*, 129-31, 179, 266-67, 299-311.

19. Ibid., 131, 266-67, 302-8; and Hasegawa, "Nuclear War-Fighting," 68-79.

20. See Primakov, "New Philosophy of Foreign Policy," 1-4; Steven Meyer, "New Thinking for an Old Bear," *Los Angeles Times*, September 22, 1987; and "Nato sees military rethink by Moscow," *Financial Times* (London), September 22, 1987.

21. "A Garthoff-Pipes Debate on Soviet Strategic Doctrine," *Strategic Review* 10 (Fall 1982): 36-63.

22. Jack Snyder, "Science and Sovietology: Bridging the Methods Gap in Soviet Foreign Policy Studies," *World Politics* 40 (January 1988): 182.

23. *Arms Control Today* 16 (November 1986): 1-5; David Ignatius, "We've Learned to Stop Worrying and Love Arms Control," *Washington Post National Weekly Edition*, September 14, 1987. For a contrasting view, see Jack Mendelsolm and James Rubin, "SDI as Negotiating Leverage," *Arms Control Today* 16 (December 1986): 6-9.

24. Snyder, "Science and Sovietology," 182.

25. See V. Petrovsky, *The Soviet Concept of Disarmament* (Moscow: Nauka Publishers, 1984), 84-86; Raymond Garthoff, "The Soviet Military and SALT," in *Soviet Decisionmaking for National Security*, ed. Jiri Valenta and William Potter (London: Allen & Unwin, 1984), 142; Zigurds L. Zile, Robert Sharlet, and Jean C. Love, *The*

Soviet Legal System and Arms Inspection: A Case Study in Policy Implementation (New York: Praeger, 1972), 308-13; Thomas B. Larson, *Disarmament and Soviet Policy: 1964-68* (Englewood Cliffs, NJ: Prentice-Hall, 1969), ch. 12; and Vigor, *Soviet View of Disarmament,* 141, 158, 165-66.

26. See Roland M. Timerbaev, "A Soviet Official on Verification," *Bulletin of the Atomic Scientists* 43 (January-February 1987): 8-10; "Summary and Text of the INF Treaty and Protocols," *Arms Control Today* 18 (January/February 1988): INF Supplement 1-16.

27. See Alvin Z. Rubinstein, *Soviet Foreign Policy Since World War II: Imperial and Global* (Cambridge, MA: Winthrop, 1981), 120-35; Ulam, *Expansion and Coexistence,* 613-19, 665-93, 701-21; 749, 761-68; Shevchenko, *Breaking with Moscow,* 93, 166-68; Einhorn, *Negotiating from Strength,* 59; B. Thomas Trout, "Soviet Policy Towards China: Implications for U.S. Policy," in *Soviet International Behavior and U.S. Policy Options,* ed. Dan Caldwell (Lexington, MA: Lexington Books, 1985); John Newhouse, *Cold Dawn: The Story of SALT* (New York: Holt, Rinehart, and Winston, 1973), 91, 235; Samuel B. Payne, Jr., *The Soviet Union and SALT* (Cambridge, MA: MIT Press, 1980), 20; U.S. Congress, House Committee on Foreign Affairs, Subcommittee on Arms Control, International Security and Science, *Fundamentals of Nuclear Arms Control,* Part 6—"Soviet Attitudes and Objectives in Negotiations," Report prepared by the Congressional Research Service, Library of Congress, 99th Cong., 2d sess., 1986, Committee Print, 16; and Dan L. Strode, "Arms Control and Sino-Soviet Relations," *Orbis* 28 (Spring 1984).

28. See Robbin F. Laird, "The Soviet Union and the Western Alliance: Elements of an Anticoalition Strategy," *Proceedings of the Academy of Political Science* 36 (1987): 106-118.

29. Ulam, *Expansion and Coexistence,* 723; Kenneth A. Myers and Dimitri Simes, *Soviet Decision Making, Strategic Policy, and SALT* (Washington, DC: Center for Strategic and International Studies at Georgetown University, 1974), 43.

30. This framework draws heavily from Breslauer, "Why Detente Failed," 330-31.

31. My contingent approach to international economic calculations is similar but not identical to ideas presented by Edward A. Hewett. See his book, *Energy, Economics, and Foreign Policy in the Soviet Union* (Washington, DC: Brookings Institution, 1984), 201-2. The difference is that my typology of relevant conditions is explicit about market shares and a trade-stimulating environment. Ideas concerning trade-stimulating and trade-restricting environments draw from John P. Hardt and Donna Gold, "Soviet Commercial Behavior with Western Industrial Nations," in *Soviet International Behavior,* ed. Caldwell, 207-210.

32. Hardt and Gold, "Soviet Commercial Behavior," 199; and Edward A. Hewett, testimony in U.S. Congress, House, Committee on Foreign Relations, *Soviet Union: Domestic Issues and Military Trends: Hearings before the Subcommittee on Europe and the Middle East,* 99th Cong., 1st sess., July 29, 1985, 61.

33. See U.S. Department of Agriculture, *USSR: Situation and Outlook Report* (Washington, DC: n.p., May 1986), 19; Marshall I. Goldman, *Gorbachev's Challenge: Economic Reform in the Age of High Technology* (New York: W. W. Norton, 1987), 36-40, 196-97.

34. See Joan E. Spero, *The Politics of International Economic Relations*, 2d ed. (New York: St. Martin's Press, 1981), 297-99; Franklyn D. Holzman and Robert Legvold, "The Economics of East-West Relations," in *Conduct of Soviet Foreign Policy*, ed. Hoffmann and Fleron, 430-31.

35. See Spero, *International Economic Relations*, 299-300; and Holzman and Legvold, "East-West Relations," 433, 437.

36. Hardt and Gold, "Soviet Commercial Behavior," 207-9.

37. For a discussion of the "Kosygin reforms" and other attmpts to reform the Soviet economy, see Spero, *International Economic Relations*, 299; Goldman, *Gorbachev's Challenge*, 48-63, 69-84; Erik P. Hoffmann and Robbin F. Laird, *The Politics of Economic Modernization in the Soviet Union* (Ithaca, N.Y.: Cornell University Press, 1982), 44-45; and Franklyn D. Holzman, *The Soviet Economy: Past, Present and Future* (New York: Foreign Policy Association, 1982), 16, 20-21.

For a discussion of CMEA, see Spero, *International Economic Relations*, 300-307; Holzman and Legvold, "East-West Relations," 430; Vladimir V. Kusin, "Gorbachev and Eastern Europe," *Problems of Communism* 35 (January-February 1986): 42-43; and Jackson Diehl, "Gorbachev Preaches Economic Togetherness," *Washington Post National Weekly Edition*, June 15, 1987.

38. See Spero, *International Economic Relations*, 315-20, and 1985 ed., 375-77, 384.

39. Ibid. (1985), 369-85.

40. See Holzman and Legvold, "East-West Relations," 472-73; and Spero, *International Economic Relations* (1985), 364, 368.

41. See Spero, *International Economic Relations* (1985), 368, 376-85.

42. See David Lane, *Politics & Society in the USSR*, 2d ed. (New York: New York University Press, 1978), 11, 125-29, 162, 229-30, 257.

43. See George W. Breslauer, "Political Succession and the Soviet Policy Agenda," *Problems of Communism* 29 (May-June 1980), and *Khrushchev and Brezhnev as Leaders: Building Authority in Soviet Politics* (London: Allen and Unwin, 1982); and Grey Hodnett, "Patterns of Leadership Politics," in *The Domestic Context of Soviet Foreign Policy*, ed. Sewern Bialer (Boulder, CO: Westview Press, 1981).

44. Breslauer, *Khrushchev and Brezhnev*, 132-33; Hodnett, "Patterns of Leadership," 89-91; Jerry Hough and Merle Fainsod, *How the Soviet Union Is Governed* (Cambridge, MA: Harvard University Press, 1979), 236; and Shevchenko, *Breaking with Moscow*, 116-18, 125-28.

45. William Oden, "A Dissenting View on the Group Approach to Soviet Politics," *World Politics* 38 (July 1976). Richard Pipes adds that all Soviet leaders are "hawks" at heart, which suggests he would think the analysis is pointless. See his *U.S.-Soviet Relations in the Era of Detente* (Boulder, CO: Westview Press, 1981), 179.

46. See Carl A. Linden, *Khrushchev and the Soviet Leadership, 1957-64* (Baltimore: John Hopkins University Press, 1966); Michael Tatu, *Power in the Kremlin: From Khrushchev to Kosygin* (New York: Viking Press, 1968); and Christer Jonsson, *The Soviet Union and the Test Ban: A Study in Soviet Negotiating Behavior* (Ph.D. diss., University of Lund, Sweden, 1975).

47. See T. H. Rigby, "Crypto-Politics," *Survey*, no. 50 (January 1964); Hough and

Fainsod, *How the Soviet Union is Governed*, 547.

48. See Gordon Skilling and William Griffiths, eds., *Interest Groups in Soviet Politics* (Princeton, NJ: Princeton University Press, 1971); Schwartz, *Domestic Factors*, 176-89.

49. See Waltz, *Theory of International Politics*, 170-74, 185, 199; Steven M. Walt, "Alliance Formation and the Balance of World Power," *International Security* 9 (Spring 1985): 35-36; Breslauer, "Why Detente Failed," 320.

50. Jonsson, *Soviet Union and Test Ban*, 177.

51. I owe special thanks to George Breslauer for pointing this out to me. See also Breslauer, "Political Succession," 35; and Hans Rogger, "How the Soviets See Us," in *Shared Destiny: Fifty Years of Soviet-American Relations*, ed. Mark Garrison and Abbott Gleason (Boston: Beacon Press, 1985), 125.

52. Sewern Bialer, "Danger in Moscow," *New York Review of Books* 31 (February 16, 1984): 6-8.

53. This analysis draws heavily from Breslauer, "Why Detente Failed."

54. See Gordon Livermore, ed., *Soviet Foreign Policy Today: reports and commentaries from the soviet press*, 2d ed., (Columbus, OH: Current Digest of the Soviet Press, 1986), 5-7, 10-23. See also Paul H. Nitze, "Living with the Soviets," *Foreign Affairs* 63 (Winter 1984/85): 366; Trout, "Soviet Policy Towards China," 87 n. 40; Rubinstein, *Soviet Foreign Policy*, 75-76, 265-71; Ulam, *Expansion and Coexistence*, 572-78, 606, 772-76; and Snyder, "Gorbachev Revolution," 99-109, 118.

55. See Livermore, *Soviet Foreign Policy*, 19-22; Breslauer, "Why Detente Failed," 320; Snyder, "Gorbachev Revolution," 93-95, 99-109, 117-130; Primakov, "New Philosophy of Foreign Policy," 1-3.

56. The higher figures are drawn from a 1974 Soviet source noted in Meyer, "Soviet Perspectives," 174 and 258 n. 13. The lower figures cite Western estimates and are mentioned in Primakov, "New Philosophy of Foreign Policy," 3.

57. See Lawrence Freedman, *The Evolution of Nuclear Strategy* (New York: St. Martin's Press), 239.

58. Desmond Ball, "Soviet Strategic Planning and the Control of Nuclear War," in *Soviet Calculus*, ed. Kolkowicz and Mickiewicz, 54-55.

59. Allison and Morris, "Armaments," 108-13.

Chapter 4

1. *Congressional Record*, 87th Cong., 2d sess., September 21, 1962, A7008.

2. Raymond Garthoff, "Banning the Bomb in Outer Space," *International Security* 5 (Winter 1980/81): 31, 34; U.S. ACDA, *Documents on Disarmament*, 1962, 193, 360.

3. Garthoff, "Outer Space," 26-31.

4. Ibid., 31.

5. U.S. ACDA, *Documents on Disarmament, 1962* II, 1122.

6. Garthoff, "Outer Space," 33-34.

7. U.S. ACDA, *Documents on Disarmament, 1963*, 523.

8. Ibid., 537.

9. Garthoff, "Outer Space," 25, 34-37; and Steinberg, *Satellite Reconnaissance,* 86, 132.

10. Garthoff, "Outer Space," 36.

11. U.S. ACDA, *Arms Control and Disarmament Agreements: Texts and Histories of Negotiations* (Washington, DC: GPO, 1980), 52.

12. Garthoff, "Outer Space," 31.

13. During 1962 the United States invited the International Atomic Energy Agency to inspect several of its small research and power reactors. See U.S. ACDA, *Documents on Disarmament, 1964,* 80. Since I found no references to this topic in *Documents on Disarmament, 1962,* I was unable to learn when the agreement was made, when inspection began, or whether or not the United States informed the Soviets of the policy. Consequently it is plausible that in 1962 the Soviets did not perceive this U.S. policy as a unilateral initiative. The United States also said it was phasing out B-47 bombers over the next several years, but this policy was not yet part of a unilateral initiative tactic. See U.S. ACDA, *Documents on Disarmament, 1963,* 22; and chapter 6 in this book.

14. In all my case studies, *Documents on Disarmament* is the source for evidence on the topics of accompanying historical and political-military contexts. See, for example, U.S. ACDA, *Documents on Disarmament, 1963,* 17-21.

15. Ibid., 215-22.

16. See Garthoff, "Outer Space," 35; and U.S. Congress, Senate Committee on Foreign Relations, Hearings, *Treaty on Outer Space,* 90th Cong., 1st sess., March 7, 13, and April 12, 1967 (Washington, DC: GPO, 1967), 81.

17. Scott and Scott, *Soviet Art of War,* 168-70.

18. Garthoff, "Outer Space," 38; and John J. Kruzel, *The Preconditions and Consequences of Arms Control Agreements* (Ph.D. diss., Harvard University, 1975), 255, 270-71.

19. Kruzel, *Arms Control Agreements,* 251.

20. Steinberg, *Satellite Reconnaissance,* 30-35, 71-87.

21. *Congressional Record,* A7008.

22. Kruzel, *Arms Control Agreements,* 255-56.

23. See Ulam, *Expansion and Coexistence,* 613, 619, 660.

24. Ibid., 629-90.

25. U.S. ACDA, *Documents on Disarmament, 1963,* 239-42.

26. Ibid., 538.

27. Spero, *International Economic Relations* (1981), 297-98.

28. Marshall I. Goldman, *Detente and Dollars: Doing Business with the Soviets* (New York: Basic Books, 1975), 30-31.

29. Ibid., Goldman, *Gorbachev's Challenge,* 32.

30. Spero, *International Economic Relations* (1981), 308, 314.

31. Statistics on U.S. market shares and the mix of Soviet grain imports are drawn from reports by the U.S. Department of Agriculture: *World Food Grain Trade, 1962-83: Wheat, Rice, and Wheat Flour* (Washington, DC: n.p., October 1985), 15-36; *USSR: Situation and Outlook,* 29-30; and *World Agriculture: Outlook and Situation* (Washington, DC: n.p., November 1982). See also U.S. Central Intelligence Agency, *Soviet*

Agricultural Commodity Trade, 1960-76: A Statistical Survey (Washington, DC: n.p., September 1978), 10-11, 216-17; and U.S. General Accounting Office, *Agriculture Review: U.S. Food/Agriculture in a Volatile World Economy,* Briefing Report to the Congress (Washington, DC: GAO, November 1985), 3, 32.

32. See Ted Greenwood, *Making the MIRV* (Cambridge, MA: Ballinger, 1975), 98-99; Jerome Kahan, *Security in the Nuclear Age: Developing U.S. Strategic Arms Policy* (Washington, DC: Brookings Institution, 1975), 110-13; Thomas W. Wolfe, *Soviet Power in Europe, 1945-1970* (Baltimore: John Hopkins University Press, 1970), 187.

33. Breslauer, *Khrushchev and Brezhnev,* 132; Hough and Fainsod, *How the Soviet Union is Governed,* 233-36.

34. Richard Smoke, *National Security and the Nuclear Dilemma* (Reading, MA: Addison-Wesley, 1984), 145; Ulam, *Expansion and Coexistence,* 633, 652, 666; Christer Jonsson, *Soviet Bargaining Behavior: The Test Ban Case* (New York: Columbia University Press, 1979), 162, 178, 185; George W. Breslauer, "Do Soviet Leaders Test New Presidents?" *International Security* 8 (Winter 1983-84): 89-90.

35. Jonsson, *Soviet Union and Test Ban,* 177-79, 202, and *Soviet Bargaining Behavior,* 178-81.

36. Jonsson, *Soviet Union and Test Ban,* 202, and *Soviet Bargaining Behavior,* 195-203; Smoke, *National Security,* 145.

37. See Morton Schwartz, *Soviet Perceptions of the United States,* (Berkeley: University of California Press, 1978), 122; Etzioni, "The Kennedy Experiment," 365-6; Harold K. Jacobson and Erik Stein, *Diplomats, Scientists, and Politicians: The United States and the Nuclear Test Ban Negotiations* (Ann Arbor: University of Michigan Press, 1966), 453; Arthur H. Dean, *The Test Ban and Disarmament* (New York: Harper and Row, 1966), 111-12; and Abram Chayes, T. Ehrlich, and A. Lowenfeld, *International Legal Process,* Vol. II (Boston: Little, Brown, 1969), 995.

38. U.S. ACDA, *Documents on Disarmament, 1963,* 509.

39. International Institute for Strategic Studies, *The Military Balance, 1969-70* (London: IISS, 1969), 55, and *1970-71,* 105-106; Smoke, *National Security,* 99; and "Soviet slip suggested in '62 missile crisis," *Boston Globe,* October 14, 1987, 12. One author cites two figures for the number of Soviet ICBMs in 1962: 75 (p. 309) and 30 (p. 306). See Bruce G. Blair, *Strategic Command and Control: Redefining the Nuclear Threat* (Washington, DC: Brookings Institution, 1985).

40. See IISS, *Military Balance, 1969-70,* 55; Blair, *Command and Control,* 306-9; Meyer, "Soviet Perspectives," 175.

41. Richard K. Betts, "A Golden Nuclear Age? The Balance Before Parity," *International Security* 11 (Winter 1986-87): 17-22.

42. Ibid., 27-28; and Kahan, *Security in the Nuclear Age,* 52.

43. Betts, "Balance Before Parity," 28.

44. Kahan, *Security in the Nuclear Age,* 112.

45. IISS, *The Military Balance, 1969-70,* 55, *1962-63,* 4, and *1963-64,* 3; Blair, *Command and Control,* 306; Meyer, "Soviet Perspectives," 173.

46. See Robert McNamara, in Kahan, *Security in the Nuclear Age,* 93.

47. IISS, *The Military Balance, 1969-70,* 55; Blair, *Command and Control,* 306; Meyer, "Soviet Perspectives," 173.

48. Meyer, "Soviet Perspectives," 171, 257 n. 6.

49. Ibid., 175; Freedman, *Evolution of Nuclear Strategy*, 166-71; and IISS, *The Military Balance, 1962-63*, 4, and *1963-64*, 3.

50. IISS, *The Military Balance, 1960*, 7 and 14.

51. IISS, *The Military Balance, 1963-64*, 34.

52. Meyer, "Soviet Perspectives," 173.

53. Kahan, *Security in the Nuclear Age*, 91; Freedman, *Evolution of Nuclear Strategy*, 239; Ball, "Soviet Strategic Planning," 54-55.

54. IISS, *Military Balance, 1963–64*, 11, 34; Freedman, *Evolution of Nuclear Strategy*, 246.

55. Arthur J. Goldberg, March 7, 1967, in U.S. Congress, Senate, *Treaty on Outer Space*, 8.

Chapter 5

1. James H. McBride, *The Test Ban Treaty* (Chicago: Henry Regnery, 1967), 27-31, 79-80; Kruzel, *Arms Control Agreements*, 222-23.

2. Kruzel, *Arms Control Agreements*, 39.

3. Ibid., 216-18; Robert A. Divine, *Blowing in the Wind: The Nuclear Test Ban Debate, 1954–60* (New York: Oxford University Press, 1978), 178-322.

4. Dean, *Test Ban and Disarmament*, 90-91.

5. U.S. ACDA, *Documents on Disarmament, 1962*, 1047-55, 1184-85, 1241, 1299-1301; Jonsson, *Soviet Union and Test Ban*, 125, 189.

6. U.S. ACDA, *Documents on Disarmament, 1962*, 1301, and *1963*, 4, 16.

7. U.S. ACDA, *Documents on Disarmament, 1963*, 16. See also McBride, *Test Ban Treaty*, 16-17; and Glenn Seaborg, *Kennedy, Khrushchev, and the Test Ban* (Berkeley: University of California Press, 1981), 183-85.

8. Murrey Marder, "Kennedy Calls Halt to Nevada A-Test," *Washington Post*, January 27, 1963.

9. U.S. ACDA, *Documents on Disarmament, 1963*, 16, 31; Seaborg, *Test Ban*, 183-85.

10. U.S. ACDA, *Documents on Disarmament, 1963*, 40, 50-56.

11. Ibid., 32-38.

12. Divine, *Blowing in the Wind*, 210.

13. U.S. ACDA, *Documents on Disarmament, 1963*, 99.

14. Divine, *Blowing in the Wind*, 204.

15. Shevchenko, *Breaking with Moscow*, 86-87.

16. Greenwood, *Making the MIRV*, 4-7.

17. Ulam, *Expansion and Coexistence*, 661-77.

18. U.S. ACDA, *Documents on Disarmament, 1963*, 36, 193.

19. Ibid., 226.

20. Ulam, *Expansion and Coexistence*, 685-90; Horelick and Rush, *Strategic Power*, 154.

21. U.S. ACDA, *Documents on Disarmament, 1963*, 9.

22. Ibid., 206-14.

23. Shevchenko, *Breaking with Moscow*, 117-18.

24. See Goldman, *Detente and Dollars*, 30-31; Hardt and Gold, "Soviet Commercial Behavior," 207-210; Spero, *International Economic Relations* (1981), 297-300.

25. Jonsson, *Soviet Bargaining Behavior*, 146, 196-97; Shevchenko, *Breaking with Moscow*, 92, 112.

26. U.S. ACDA, *Documents on Disarmament, 1963*, 28, 34.

27. Seaborg, *Test Ban*, 185. See also McBride, *Test Ban Treaty*, 16.

28. U.S. ACDA, *Documents on Disarmament, 1963*, 28.

29. U.S. ACDA, *Documents on Disarmament, 1963*, 220-21.

30. Sources detailing the formulation of the U.S. policy include Kruzel, *Arms Control Agreements*, 222-29; McBride, *Test Ban Treaty*, 27; Steinberg, *Satellite Reconnaissance*, 161; James T. Terchek, *The Making of the Test Ban Treaty* (The Hague: Marinus Nijhoff, 1970), 19, 118; and Jacobson and Stein, *Diplomats, Scientists, and Politicians*, 447-48.

31. U.S. ACDA, *Documents on Disarmament, 1963*, 220-21; and see ch. 4, n. 39.

32. U.S. ACDA, *Documents on Disarmament, 1963*, 244-46; and see Kruzel, *Arms Control Agreements*, 219.

33. U.S. ACDA, *Documents on Disarmament, 1963*, 249.

34. McBride, *Test Ban Treaty*, 19-21.

35. Jonsson, *Soviet Union and Test Ban*, 121.

36. U.S. ACDA, *Documents on Disarmament, 1963*, 286.

37. Ibid., 321-24.

38. Once again, France is the partial exception. See ibid., 267-68.

39. Ibid., 428-30, 505-6.

40. Ibid., 269.

41. Ibid., 281.

42. McBride, *Test Ban Treaty*, 19-21.

43. Steinberg, *Satellite Reconnaissance*, 151-52, 164.

44. Jacobson and Stein, *Diplomats*, 449; Jonsson, *Soviet Bargaining Behavior*, 195-96.

45. See Shevchenko, *Breaking with Moscow*, 125-28; and Breslauer, *Khrushchev and Brezhnev*, 132.

46. Schwartz, *Soviet Perceptions*, 122.

47. See Etzioni, "The Kennedy Experiment."

Chapter 6

1. See Michael E. Brown, *Flying Blind: Decision Making in the U.S. Strategic Bomber Program* (Ph.D. diss., Cornell University, 1983), chs. 2 and 3; Smoke, *National Security*, 68-70, 92; and Wolfe, *Soviet Power in Europe*, 94, 179.

2. Jeremy Stone, "Bomber Disarmament," *World Politics* 17 (October 1964): 13.

3. U.S. ACDA, *Documents on Disarmament, 1964*, 2.

4. Ibid., 16.

5. Ibid., 73.

6. Ibid., 102-3.

7. Ibid., 103.

8. Ibid., 137-38, 284-88.

9. Ibid., 290.

10. Ibid., 515.

11. U.S. ACDA, *Documents on Disarmament, 1965,* 69- 70.

12. Ibid., 75-76.

13. Ibid., 82.

14. Ibid., 109-110; idem, *Documents on Disarmament, 1966,* 164, 234.

15. Stone, "Bomber Disarmament," 16; Kahan, *Nuclear Age,* 97-98.

16. Robert P. Berman, *Soviet Air Power in Transition* (Washington, DC: Brookings Institution, 1978), 23-27.

17. U.S. ACDA, *Documents on Disarmament, 1966,* 144.

18. U.S. ACDA, *Documents on Disarmament, 1964,* 14. See also Chapter 2 of this book, note 41b.

19. U.S. ACDA, *Documents on Disarmament, 1964,* 36. See also Chapter 2, note 43a.

20. U.S. ACDA, *Documents on Disarmament, 1964,* 82. See also Chapter 2, note 41a.

21. U.S. ACDA, *Documents on Disarmament, 1964,* 152.

22. Ibid., 166-69.

23. Ibid., 75-76.

24. Ibid., 103.

25. Ibid., 292-93.

26. Ibid., 138-39. See also pages 509-10.

27. Ibid., 50.

28. Ibid., 311, 535, and notes 18-20 above.

29. Ibid., 138.

30. Ibid., 103, 292-93.

31. Mark E. Miller, *Soviet Strategic Power and Doctrine: The Quest for Superiority* (Miami: Advanced International Studies Institute, 1982), 83-84; David Holloway, *The Soviet Union and the Arms Race,* 2d ed. (Washington, DC: Brookings Institution, 1978), 67.

32. IISS, *The Military Balance, 1965–66,* 3.

33. IISS, *The Military Balance, 1964-65,* 3, 36; Miller, *Soviet Power and Doctrine,* 72; Horelick and Rush, *Strategic Power,* 163.

34. U.S. ACDA, *Documents on Disarmament, 1964,* 448.

35. IISS, *The Military Balance: 1963–64,* 12; *1964-65,* 17, 22; and *1965-66,* 9, 17.

36. U.S. ACDA, *Documents on Disarmament, 1964,* 291.

37. Ibid., 287.

38. Ibid., 292.

39. Ulam, *Expansion and Coexistence,* 676-77, 702-21.

40. U.S. ACDA, *Documents on Disarmament, 1964,* 59.

41. Ibid., 130, 147, 189.

42. Kahan, *Security in the Nuclear Age,* 120.

43. Wolfe, *Soviet Power in Europe,* 180.

44. See Chapter 3, Table 2.

45. IISS, *Military Balance, 1964–65,* 3; Miller, *Soviet Power and Doctrine,* 43, 83; Berman, *Soviet Air Power,* 13-14, 21-27, 44.

46. Breslauer, "Political Succession and the Soviet Policy Agenda," 36, 40-41.

47. Shevchenko, *Breaking with Moscow*, 124-28.

48. U.S. ACDA, *Documents on Disarmament, 1964*, 73-74, 509.

49. Ulam, *Expansion and Coexistence*, 699-701.

50. Ibid., 701-5; John G. Stoessinger, *Why Nations Go To War*, 4th ed. (New York: St. Martin's Press, 1985), 101-2; Breslauer, "Soviets Test New Presidents?," 95; Thomas W. Wolfe, "Soviet Military Policy After Khrushchev," in *Soviet Politics Since Khrushchev*, ed. Alexander Dallin and Thomas B. Larson (Englewood Cliffs, NJ: Prentice Hall, 1968), 115.

51. In Dallin and Larson, *Soviet Policies*, see Vernon V. Aspaturian, "Foreign Policy Perspectives in the Sixties," 146, and William Zimmerman, "Soviet Perceptions of the U.S.,"163-74.

52. U.S. ACDA, *Documents on Disarmament, 1965*, 188.

53. Meyer, "Soviet Perspectives," 176.

54. Kahan, *Security in the Nuclear Age*, 94-96.

55. Betts, "Balance Before Parity," 19.

Chapter 7

1. Wolfe, *Soviet Power*, 184-86; Johan J. Holst and William Schneider, Jr., *Why ABM?* (New York: Pergamon Press,1969), 147-50.

2. Kahan, *Security in the Nuclear Age*, 28-29; Benson D. Adams, *Ballistic Missile Defense* (New York: American Elsevier, 1971), 20-34; Ernest J. Yanarella, *The Missile Defense Controversy* (Lexington: University of Kentucky Press, 1977), 60.

3. Kahan, *Security in the Nuclear Age*, 98; Greenwood, *Making the MIRV*, 97.

4. See Wolfe, *Soviet Power*, 186-87, 439; Holst and Schneider, *Why ABM?*, 150.

5. Adams, *Ballistic Missile Defense*, 44, 52, 63, 85.

6. Greenwood, *Making the MIRV*, 4.

7. Kahan, *Security in the Nuclear Age*, 110-13; Wolfe, *Soviet Power*, 187; Horelick and Rush, *Strategic Power*, 155.

8. Kahan, *Security in the Nuclear Age*, 119-20; U.S. ACDA, *Documents on Disarmament, 1964*, 27-28, 544.

9. Holst and Schneider, *Why ABM?*, 151; Wolfe, *Soviet Power*, 438-39; Greenwood, *Making the MIRV*, 99-103.

10. Adams, *Ballistic Missile Defense*, 112-13; Kahan, *Security in the Nuclear Age*, 94-98, 121.

11. Holst and Schneider, *Why ABM?*, 154-55; Sayer Stevens, "The Soviet BMD Program," in *Ballistic Missile Defense*, ed. Ashton B. Carter and David N. Schwartz (Washington, DC: Brookings Institution, 1984), 189-94, 200-201; Lawrence Freedman, *United States Intelligence and the Soviet Strategic Threat* (London: Macmillan, 1977), pp. 87-90; Greenwood, *Making the MIRV*, 76-77.

12. Adams, *Ballistic Missile Defense*, 145; Newhouse, *Cold Dawn*, 81-102; Halperin, *Bureaucratic Politics*, 297-310.

13. U.S. ACDA, Disarmament Document Series, no. 444, *Selected Statements by President Johnson on Disarmament and Related Matters, July 1, 1966–June 30, 1967*

(Washington, DC: GPO, 1967), 42. See also Lyndon B. Johnson, *The Vantage Point: Perspectives of the Presidency, 1963-69* (New York: Holt, Rinehart and Winston, 1971), 179; Halperin, *Bureaucratic Politics*, 301; Newhouse, *Cold Dawn*, 87; Adams, *Ballistic Missile Defense*, 145-46.

14. U.S. ACDA, *Documents on Disarmament, 1967*, 7, 11.

15. Adams, *Ballistic Missile Defense*, 145-146.

16. U.S. ACDA, *Documents on Disarmament, 1967*, 60, 270; Newhouse, *Cold Dawn*, 89-94; Johnson, *Vantage Point*, 480-84.

17. Halperin, *Bureaucratic Politics*, 303.

18. U.S. ACDA, *Documents on Disarmament, 1967*, 382-394.

19. Ibid., 402-5, 454-59.

20. "Defense Fantasy Comes True: In an Exclusive Interview, Secretary McNamara Explains in Full the Logic Behind the ABM System," *Life*, September 29, 1967: 28 A-C.

21. Halperin, *Bureaucratic Politics*, 3, 236, 302; Newhouse, *Cold Dawn*, 96-98.

22. Newhouse, *Cold Dawn*, 97; U.S. ACDA, *Documents on Disarmament, 1968*, 261; Adams, *Ballistic Missile Defense*, 177; Halperin, *Bureaucratic Politics*, 304-310.

23. Holst and Schneider, *Why ABM?*, 159; Wolfe, *Soviet Power*, 440.

24. Newhouse, *Cold Dawn*, 98-103; Kahan, *Security in the Nuclear Age*, 124; Wolfe, *Soviet Power*, 270-73; Johnson, *Vantage Point*, 485-87.

25. Freedman, *U.S. Intelligence*, 90; Payne, *Soviet Union and SALT*, 19-20; Wolfe, *Soviet Power*, 441.

26. Myers and Simes, *Soviet Decision Making*, 44-46; Johnson, *Vantage Point*, 487.

27. U.S. ACDA, *Documents on Disarmament, 1969*, 102-5. See also Adams, *Ballistic Missile Defense*, 194-203; Henry Kissinger, *The White House Years* (Boston: Little, Brown, 1979), 209, 535, 799.

28. U.S. ACDA, *Documents on Disarmament, 1969*, 103, 130; Kissinger, *White House Years*, 208, 799; Adams, *Ballistic Missile Defense*, 207; Kahan, *Security in the Nuclear Age*, 150, 157, 175, 297.

29. My sources disagree on the date. Contrast Newhouse (*Cold Dawn*, 214-18) and Kahan (*Security in the Nuclear Age*, 184) with Gerard C. Smith, *Doubletalk: The Story of the First Strategic Arms Limitation Talks* (Garden City, NY: Doubleday, 1980), 192-95, 233.

30. See Newhouse, *Cold Dawn*, ch. 5; Kahan, *Security in the Nuclear Age*, 182-87.

31. See Einhorn, *Negotiating from Strength*, 2-3, 15-16, 39, 54; Newhouse, *Cold Dawn*, 188; Kahan, *Security in the Nuclear Age*, 174-75, 183-87; Payne, *Soviet Union and SALT*, 109.

32. U.S. ACDA, *Documents on Disarmament, 1967*, 60, 270.

33. Wolfe, *Soviet Power*, 439.

34. Newhouse, *Cold Dawn*, 91-92.

35. Wolfe, *Soviet Power*, 439.

36. Ibid.

37. Shevchenko, *Breaking with Moscow*, 201-2.

38. Wolfe, *Soviet Power*, 439.

39. Ibid.

40. Ibid.

41. Ibid.

42. Freedman, *U.S. Intelligence*, 90.

43. Shevchenko, *Breaking with Moscow*, 37; Stevens, "Soviet BMD Program," 201; Einhorn, *Negotiating from Strength*, 54; Wolfe, *Soviet Power*, 441.

44. Newhouse, *Cold Dawn*, 101, 107, 156-57; Myers and Simes, *Soviet Decision Making*, 44-46; Ulam, *Expansion and Coexistence* (1963), 772; Payne, *Soviet Union and SALT*, 11, 19-20.

45. See Myers and Simes, *Soviet Decision Making*, 54.

46. Einhorn, *Negotiating from Strength*, 15-16, 54.

47. U.S. ACDA, *Documents on Disarmament, 1969*, 103.

48. Newhouse, *Cold Dawn*, 90-94.

49. U.S. ACDA, *Documents on Disarmament, 1967*, 459, 751.

50. Ibid., 650.

51. See Ulam, *Expansion and Coexistence*, 676-77; Newhouse, *Cold Dawn*, 91, 235.

52. Myers and Simes, *Soviet Decision Making*, 43; Ulam, *Expansion and Coexistence*, 723.

53. U.S. ACDA, *Documents on Disarmament, 1967*, 50, 318-19, 471.

54. See ibid., 602-3, 621, 567-71.

55. Ibid., 693, and *1968*, 49, 116, 330.

56. Payne, *Soviet Union and SALT*, 20.

57. Myers and Simes, *Soviet Decision Making*, 44-46; Johnson, *Vantage Point*, 487.

58. IISS, *Military Balance, 1969-70*, 55; Wolfe, *Soviet Power*, 433-34.

59. U.S. Central Intelligence Agency, *Handbook of Economic Statistics, 1985* (Washington, DC: CIA, 1985), 64; U.S. Congress, *Fundamentals of Nuclear Arms Control*, pt. 6, 14 n. 13; Shevchenko, *Breaking with Moscow*, 47.

60. See chapter 3, Table 2.

61. Spero, *International Economic Relations* (1981), 308.

62. See chapter 4, note 31.

63. Newhouse, *Cold Dawn*, 92; Wolfe, *Soviet Power*, 270-74.

64. Shevchenko, *Breaking with Moscow*, 202. See also Wolfe, *Soviet Power*, 441; Newhouse, *Cold Dawn*, 92.

65. Breslauer, "Political Succession," 36-39, and *Khrushchev and Brezhnev*, 142-52, 246, 252, 257.

66. Breslauer, "Political Succession," 35; Kissinger, *White House Years*, 527-28.

67. See chapter 6, note 50.

68. U.S. ACDA, *Documents on Disarmament, 1967*, 217.

69. Ibid., 351.

70. Ibid., 631.

71. In Dallin and Larson, *Soviet Politics*, see Aspaturian, "Foreign Policy Perspectives," 146, and Zimmerman, "Soviet Perceptions," 163-74.

72. See Ulam, *Expansion and Coexistence*, 676-77; Newhouse, *Cold Dawn*, 91, 235; and chapter 3, note 51.

73. Myers and Simes, *Soviet Decision Making*, 44-46.

74. Blair, *Command and Control*, 306-8.

75. See Meyer, "Soviet Perspectives," 173, 178, 182; Ball, "Soviet Strategic Planning," 54-55; Michael MccGwire, *Military Objectives in Soviet Foreign Policy* (Washington, DC: Brookings Institution, 1986) 27-30.

76. Blair, *Command and Control*, 307-12.

77. See Freedman, *Evolution of Nuclear Strategy*, 261; and Paul Bracken, "Accidental Nuclear War," in *Hawks, Doves, & Owls*, ed. Allison, Carnesale, and Nye, 43.

78. Kahan, *Security in the Nuclear Age*, 106-8.

79. Betts, "Balance Before Parity," 19.

80. Ibid.; Allison and Morris, "Armaments and Arms Control," 105, 111; U.S. ACDA, *Documents on Disarmament, 1969*, 103.

Chapter 8

1. Fred M. Kaplan, "Enhanced Radiation Weapons," *Scientific American* 238 (May 1978): 46-47; SIPRI, *World Armaments and Disarmament: SIPRI Yearbook 1982* (London: Taylor and Francis, 1982), ch. 3.

2. Samuel T. Cohen, *The Truth About the Neutron Bomb: The Inventor of the Bomb Speaks Out* (New York: William Morrow, 1983), 158-60.

3. Sherri L. Wasserman, *The Neutron Bomb Controversy: A Study in Alliance Politics* (New York: Praeger, 1983), 21.

4. Ibid., 22.

5. Ibid., 25.

6. A neutron bomb was, for example, a warhead for the short-range Sprint ABM. Its reduced blast, heat, and fallout meant that it would cause less damage to U.S. cities than standard warheads, while the neutrons could disable an incoming enemy warhead. See Wasserman, *Neutron Bomb Controversy*, 27.

7. Freedman, *Evolution of Nuclear Strategy*, 285-93.

8. Harold Brown, *Thinking About National Security: Defense and Foreign Policy in a Dangerous World* (Boulder, CO: Westview, 1983), 108.

9. Wasserman, *Neutron Bomb Controversy*, 23.

10. Strobe Talbott, *Deadly Gambits* (New York: Vintage Books, 1985), 27-28; SIPRI, *Yearbook 1982*, 65-66.

11. Pat Towell, "NATO Role Hit: Members of Congress Fault Carter for Failure to Decide Future of Neutron Bomb," *Congressional Quarterly Weekly Reports*, April 15, 1978, 885.

12. James Schlesinger, *Report of Secretary of Defense James R. Schlesinger to the Congress on the FY 1976 Budget* (Washington, DC: GPO, 1975), 2-11; David N. Schwartz, *NATO's Nuclear Dilemma* (Washington, DC: Brookings Institution, 1983), 73-75.

13. Towell, "NATO Role Hit," 885.

14. Kaplan, "Enhanced Radiation Weapons," 46.

15. For a discussion of the debate in Congress preceding authorization for ERDA funds, see Cyrus Vance, *Hard Choices: Critical Years in America's Foreign Policy* (New York: Simon and Schuster, 1983), 67-68; and Towell, "NATO Role Hit," 885.

16. For a discussion of Soviet propaganda efforts and their effect on Schmidt, see Wasserman, *Neutron Bomb Controversy*, 103-104; and Chapman Pincher, *The Secret Offensive* (New York: St. Martin's Press, 1985), 210-13.

17. Zbigniew K. Brzezinski, *Power and Principle: Memoirs of the National Security Advisor, 1977–81* (New York: Farrar, Straus, Giroux; 1983), 301-6; Jimmy Carter, *Keeping Faith: Memoirs of a President* (New York: Bantam Books, 1982), 226; and Vance, *Hard Choices*, 68-69.

18. IISS, *The Military Balance, 1977–78*, 3-8, 106, and *1978–79*, 8, 111.

19. Wasserman, *Neutron Bomb Controversy*, 91; Theodor H. Winkler, "Arms Control and the Politics of European Security," in *Arms Control and European Security*, ed. Jonathan Alford (New York: St. Martin's Press for the IISS, 1984), 27; and Lothar Ruehl, "MBFR: Lessons and Problems," also in Alford, 47.

20. Wasserman, *Neutron Bomb Controversy*, 92-95.

21. Ibid., 98.

22. Ibid., 108.

23. "Aids Report Carter Bans Neutron Bomb," *New York Times*, April 4, 1978; "Carter is Reported Reconsidering a Ban on the Neutron Bomb," *New York Times*, April 5, 1978.

24. In his memoirs, Carter did not say he planned to produce ERWs in the absence of Soviet concessions. Instead he emphasized his resentment at not hearing about an allied consensus earlier and at West German timidity, and he said deployment was doubtful in any case because of the weapon's political liabilities. In addition, neither Brzezinski nor Vance said Carter intended to fulfill the conditional nature of the initiative. Since they emphasized how the initiative was a way out of political trouble, we can reasonably conclude that this explanation was Carter's principal motive. See Carter, *Keeping the Faith*, 220-29; Brzezinski, *Power and Principle*, 302-4; Vance, *Hard Choices*, 92-95; and *Congressional Quarterly Almanac*, vol. 2, 95th Cong., 2d sess., 1978, 372.

25. U.S. ACDA, *Documents on Disarmament, 1978*, 230.

26. Ibid., 232-33.

27. Ibid., 237.

28. Ibid., 257-58.

29. Jimmy Carter, *Public Papers of the President of the United States, 1978* I (Washington, DC: GPO, 1979), 777.

30. Blacker and Duffy, eds., *International Arms Control: Issues and Agreements*, 300-304.

31. U.S. ACDA, *Documents on Disarmament, 1979*, 606.

32. Ibid.

33. Ibid., 609.

34. Blacker and Duffy, *International Arms Control*, 305-11.

35. U.S. ACDA, *Documents on Disarmament, 1979*, 806.

36. See IISS, *The Military Balance, 1977–78*, 3, 8, *1978–79*, 8, *1979–80*, 9, *1980-81*, 9, and *1981–82*, 11.

37. U.S. ACDA, *Documents on Disarmament, 1980*, 268-69.

38. Ibid., 431.

39. U.S. ACDA, *Documents on Disarmament, 1978*, 230.

40. See Cohen, *Truth About Neutron Bomb*, 118; and Wasserman, *Neutron Bomb Controversy*, 139.

41. Blacker and Duffy, *International Arms Control*, 305.

42. U.S. ACDA, *Documents on Disarmament, 1978*, 233.

43. Wasserman, *Neutron Bomb Controversy*, 91, 92-95; Winkler, "Arms Control," 27; Ruehl, "MBFR," 47.

44. U.S. ACDA, *Documents on Disarmament, 1978*, 230.

45. Carter, *Papers of the President*, 875.

46. U.S. ACDA, *Documents on Disarmament, 1979*, 609.

47. *Congressional Quarterly Almanac* 34 (1978), 375.

48. Richard Burt, "President Decides to Defer Production of Neutron Weapons," *New York Times*, April 8, 1978.

49. *Congressional Quarterly Almanac* 35 (1979), 437.

50. *Congressional Quarterly Almanac* 34 (1978), 373-74.

51. Harold Brown, *Department of Defense Annual Report for Fiscal Year 1980* (Washington, DC: GPO, 1979), 137.

52. Harold Brown, *Department of Defense Annual Report for FY 81* (1980), 146; *Department of Defense Annual Report for FY 82* (1981), 127.

53. *Congressional Quarterly Almanac* 36 (1980), 84.

54. Brown, *Annual Report for FY 82*, 127.

55. See chapter 2, note 41c.

56. *Congressional Quarterly Almanac* 33 (1977), 33.

57. U.S. ACDA, *Documents on Disarmament, 1979*, 806.

58. John J. Binder and Robert W. Clawson, "Warsaw Pact Ground Forces: Formations, Combat Doctrine, and Capabilities," in *The Warsaw Pact: Political Purposes and Military Means*, ed. Robert W. Clawson and Lawrence S. Kaplan (Wilmington, DE: Scholarly Resources, 1982), 229; Condoleezza Rice, "The Party, the Military, and Decision Authority in the Soviet Union," *World Politics* 40 (October 1987): 62, 78.

59. Binder and Clawson, "Warsaw Pact Ground Forces," 234.

60. Brown, *Thinking About National Security*, 89.

61. For a related argument, see Christopher D. Jones, "Soviet Hegemony in Eastern Europe: The Dynamics of Political Autonomy and Military Intervention," *World Politics* 29 (January 1977): 216-41. Jack Snyder does not see this factor as decisive. See his "Limiting Offensive Conventional Forces: Soviet Proposals and Western Options," *International Security* 12 (Spring 1988): 61 n. 50.

62. William J. Lewis, *The Warsaw Pact: Arms, Doctrine, and Strategy* (New York: McGraw-Hill, 1982), 219, 233; John P. Rose, "U.S. Army Doctrine and the Nuclear Threat," in *NATO's Strategic Options: Arms Control and Defense*, ed. David S. Yost (New York: Pergamon Press, 1981), 29; Binder and Clawson, "Warsaw Pact Ground Forces," 235.

63. Binder and Clawson, "Warsaw Pact Ground Forces," 235.

64. Ibid.

65. IISS, *Military Balance: 1978–79*, 111.

66. See Cohen, *Truth About Neutron Bomb*, 161.

67. See Samuel Cohen, "The Neutron Bomb: The Potential Contributions of ERWs," in Yost, *NATO's Options*, 154.

68. See Rose, "U.S. Army Doctrine," 39.

69. This analysis draws heavily from Steven J. Zaloga, "NBC Defense: Protecting Soviet Armored Vehicles," *NBC Defense and Technology International* 1 (September 1986): 26-30.

70. Ibid., 28.

71. Kent Wisner, "Military Aspects of Enhanced Radiation Weapons," *Survival*, November/December 1981: 246-50.

72. G. Ivanov, "Neutron Weapons," *Zarubezhnoye Voyennoye Obozreniye*, no. 12 (Moscow: December 1982): 53-54, in William V. Garner, *Soviet Threat Perceptions of NATO's Eurostrategic Missiles* (Ph.D. dissertation, Georgetown University, 1985), 30.

73. Wisner, "Enhanced Radiation Weapons," 250.

74. See Ibid.; Cohen, "The Neutron Bomb," 165-66; Rose, "U.S. Army Doctrine," 40; Kaplan, "Enhanced Radiation Weapons," 49; Wisner, "Military Aspects of ERWs," 250; and "NATO and the Neutron Bomb," in *The Defense Monitor* 7 (June 1978), 1.

75. I found no direct quotation by Brown, but two sources referred to his statement: *Documents on Disarmament, 1978*, 236; and Alton Frye, "Slow Fuse on the Neutron Bomb," *Foreign Policy*, No. 31 (Summer 1978): 95. Vance added that the military consequence of the neutron bomb fiasco was low (*Hard Choices*, 96).

76. See Binder and Clawson, "Warsaw Pact Ground Forces," 236-37; and Lewis, *The Warsaw Pact*, 219-33.

77. Hasagawa, "Nuclear War-Fighting," 70-71; Meyer, "Paths to Nuclear War," 178-80, 196-204; Einhorn, *Negotiating from Strength*, 48.

78. John G. Keliher, "Does MBFR Have a Future?," in Yost, *NATO's Strategic Options*, 92; Blacker and Duffy, *International Arms Control*, 304.

79. Blacker and Duffy, *International Arms Control*, 302-4.

80. See Talbott, *Deadly Gambits*, 70, 212, 238, 287-88; and Gregory Treverton, "Nuclear Weapons in Europe," *Adelphi Papers* (London: IISS, 1981), 19-20.

81. Trout, "Soviet Policy Towards China," 61-66, 76, 81; Rubinstein, *Soviet Foreign Policy*, 127-31.

82. For a theoretical discussion of this "fear of entrapment," see Glenn H. Snyder, "The Security Dilemma in Alliance Politics," *World Politics* 36 (July 1984): 461-95.

83. In the 1978 volume of *Documents on Disarmament*, the only country not a member of either alliance to mention ERWs was Sweden. Although the Swedish representative, Mr. Thorsson, raised a concern about Soviet SS-20s, his opposition to ERWs was clear: "As my government sees it, the terrible neutron weapon is a specialized nuclear weapon which might very well lower the nuclear threshold" (p. 463).

84. The U.S. MFR delegation also opposed introducing ERW because of this asymmetry. See Wasserman, *Neutron Bomb Controversy*, 91, 94.

85. U.S. Congress, *Fundamentals of Nuclear Arms Control*, pt. 6, 14 n. 13; Shevchenko, *Breaking with Moscow*, 47.

86. See chapter 3, Table 2.

87. Spero, *International Economic Relations* (1981), 308, 314, 318-20, and 1985 ed., 377, 384.

88. Wasserman, *Neutron Bomb Controversy*, 91.

89. See index of statements on the neutron bomb and MFR in U.S. ACDA, *Documents on Disarmament, 1978*, 847.

90. Breslauer, "Political Succession," 35-39, and *Khrushchev and Brezhnev,* 257; Kissinger, *White House Years,* 527-28.

91. Breslauer, "Soviets Test New Presidents?," 100-102.

92. IISS, *Strategic Survey, 1979* (London: IISS, 1980), 34; MccGwire, *Soviet Military Objectives,* 287.

93. Schwartz, *Soviet Perceptions,* 50, 114, 129-37.

94. IISS, *Strategic Survey, 1982/83,* 36.

95. IISS, *Strategic Survey, 1981/82,* 39; Harold A. Feiveson and John Duffield, "Stopping the Sea-Based Counterforce Threat," *International Security* 9 (Summer 1984): 187-202.

96. IISS, *Strategic Survey, 1981/82,* 40, 128.

97. Ibid., 39.

98. James R. Schlesinger, *Report of the Secretary of Defense James R. Schlesinger to the Congress on the FY 1975 Defense Budget and the FY 1975-79 Defense Program* (Washington, DC: GPO, 1974), 4-6, 32-45.

99. Freedman, *Evolution of Nuclear Strategy,* 380-81.

100. Blair, *Command and Control,* 309-11.

101. IISS, *Strategic Survey, 1977,* 57, 94.

102. Harold Brown, *Department of Defense Annual Report for Fiscal Year 1979* (Washington, DC: GPO, 1978), 107-109, and *Annual Report for FY 1980,* 122.

103. IISS, *Strategic Survey, 1979,* 34. See also Brown, *Annual Report for FY 1982,* 5, 40-49.

104. IISS, *Strategic Survey, 1979,* 34-35, 125.

105. IISS, *Strategic Survey, 1980/81,* 121.

106. Blacker and Duffy, *International Arms Control,* 307-11; Smoke, *National Security,* 191-92.

Chapter 9

1. I am grateful to Robert Jervis who, after reading parts of chapters 2 and 3 that dealt with the strategic environment, suggested these two ideas to me.

2. Steinberg, *Satellite Reconnaissance,* 25.

3. Bresler and Gray, "Bargaining Chip," 66-70.

4. Ibid., 88.

5. Scoville, "Reciprocal National Restraint," 6.

6. Einhorn, *Negotiating from Strength,* 6; Greenwood, *Making the MIRV,* 127-28; Kahan, *Security in the Nuclear Age,* 178-82; Newhouse, *Cold Dawn,* 123, 158-59, 183-92; Smith, *Doubletalk,* 155-56.

7. Einhorn, *Negotiating from Strength,* 2-3, 8, 15. See also chapter 7 of this book.

8. Einhorn, *Negotiating from Strength;* and William Rose, "MX as a Bargaining Chip," *Arms Control* (London, May 1984).

9. See chapter 2, note 41.

10. See chapter 2, note 42.

11. An excellect start is made by Jack Snyder, "Gorbachev Revolution."

12. Some potentially relevant cases are listed in William Rose, *Bargaining Tactics for Arms Control*, 296-99.

13. Einhorn, *Negotiating from Strength*, 50; Greenwood, *Making the MIRV*, 113-28.

Chapter 10

1. *Congressional Quarterly Weekly Report* 42 (August 25, 1984): 2116.

2. For an earlier draft of this essay, see William M. Rose, "Beware of 'Counterfeit' Unilateral Initiatives," *Arms Control* 7 (London, May 1986): 47-58.

3. In 1906 Britain may have implemented a counterfeit unilateral initiative that was justifiable from a geopolitical perspective. For eight years, Germany had been escalating the naval arms competition. To maintain a margin of safety in the naval balance, the British foreign secretary wanted to demonstrate to the public it would be Germany's fault if, as expected, additional naval expenditures became necessary. See Woodward, *Great Britain and the German Navy*, 121-32.

4. Hedrick Smith, "US Presses Soviet for Big Reductions in its ICBM Forces," *New York Times*, June 22, 1983.

5. Fred Kaplan, "Aspin Says MX Missile Program is Dead," *Boston Globe*, July 27, 1985.

6. Ibid.

7. Bill Keller, "Revised Military Budget: Pentagon Gets Everything, But Not More," *New York Times*, July 27, 1985.

8. Bill Keller, "Pentagon Weighs New Plan to Armor and Conceal Missiles," *Boston Globe*, September 28, 1985.

9. Fred Kaplan, "In a Reagan-era first, arms budget growth is less than inflation," *Boston Globe*, February 19, 1988.

10. Ibid.

11. Stares, "Deja vu," and Snyder, "Gorbachev Revolution."

12. See Einhorn, *Negotiating from Strength*, 18-19, 33, 49, 98; Article IV of the SALT II Treaty; Article I of the Protocol; and Cyrus Vance's "Annex" in U.S. Department of State, *SALT II Agreement* (June 1979), 23.

13. See *Congressional Record*, 98th Cong., 1st sess., 23 May 1983, H3153.

14. See Murrey Marder, "Kennedy Calls Halt to Nevada A-Test," *Washington Post*, January 27, 1963.

15. IISS, *The Military Balance, 1987–88*, 205, 225; "U.S. and Soviet strategic nuclear forces, end of 1987," *Bulletin of the Atomic Scientists* 44 (January/February 1988): 56.

16. IISS, *Military Balance, 1987–88*, 34.

17. See Feiveson and Duffield, "Stopping the Sea-Based Counterforce Threat," 188-90.

18. See McGeorge Bundy, George F. Kennan, Robert S. McNamara, and Gerard Smith, "The President's Choice: Star Wars or Arms Control," *Foreign Affairs* 63 (Winter 1984-85): 267-74.

19. Edward A. Gargan, "Chinese Official Lists 6 Grievances Against U.S.," *New York Times*, February 16, 1988.

20. See Snyder, "Gorbachev Revolution," 117-20; Bill Keller, "In Moscow, a Rosy New Glow Is Cast Over the Official Portrait of America," *New York Times*, December 9, 1987; and Philip Taubman, "Gorbachev Urges Party to Update Communist Theory," *New York Times*, February 19, 1988.

21. Goldman, *Gorbachev's Challenge*, 248-52, 261-62.

22. Georgi A. Arbatov, "It Takes Two to Make a Cold War," *New York Times*, December 8, 1987.

23. For similar arguments that focus on MX as part of a bargaining chip tactic, see William M. Rose, "MX as a Bargaining Chip," 60-70; and Einhorn, *Negotiating from Strenth*, 90-101.

24. Cushman, "299 Billion Budget."

25. Snyder, "Science and Sovietology," 182.

26. *Time*, August 28, 1985; quoted in Snyder, "Gorbachev Revolution," 119-20.

27. Greenwood, *Making the MIRV*, 93, 124-39; Newhouse, *Cold Dawn*, 158-62; Kissinger, *White House Years*, 210-12.

28. Greenwood, *Making the MIRV*, 107-28; Einhorn, *Negotiating from Strength*, 50.

29. Allison and Morris, "Armaments and Arms Control," 117-21; Greenwood, *Making the MIRV*, 138-39; Kissinger, *White House Years*, 210.

30. For a similar argument about the B-47 case, see Rathjens, "Unilateral Initiatives," 176.

31. Van Evera, phone conversation, and "Why Cooperation Failed," 81-83, 112-117.

32. See Snyder, "Science and Sovietology," 181-5.

33. See Snyder, "The Gorbachev Revolution," 107-131; Primakov, "New Philosohy of Foreign Policy"; Meyer, "New Thinking for an Old Bear"; and *Financial Times*, September 22, 1987.

34. See "Agriculture's vital signs," table accompanying "America's Farm Crisis: The Weather, Economic and Otherwise, Is Improving," *New York Times*, Sunday, Febrary 14, 1988, sec. E.

35. See Breslauer, "Why Detente Failed," 328-29.

36. See Snyder, "Gorbachev Revolution," 109-131.

37. See Breslauer, "Dynamics of Soviet Policy," 131-36; and Sarah M. Terry, "The Soviet Union and Eastern Europe: Implications for U.S. Policy," also in *Soviet International Behavior*, ed. Caldwell, 34-36.

38. For an overview of the arguments, see Jonathan E. Medalia, "Trident Program," prepared for the Congressional Research Service, Issue Brief no. 73001 (July 30, 1985). Ideas for these proposals draw heavily from Feiveson and Duffield, "Stopping the Sea-Based Counterforce Threat," 194-202.

39. See "Test Flight of Navy's Missile Called a Success," *New York Times*, January 16, 1987; and Congressional Budget Office, "Trident II Missile Test Program," February 1986.

40. Epstein, "Time is Ripe for a Cutoff" (see ch. 2, n. 43a); Frank von Hippel, David H. Albright, and Barbara G. Levi, "Stopping the Production of Fissile Materials for Weapons," *Scientific American* 253 (September 1985).

41. See chapter 2, note 43a.

42. Josept Slovinec, "Uniform Reporting of Military Expenditures" (Chicago: World Without War Council, 1985).

43. The most extensive list of possible U.S. initiatives is "An American Strategy of Peace," published by the World Without War Council–Midwest (421 South Wabash Avenue; Chicago, IL 60605; 312-663-4250). New editions of the pamphlet are published during presidential election years. It covers initiatives designed to facilitate arms control and disarmament, to strengthen international institutions that could serve as alternatives to war in the resolution of international conflict, to help build a sense of world community, and to promote economic well-being. For additional sources, see chapter 1, notes 1-5 and 10.

Selected Bibliography

This selected bibliography is intended to assist anyone who would like to do further research on unilateral initiatives. I list here only my major sources. Those who want to examine case studies not covered in this book should consult the sources cited in chapter 2, notes 40-43.

The bibliography is divided into the following sections: (1) Unilateral Initiatives and Bargaining; (2) Related Works—Theory, Method, and History; (3) Soviet Foreign Policy and U.S.-Soviet Relations; and (4) the five Case Studies.

UNILATERAL INITIATIVES AND BARGAINING

Adelman, Kenneth. "Arms Control With and Without Agreements." *Foreign Affairs* 63 (Winter 1984/85): 250-60

Axelrod, Robert. *The Evolution of Cooperation.* New York: Basic Books, 1984.

Downs, George W. and David M. Rocke. "Tacit Bargaining and Arms Control." *World Politics* 39 (April 1987): 297-325.

Downs, George W., David M. Rocke, and Randolph M. Siverson. "Arms Races and Cooperation." *World Politics* 38 (October 1985): 118-46.

Etzioni, Amitai. *The Hard Way to Peace: A New Strategy.* New York: Collier Books, 1962.

George, Alexander L. "Strategies for Facilitating Cooperation." In *U.S.-Soviet Security Cooperation: Achievements, Failures, Lessons,* ed. Alexander L. George, Philip J. Farley, and Alexander Dallin. New York: Oxford University Press, 1988.

Gowa, Joanne. "Anarchy, Egoism, and Third Images." *International Organization* 40 (Winter 1986): 167-86.

Larson, Deborah. "Crisis Prevention and the Austrian State Treaty." *International Organization* 41 (Winter 1987): 27-61.

Osgood, Charles E. *An Alternative to War or Surrender.* Urbana, IL: University of Illinois Press, 1962.

Rathjens, George. "Unilateral Initiatives for Limiting and Reducing Arms." In *New Directions in Disarmament*, ed. William Epstein and Bernard T. Feld. New York: Praeger, 1981.

Schelling, Thomas C. "Reciprocal Measures for Arms Stabilization." In *Arms Control, Disarmament, and National Security*, ed. Donald G. Brennan. New York: Braziller, 1961.

_____. *The Strategy of Conflict*. New York: Oxford University Press, 1963.

_____. *Arms and Influence*. New Haven, CT: Yale University Press, 1966.

Scoville, Herbert, Jr. "Reciprocal National Restraint: An Alternative Path." *Arms Control Today* 15 (June 1985).

Woito, Robert. *To End War*. New York: Pilgram Press, 1982.

RELATED WORKS—THEORY, METHOD, AND HISTORY

Allison, Graham and Frederic Morris. "Armaments and Arms Control: Exploring the Determinants of Military Weapons." *Daedalus* 104 (Summer 1975): 99-129.

Betts, Richard K. "A Golden Nuclear Age? The Balance Before Parity." *International Security* 11 (Winter 1986-87): 3-32.

George, Alexander L. "Case Studies and Theory Development: The Method of Structured, Focused Comparison." In *Diplomatic History: New Approaches in History, Theory, and Policy*, ed. Paul G. Lauren. New York: The Free Press, 1979.

Jervis, Robert. "Cooperation Under the Security Dilemma." *World Politics* 30 (January 1978): 167-214.

Van Evera, Steven. "Why Cooperation Failed in 1914." *World Politics* 38 (October 1985):81-117.

Waltz, Kenneth N. *Theory of International Politics*. Reading, MA: Addison-Wesley, 1979.

SOVIET FOREIGN POLICY AND U.S.-SOVIET RELATIONS

Breslauer, George W. "Political Succession and the Soviet Policy Agenda." *Problems of Communism* 29 (May-June 1980): 34-52.

_____. "Why Detente Failed: An Interpretation." In *Managing the United States-Soviet Rivalry*, ed. Alexander L. George. Boulder, CO: Westview Press, 1983.

_____. "Do Soviet Leaders Test New Presidents?" *International Security* 8 (Winter 1983-84): 83-107.

Einhorn, Robert J. *Negotiating from Strength: Leverage in U.S.-Soviet Arms Control Negotiations*. New York: Praeger, 1985.

"A Garthoff-Pipes Debate on Soviet Strategic Doctrine." *Strategic Review* 10 (Fall 1982): 36-63.

Garthoff, Raymond. *Soviet Military Policy: An Historical Analysis*. New York: Praeger, 1966.

Goldman, Marshall I. *Gorbachev's Challenge: Economic Reform in the Age of High Technology*. New York: W. W. Norton, 1987.

Hasegawa, Tsuyoshi. "Soviets on Nuclear War-Fighting." *Problems of Communism* 35 (July–August 1986): 68-79.

Kolkowicz, Roman and Ellen P. Mickiewicz, eds. *The Soviet Calculus of Nuclear War.* Lexington, MA: Lexington Books, 1986.

Lowenthal, Richard. "The Logic of One-Party Rule." In *The Conduct of Soviet Foreign Policy*, 2d edition, ed. Erik P. Hoffmann and Frederik Fleron, Jr. New York: Aldine, 1980.

Meyer, Steven. "Soviet Perspectives on the Paths to Nuclear War." In *Hawks, Doves, & Owls: An Agenda for Avoiding Nuclear War*, ed. Graham Allison, Albert Carnesale, and Joseph Nye, Jr. New York: W. W. Norton, 1985.

Rubinstein, Alvin Z. *Soviet Foreign Policy Since World War II: Imperial and Global.* Cambridge, MA: Winthrop, 1981.

Schwartz, Morton. *Soviet Perceptions of the United States.* Berkeley: University of California Press, 1978.

Shevchenko, Arkady N. *Breaking with Moscow.* New York: Knopf, 1985.

Sloss, Leon and M. Scott Davis. *A Game for High Stakes: Lessons Learned in Negotiating with the Soviet Union.* Cambridge, MA: Ballinger, 1986.

Snyder, Jack. "The Gorbachev Revolution: A Waning of Soviet Expansionism?" *International Security* 12 (Winter 1987/88): 93-131.

_____. "Science and Sovietology: Bridging the Methods Gap in Soviet Foreign Policy Studies." *World Politics* 40 (January 1988): 169-93.

Ulam, Adam. *Expansion and Coexistence: The History of Soviet Foreign Policy 1917-67.* New York: Praeger, 1968.

CASE STUDIES

General Sources on Military Issues

International Institute for Strategic Studies. *The Military Balance.* London: IISS, annual.

_____. *Strategic Survey.* London: IISS, annual.

U.S. Arms Control and Disarmament Agency. *Documents on Disarmament.* Washington, DC: GPO, annual.

U.S. Department of Defense. *Report of the Secretary of Defense to the Congress on the Defense Budget.* Washington, DC: GPO, annual.

Orbiting Nuclear Weapons

Garthoff, Raymond L. "Banning the Bomb in Outer Space." *International Security* 5 (Winter 1980-81): 25-40.

Kruzel, John J. *The Preconditions and Consequences of Arms Control Agreements.* Ph.D. diss., Harvard University, 1975.

Steinberg, Gerald M. *Satellite Reconnaissance: The Role of Informal Bargaining.* New York: Praeger, 1983.

Nuclear Test Ban

Divine, Robert A. *Blowing in the Wind: The Nuclear Test Ban Debate, 1954-60.* New York: Oxford University Press, 1978.

Etzioni, Amitai. "The Kennedy Experiment." *Western Political Science Quarterly* 20 (June 1967): 361-80.

McBride, James H. *The Test Ban Treaty.* Chicago: Henry Regnery, 1967.

Jonsson, Christer. *Soviet Bargaining Behavior: The Test Ban Case.* New York: Columbia University Press, 1979.

Seaborg, Glenn. *Kennedy, Khrushchev, and the Test Ban.* Berkeley: University of California Press, 1981.

Medium-Range Bombers

Berman, Robert P. *Soviet Air Power in Transition.* Washington, DC: Brookings Institution, 1978.

Kahan, Jerome H. *Security in the Nuclear Age: Developing U.S. Strategic Arms Policy.* Washington, DC: Brookings Institution, 1975.

Miller, Mark E. *Soviet Strategic Power and Doctrine: The Quest for Superiority.* Miami: Advanced International Studies Institute, 1982.

Stone, Jeremy. "Bomber Disarmament." *World Politics* 17 (October 1964): 13-39.

Antiballistic Missiles

Adams, Benson D. *Ballistic Missile Defense.* New York: American Elsevier, 1971.

Freedman, Lawrence. *United States Intelligence and the Soviet Strategic Threat.* London: Macmillan, 1977.

Halperin, Morton. *Bureaucratic Politics and Foreign Policy.* Washington, DC: Brookings Institution, 1974.

Holst, Johan J. and William Schneider, Jr. *Why ABM?.* New York: Pergamon Press, 1969.

Johnson, Lyndon B. *The Vantage Point: Perspectives of the Presidency, 1963-69.* New York: Holt, Rinehart, and Winston, 1971.

Myers, Kenneth A. and Dimitri Simes. *Soviet Decision Making, Strategic Policy, and SALT.* Washington, DC: Center for Strategic and International Studies at Georgetown University, 1974.

Newhouse, John. *Cold Dawn: The Story of SALT.* New York: Holt, Rinehart, and Winston, 1973.

Payne, Samuel B., Jr. *The Soviet Union and SALT.* Cambridge, MA: MIT Press, 1980.

Wolfe, Thomas W. *Soviet Power in Europe, 1945-1970.* Baltimore: John Hopkins University Press, 1970.

Neutron Bombs

Blacker, Coit D. and Gloria Duffy. *International Arms Control: Issues and Agreements,* 2nd ed. Stanford, CA: Stanford University Press, 1984.

Carter, Jimmy. *Keeping Faith: Memoirs of a President.* New York: Bantam Books, 1982.

Clawson, Robert W. and Lawrence S. Kaplan, eds. *The Warsaw Pact: Political Purposes and Military Means.* Wilmington, DE: Scholarly Resources, 1982.

Cohen, Samuel T. *The Truth About the Neutron Bomb: The Inventor of the Bomb Speaks Out.* New York: William Morrow, 1983.

Lewis, William J. *The Warsaw Pact: Arms, Doctrine, and Strategy.* New York: McGraw-Hill, 1982.

Wasserman, Sherri L. *The Neutron Bomb Controversy: A Study in Alliance Politics.* New York: Praeger, 1983.

Wisner, Kent. "Military Aspects of Enhanced Radiation Weapons." *Survival* 23 (November/December 1981): 246-51.

Zagola, Steven J. "NBC Defense: Protecting Soviet Armored Vehicles." *NBC Defense and Technology International* 1 (September 1986): 26-30.

Index

About the Author

WILLIAM ROSE is Assistant Professor of Government at Connecticut College. His articles on arms policy and arms control have appeared in *Arms Control: The Journal of Arms Control and Disarmament, Bulletin of the Atomic Scientists,* and other publications.